TODAY'S ISMS

BOOKS BY WILLIAM EBENSTEIN

POLITICAL THOUGHT IN PERSPECTIVE

TODAY'S ISMS: *Communism, Fascism, Capitalism, Socialism*

MODERN POLITICAL THOUGHT: *The Great Issues*

INTRODUCTION TO POLITICAL PHILOSOPHY

GREAT POLITICAL THINKERS: *Plato to the Present*

MAN AND THE STATE: *Modern Political Ideas*

THE GERMAN RECORD: *A Political Portrait*

THE PURE THEORY OF LAW

THE NAZI STATE

THE LAW OF PUBLIC HOUSING

FASCIST ITALY

WILLIAM
EBENSTEIN

PRINCETON
UNIVERSITY

TODAY'S

SECOND
EDITION

ISMS

PRENTICE-HALL, INC.

ENGLEWOOD CLIFFS, N. J.

1958

PRINTED IN THE UNITED STATES OF AMERICA

92448

TO THE MEMORY OF JOY

PREFACE

THE MAJOR CONFLICT of our age is the struggle between aggressive totalitarianism and the free way of life. Not long ago the chief threat to liberty was fascism; today it is communism. The violence and terror of totalitarian communism and fascism, ranging from slave labor camps to genocide, reflect a fanatical ideology that brooks no compromise.

This book is a discussion of the main representatives of each side —communism and fascism on the totalitarian side, capitalism and socialism on the democratic. In a short book, it has seemed advisable to concentrate on the isms that shape the fate of the world rather than to discuss in detail the numerous other isms that are important, but that have not been decisive, in the struggle for men's minds. These lesser isms, whether philosophical, political, social, or economic, are therefore dealt with in this book only to the extent that they are related to the four major isms. The psychological roots of totalitarianism and democracy are given particularly close attention, since it is difficult to understand either system without understanding both the personality traits and psychological motivations to which each system appeals.

The key approach in this book is through the *way of life* concept rather than through one particular aspect, such as government or economics. Totalitarianism and democracy are more than specific social, political, or economic systems: they are two diametrically opposed ways of life, with contradicting beliefs and values, based on distinct and opposite conceptions of the nature of man. The scope and gravity of the present world crisis can therefore be fully grasped only by perceiving it, not as the mere result of conflicting political or economic ideas and practices, but as a conflict between two ways of thought and action encompassing the totality of social life.

WILLIAM EBENSTEIN

Princeton University

vii

TABLE OF

CONTENTS

the totalitarian way of life

1

TOTALITARIAN COMMUNISM

The Economic Interpretation of History

Before Marx, history was interpreted in several typical fashions. Some sought the key to history in the working of divine providence, and conceived of human development as but part of the unfolding of God's design of the whole universe. The main difficulty of this *religious* interpretation of history lies in the fact that God's will is unknown and unknowable to man's direct experience, and that whereas there is only one God, there are many contrasting human conceptions of God and his plans for mankind.

A second dominant pre-Marxist approach to the understanding of human history was *political:* great emperors, kings, legislators, and soldiers were viewed as the decisive forces in history, and historical writing was largely the record of kings, parliaments, wars, and peace treaties.

This political emphasis in human affairs has one main shortcoming: it tends to exaggerate the relative role that most people assign to government and politics in the total setting of their lives. It is natural that statesmen, politicians, and political philosophers see in politics the most important single element in human relations, and in political remedies the most important answer to human troubles. But human nature and human problems are more intricate

3

than politics; politics is only one approach—and not always the most penetrating one—among many others.

A third major approach, the *hero interpretation of history* (popularized in modern times by Carlyle), is closely related to the political one, inasmuch as most heroes in world history are conventionally chosen from great kings, emperors, generals, legislators, founders of new states, and pioneering reformers and revolutionaries. The main weakness of the hero interpretation is that it overstresses the role of individuals at the expense of larger cultural, religious, social, and economic circumstances, circumstances that form the background without which there can be no meaningful exercise of leadership. Although it is undoubtedly true that leaders mold events, it is no less true that events mold leaders.

The fourth pre-Marxist approach to the understanding of history was through the impact of *ideas:* ideas were conceived (by Hegel, for example) to be the principal causes of the historical process, and the material conditions (social, economic, technological, military) of society were thought of as essentially derived from, and caused by, the great motivating ideas. This emphasis on ideas often also implied that history was progressively evolving toward the realization of *key* ideas, such as freedom and democracy.

While undoubtedly containing—like the other interpretations— much that is valid, the exclusive emphasis on ideas as the main driving force in history overlooks the fact that ideas not only generate events but also reflect them. Therefore, to isolate ideas as the chief agent of human action is to neglect the framework of circumstances; circumstances, after all, make some ideas possible and others not, and it is circumstances from which ideas derive their vitality and practical impact.

Finally, the study of history may be focused on *war:* the phenomenon of conflict is present in all phases of human development, and the birth, rise, and decline of states are often directly connected with warfare. The shortcoming of the military interpretation of history lies in its failure to see war as the result, rather than as the cause, of events. There is no doubt that war often marks a turning point in the life of nations and civilizations: yet the dramatic swiftness and decisiveness of war should not draw our attention from the multitude of psychological, ideological, and material factors that lead to war and contribute to its complexity.

Marx's main premise in the analysis of society is his *economic interpretation of history:* the production of the goods and services that support human life, and the exchange of those goods and services, are the basis of all social processes and institutions. Marx does not claim that the economic factor is the only one that goes into the making of history; he does claim that it is the most important one, the *foundation* upon which is erected the *superstructure* of culture, law, and government, buttressed by corresponding political, social, religious, literary, and artistic ideologies.

In a general way, Marx describes the relations between men's material conditions of life and their ideas by saying that *"it is not the consciousness of men which determines their existence, but, on the contrary, it is their social existence which determines their consciousness."*

In a nomadic society, for example, horses might be considered the principal means of acquiring and accumulating wealth. From Marx's viewpoint, this "foundation" of nomadic life is the clue to its "superstructure" of law, government, and dominant ideas. Thus, Marx would say that those who are the largest owners of horses in such a nomadic society would also be the political chieftains who make and interpret the law; they are also likely to receive the highest respect and deference from the members of the tribe who own no horses. In the realm of ideas, the predominant social and cultural concepts would reflect the dominant economic position of the large owners of horses. Even in religion the impact would not be missing: God might, for instance, be represented in the image of a swift and powerful rider, and the concept of divine justice and rule would be, in a sense, an extension and magnification of human justice as determined by the horse-owning chiefs.

In a settled agricultural society, the ownership of *land* would provide the clue to the political, social, legal, and cultural institutions and conceptions. In such a society, according to Marx, the landowning class is the real ruler of state and society, regardless of any divergent *formal* organization of authority. Similarly, the landowning class would also set the predominant social standards and values.

Finally, according to Marx, *in the modern industrial society of the last two hundred years the ownership of the means of industrial production is the master key:* the capitalists not only determine the economic destiny of society, but also rule it politically (regardless of formal and legal façades to the contrary), and set its social standards and values. The ultimate purpose of the law, education, the press, and artistic and literary creation is to maintain an ideology that is imbued with the sanctity and justice of capitalist property relations.

Our understanding of history has gained immensely from Marx's economic interpretation. It is virtually impossible to write history today without some attention at least to the relation of economic forces and conflicts to political, military, and international issues.

Yet Marx's economic interpretation suffers from the same defect that afflicts all theories that pretend to supply the master key to history: *excessive generalization and simplification*. Whenever a single factor (be it the hero, war, religion, the climate, race, geography, and so forth *ad infinitum*) is required to do the work of explanation and illumination that more properly can be done only by several factors, its burden proves too heavy. No single factor has been predominant throughout history as a whole, and which factor is the most important in a particular situation is a question of empirical inquiry.

There is always a complicated pattern of many factors, and it is none too easy to disentangle them in any one concrete event or series of events. It is difficult enough to state precisely what the component motivations of an action of one person are, because one person's actions are often mutually contradictory and logically inconsistent. It is even more difficult to isolate the determinant components in a single action of a small group; and it is virtually impossible to generalize about large-scale collective actions and processes throughout the whole of history.

To take one practical illustration: the Marxist interpretation of *imperialism* is that it is primarily caused by economic interests and rivalries, and that war in the capitalist era is the culmination of such imperialist rivalries. There have undoubtedly been manifestations of imperialism in history, ancient as well as modern, whose origins can be traced to economic factors—some of the classical imperialist expansion of advanced capitalist nations like Holland, England, and France in the eighteenth and early nineteenth centuries may be traced chiefly to economic forces. It is also possible to find minor wars, in antiquity as in more recent times, that have been primarily motivated by economic interests and conflicts.

Yet the economic interpretation misses the core, where the great and vital conflicts of history are concerned.

The Greeks who fought Persia almost 2500 years ago did so not primarily to protect Athenian *investments* and trade interests in Asia Minor, but because they knew that the victory of Persia would mean the end of Greek civilization. Persian victory would undoubtedly have entailed serious economic and financial losses for the Greeks, but the main effect would have been the destruction of the *Greek way of life,* with its devotion to the search for truth and its appreciation of human values. Because the whole fabric of western civilization is unthinkable without its Greek source, Persian victory over Greece would have meant the spiritual and intellectual "Asianization" of Europe.

To take more recent illustrations, the core of the conflict in World Wars I and II was not the protection of British investments in Africa or of American loans to Britain and France, but the more fundamental issue of whether freedom—religious, intellectual, political, racial—was to survive, or whether totalitarian militarism was to rule the world. Again, there is no doubt that a German victory in World War I or II would have entailed profound economic losses for the vanquished, but the economic effects would have been relatively ~~or compared~~ with the effects of reverting to a way of life based ~~al denial of the western tradition.~~

~~resent conflict between communist imperialism and not be explained in Marxian economic terms, perialism is the last phase of an advanced and abundance of capital that it seeks to invest from the economic viewpoint, the Soviet hungry for capital, suffering from its Their imperialism is motivated by im of world domination by force. rmed might and fanatical ide- economic expansion, there ussian or Chinese imperi-~~

~~is a concern to the ist logic—its non- eapons are tanks and~~

subversion. The Hungarian Revolution of 1956 clearly showed that Soviet imperialism can ultimately rely only on tanks and guns, and not on economic, or much less ideological, penetration.

What the Marxist-communist interpretation misses in the analyses of such major conflicts is, first, the element of *power* (which is often the cause rather than the effect of economic advantage), and second, the clash of *value systems,* which are frequently more important to people than economic interests, regardless of whether the values concerned are specifically political, religious, intellectual, or—in a wider sense—the symbolic expression of a whole way of life.

In fact, where conflicts of interest are primarily economic, compromise will usually be relatively easy; it is where more deeply felt values are at stake, such as individiual liberty, freedom of religion, or national independence, that compromise becomes more difficult.

DYNAMICS OF SOCIAL CHANGE

Before Marx, basic social change was conceived of as largely the work of great political leaders, legislators, and pioneering reformers. Marx rejects the traditional emphasis on the force of personality as the principal agent of important social change, and looks for an explanation in impersonal economic causes. The two key concepts that Marx uses in approaching the problem of basic social change are, first, the *forces of production,* and second, the *relations of production.* The clash between these two is the deeper cause of b social change, as expressed by Marx in his *Critique of Political Economy* (1859): "At a certain stage of their development the m productive forces of society come into contradiction with the ing productive relationships, or, what is but a legal expres these, with the property relationships within which they ha before. From forms of development of the productive f relationships are transformed into their fetters. Then a social revolution opens. With the change in the economi the whole vast superstructure is more or less rapidly

The Marxist conception of the *forces of produc man's relation to nature,* and is essentially what we technological and scientific *know-how.* Marx's no *tions of production* expresses *man's relation to* passes all that we would include today under the term *social institutions*. Seen in these more modern terms, what Marx roughly suggests is that in every social-economic system there is at first a balance between knowledge and social organization, but gradually a disequilibrium or lag develops between available scientific knowledge and existent social institutions. *Our scientific knowledge grows faster than our social wisdom.*

This lag is the more modern, and broader, version of Marx's more specific lag between the forces of production and the relations of production. Since the economic aspects of society are for Marx its chief determining factor, it is not surprising that he reduces the general phenomenon of the lag between knowledge and wisdom to the more specific lag between forces of production and relations of production.

Thus, to provide an illustration in line with the Marxist pattern, when new productive forces developed within the productive relations of the feudal system, social revolution was, according to Marx, inevitable, because the productive relations of feudalism (property relations, market controls, internal customs and tariffs, monetary instability) did not permit the utilization of the newly developing productive forces of industrial capitalism.

The capitalist system, having run its cycle, now shows the same tendency to rigidity, Marx holds, and it is due to meet the same fate when its productive forces (the capacity to produce) have outstripped its productive relations (law of private property, production for private profit). Like the social systems preceding it, capitalism thus will eventually stand in the way of scientific knowledge and will not permit technological resources to be fully employed.

What has doomed all historically known forms of economic organization, according to Marx, is the fact that when new productive forces develop, the existing productive relations—i.e., the existing social institutions—stand in the way of their proper utilization. Each system thus eventually becomes wasteful in terms of the creative potentialities that have developed in its womb but are not permitted to be born and grow. Only public ownership of the means of production can, according to Marx, bring into existence a new system of productive relations based on production for common use rather than for private profit that will match the tremendous forces of production actually or potentially known to man. In other words, man's capacity to produce will find full expression only in a social system in which production is limited by scarce resources and incomplete knowledge, and not by such faulty social institutions as production for private profit based on the private ownership of the means of production.

Marx's insight that man's knowledge of physical nature ("forces of production") grows faster than his wisdom in creating social institutions ("relations of production") is highly important in understanding a vital source of social tension and conflict both within and between nations.

What distinguishes Marx from non-Marxists is his insistence that *basic social change*—caused by the excessive lag between advanced scientific knowledge and retrograde social institutions—can be brought about *only by revolution,* whereas non-Marxists affirm that the necessary changes can be effected by peaceful means.

REVOLUTION THE ONLY WAY OUT

In the *Communist Manifesto,* Marx explains why revolution is the only method of basic social transformation. When technological know-how ("forces of production") begins to outstrip the existing social, legal, and political institutions ("relations of production"), the owners of the means of production do not politely step aside to allow history to run its inevitable course. Since the ideology of the ruling class reflects the existing economic system, the owners of the means of production sincerely believe that the existing system is economically the most efficient, socially the most equitable, and philosophically the most harmonious with the laws of nature and the will of whatever god they venerate.

Marx penetratingly denies that the individual feudal landowner or industrial capitalist obstructs social change out of selfish greed: the resistance of the ruling class to change is so obstinate—making revolution finally inevitable—precisely because it identifies its own values with universally valid ones. The ruling class will therefore mobilize all the instruments of the legal, political, and ideological superstructure to block the growth of the forces that represent the potentially more progressive economic system. For this reason Marx states early in the *Communist Manifesto* that the "history of all hitherto existing society is the history of class struggles."

Marx could find no instance in history in which a major social and economic system freely abdicated to its successor. On the assumption that the future will resemble the past, the communists, as the *Communist Manifesto* says, "openly declare that their ends can be attained only by the forcible overthrow of all existing social conditions."

This is the crucial tenet of Marxism-Leninism, and the one that most clearly and irreconcilably distinguishes it from democracy.

Marx had no clear-cut notion of how the political transformation from capitalism to communism would come about. Though in the *Communist Manifesto,* as throughout most of his other statements on the problem, he believed in the need for revolution, he was occasionally less dogmatic. Speaking in 1872 at a public meeting in Amsterdam following the Congress of the International, Marx conceded that the working class can travel on different roads in its quest for power: "We know that we must take into consideration the institutions, the habits and customs of different regions, and we do not deny that there are countries like America, England, and—if I knew your institutions better I would perhaps add Holland—where the workers can attain their objective by peaceful means. But such is not the case in all other countries."

Marx never fully pursued the implications of this distinction, and the orthodox opinion of Marxism-communism has remained that fundamental social and economic change is impossible except by class war, violence, and revolution.

In the early eighteen thirties there occurred two major revolutions that Marx failed to appraise properly. In 1832, the passage of the Reform Act in England meant that the government of the nation would henceforth be shared by the aristocracy and the middle classes, with the weight constantly shifting in favor of the latter.

At about the same time, the Jacksonian revolution in the United States effected a similar peaceful shift in class power, by bringing the men from the backwoods into American politics and successfully challenging the supremacy of the gentlemen from Virginia and New England who had treated the government of the United States as their God-given preserve.

These changes in Britain and the United States were more than just political victories: they inaugurated a permanent shift in the distribution of social and economic power in both nations, the kind of basic change that Marx had in mind. When revolution swept all over Europe in 1848, England was spared, because the aims of the revolutions of 1848—winning for the middle class its proper share of social and political power—had already been peacefully obtained by the British middle class in 1832.

If Marx had accorded the political factor its due weight, if he had fully grasped the importance of the Reform Act in England and of the Jacksonian revolution in the United States, he might have realized that socialism, too, might be accomplished without violence in countries that possessed democratic traditions strong enough to absorb far-reaching social and economic changes without resorting to civil war. A recognition of the cultural and political factors in the equation of social change would have amounted, however, to a virtual abandonment of the central position of Marx: that history is the history of class wars, and that ruling classes always defend their positions to the bitter end.

When Marx allowed, occasionally, that in countries like England, the United States, or Holland violent revolution would be unnecessary in transforming capitalism into the classless proletarian society, it was obvious that what the three countries had in common was *political democracy,* supported by democratic habits and institutions in all kinds of human relations, whether political or not. Whether the range of Marx's exceptions should now be enlarged or not would thus depend on whether democracy has spread in the world since Marx's death.

In any case, Marx's concession that in a few politically advanced countries revolution might be unnecessary has always caused the communists a good deal of headache. Lenin took up the question in *State and Revolution* (1918), his best known and most influential political tract, claiming that by 1917 "this exception made by Marx is no longer valid," because England and the United States had developed bureaucratic institutions "to which everything is subordinated and which trample everything under foot." Between 1872 and 1917, both England and the United States broadened the suffrage, and moved steadily in the direction of more political and social reform. Only one year after Marx's death, a British Liberal leader, Sir

William Harcourt, stated in 1884 "We are all socialists now," indicating the acceptance of basic social and economic reform by all parties.

Since the plain historical record of the years 1872-1917 seemed to contradict Lenin's dogma, it was necessary to rewrite history. Far from admitting that England and the United States had moved toward more political and social democracy since 1872, Lenin maintained that both countries had become more repressive, authoritarian, and plutocratic. To Sir William Harcourt's "We are all socialists now," Lenin would have replied "You are all bloodthirsty militaristic lackeys of Wall Street."

Since 1917, the communist case has progressively become weaker. In the United States, there has been the peaceful revolution of social reform, which started early in the century with Theodore Roosevelt's Square Deal, was continued by Woodrow Wilson's New Freedom, and culminated in Franklin D. Roosevelt's New Deal.

In Britain, Lloyd George's "People's Budget" of 1909 gave the propertied classes a foretaste of things to come. In 1945, the victory of the Labor Party at the polls was more than a mere electoral triumph. Just as 1832 meant the incorporation of the middle classes into the government of the nation, 1945 meant the same thing for the working classes in Britain. Whether the Labor Party is henceforth in office or in opposition, the British working class is going to remain an active partner in the business of governing the nation.

In the light of these facts, the only way left open to communist interpretation is to rewrite history. In the communist mythology, the New Deal was not the revolt of the little man against Big Business, but a clever plot of Big Business to keep itself in power. Similarly, the communists deny that the British Labor Party is socialist, and claim that it is actually a front for the propertied classes.

The relentless communist insistence on revolution as the only way of basic social change violates Marxist doctrine in one central point. According to Marx, the conditions of man's existence determine his consciousness, and social change is therefore not the product of mere will and free choice. Where the conditions of society permit peaceful change from private to public ownership of the means of production, the use of force and subversion is, in a deeply Marxian sense, un-Marxian.

The communist dogma of universal revolution and dictatorship is in harmony with Marx's theory of consciousness only in societies in which the conditions of social and political life have created a general distrust in the possibility of peaceful change; it is out of harmony in nations whose democratic consciousness is the result, not of paper constitutions, but of the conditions of their existence. By insisting on universal revolution and dictatorship as the one and only method of change, communists in fact proclaim the un-Marxian doctrine that regardless of the historical, cultural, social, economic, and political conditions a uniform consciousness—the creed of communism—can be imposed everywhere by sheer force.

There is a similar dogmatism in reverse, maintained by anti-communist adherents of free enterprise, who would like to see it practiced in the whole world. They, too, violate elementary common sense and historical experience: Whether a society is likely to operate a capitalist economy is not a matter of pure logic and choice, but the result of historical environment, cultural heritage, social institutions, and political ideologies. Thus, in 1900 it would have been easy to predict that basic changes in Britain or the United States would occur without revolution, and that such changes would be accompanied by violence and revolution in countries like Russia or China.

At present, it is often possible to predict whether change will be possible with or without violence. Yet there are countries, such as Italy in Europe, or India in Asia, where prediction is difficult because the balance of democratic versus undemocratic habits and traditions is not easy to define. Clearly, in view of the fact that such border-line countries exist, no general prediction based on dogma—be it communist or anticommunist dogma—is likely to be accurate. Every prediction is a question of investigating each particular situation rather than of applying preconceived universal laws of development.

Usually, correct theory is a guide to effective policy, and faulty theory is punished by practical failure. Where the communist concept of revolutionary change is supported by the underlying facts of social and cultural development—as in the economically and politically backward areas of Europe, Asia, Africa, and South America—either communist revolution has succeeded, or else communist spearheads have penetrated the body politic in preparation for the conquest of power. Where the anticommunist position has been theoretically sound, where democratic conditions of existence make revolutionary change unappealing and unnecessary—as in

northwestern Europe, North America, Australia, New Zealand,
Uruguay, and Israel—anticommunist policy has been successful.

If the world today is divided into two, with one orbit led by the
United States and the other by the Soviet Union, this *political division* generally follows the division into *two ways of life:* in one
orbit, social change can be transacted more or less peacefully,
whereas in the other, human relations are not yet established on a
basis of consent. Where—as in Italy or India—these internal conditions are not clearly defined, the external political commitment is
uncertain also.

The Point IV program is the indirect method of the United States
to counteract communism by helping economically retarded nations,
so that they do not have to look to communist revolution as the way
out. Subversion, infiltration, and civil war are the communist methods of preventing underdeveloped societies from evolving peacefully
into more advanced social and economic conditions. If India, for
example, can show the backward areas throughout the world that
it can develop economically while retaining political liberty, it will
win the race with China for leadership in Asia. If India stagnates
economically, and China progresses, the communists will have convinced Asia that peaceful progress is impossible, and that totalitarian communism is the only road to economic and political-military
power.

ECONOMIC CONTRADICTIONS OF CAPITALISM

The end of capitalism will be brought about, Marx argues, not by
"subversive conspiracies" of professional revolutionaries, but by the
same inexorable laws of social development and change that destroyed previous systems. Marx uses, first, the "grave-digger" theory:
the more capitalism succeeds, the more capitalist enterprise is organized in *large-scale* units, and the more it inevitably creates its own
grave-digger: a class-conscious proletariat. Big Labor inevitably follows Big Business.

The capitalist class has no way of escaping the dilemma of rear-
ing its own destroyer as it goes along: the *law of the falling profit
rate* (which is not to be confused with the absolute *amount* of
profit) makes that impossible. Marx's prediction of the declining

profit rate was based on the assumption that, under the capitalist system of production, the entrepreneurial class would steadily accumulate more and more capital: the lessened scarcity of capital would then inevitably be reflected in the decline of the price (interest) and return (profit) of capital.

There can be no disagreement—because the facts speak too plainly—that the absolute amount of profits has risen immensely since Marx, and is constantly rising.

What about Marx's prediction that the *rate* of profit (and of interest) would go down because capital would become more abundant?

Here, too, the prediction has not come true. During the depression of the 1930's, the rates of profit and interest were low, and seemed to confirm Marx's forecast. Yet in the 1950's, as in earlier periods of prosperity, the rates of interest and profit have again reached new highs, thus disproving Marx.

Contrary to Marx, the facts of economic history do not support his "law of the falling profit rate." Marx made his erroneous prediction because he looked primarily at the *supply* side of capital: more and more capital is constantly created and accumulated in the capitalist system, and increased supply of a good leads to a lower price—provided the demand remains the same. Yet this is exactly what did not happen. The reason for the high interest rates (price of capital) in the 1950's is that, despite an all-time high in the supply of capital, the *demand for capital has grown even faster,* since too many companies simultaneously want fresh capital for the improvement, expansion, and building of productive facilities.

The price of capital (interest) or return of capital (profit) are subject to the classical economic law of supply and demand, and not to any predetermined Marxian law of constant decline. Whenever the demand for capital outruns the supply, the rate of interest goes up, and the price of capital behaves like any other price.

The reason Marx overlooked the importance of the demand side in the capital market was his expectation (and hope) that the capitalist system would gradually lose its vitality and growth, thus requiring less new capital for investment. This, however, has not happened.

Finally, Marx also underestimated the role of technological progress. Capitalism not only constantly produces more capital, but *more efficient capital*. More abundantly available capital therefore need not lead to lower rates of profit if the capital is more efficient.

In a stationary economy, in which there is little or no technological innovation, more capital might automatically lead to lower rates of profit and interest. In a progressive economy, in which the productivity of capital is constantly raised, profits and the rate of profit may go up, although the absolute amount of available capital is also rising.

Moreover, *technological innovation strengthens the demand side in the capital market,* because new technologies require large capital investments, thus counterbalancing the effects of increased capital on the supply side. As long, therefore, as capitalism will continue to progress technologically, the effects of increased capital resources will not, as Marx assumed, either depress the absolute volume of profit or the rate of profit.

Since Marx's main objection to capitalism was its inefficiency as well as its injustice, experience has contradicted his forecasts on that score, too. The per capita income in the United States is still about 5-6 times higher than in the Soviet Union. As to technological innovation, the capitalist countries still are the creators, and the communist, the borrowers and imitators.

Marx also stated that capitalists would seek to stem the impact of the law of the falling profit rate in two ways: first, they would constantly seek to "rationalize" industry, or make it technologically more efficient—this would eliminate the less efficient enterprises, and would lead to the *concentration of economic power,* large-scale industrial organization, and increasing proletarianization. Second, they would *invest capital in underdeveloped countries,* where the return for capital, or profit, is still very high. This device, Marx points out, only delays, but does not avert, the inevitable doom: in the colonial country, too, capital becomes increasingly more abundant, a native capitalist class develops, threatened by its own proletariat, and the law of the falling profit rate makes the imperialist solution of the capitalist dilemma at home unfeasible.

Another source of tension that undermines the vitality of the capitalist system, according to Marx, is *unemployment.* In Marx's own time, industry expanded at an enormous rate, and there was a chronic shortage of labor. Yet Marx foresaw that the maldistribution of wealth and income under capitalism would lead to periodical crises of unemployment. The depression decade of 1929-1939 seemed to confirm Marx's prediction, and there was severe unemployment right up to 1939, when the preparation for war gradually eliminated it.

After World War II, the growth of welfare state policies in the major capitalist countries led to the recognition of full employment as a primary social objective. Also, the cold war, followed by hot war in Korea, inevitably led to full employment based, to a considerable extent, on rearmament. Should the western liberal capitalist societies be freed some day from the burden of rearmament, it will be seen whether the lessons of Keynesian economics combined with the objectives of welfare state policies will suffice to banish the scourge of unemployment from free societies.

Marx also predicted that two other developments would disintegrate the capitalist system: the *concentration of economic power* and, as a direct result, the *increasing proletarianization* of society. There is little doubt that, compared with earlier stages of industrial development, the contemporary capitalist economy shows impressive features of concentration. Yet it is doubtful whether the tendency toward concentration in the capitalist system keeps on forever, or whether after a certain point the forces of competition begin to catch up with excessive concentration.

Also, Marx did not foresee that in advanced capitalist nations concentration of management might be mitigated by important counterforces: the spreading ownership of industry among large numbers of persons through the holding of shares of corporate businesses, and, second, the growing control of business managements by government, public opinion, and labor unions.

The Role of the Salariat

Marx's prediction of the inevitable proletarianization of society in a capitalist economy has been very largely disproved by events.

In the initial phases of industrial development, under capitalism or any other system, the industrial working class, Marx's "proletariat," constantly increases at the expense of artisans, landless peasants, and other social groups whose members seek employment in the expanding factories and mines. In a later and more advanced phase of industrial development, however, the *industrial working class* begins to *decline in proportion to the total population,* though it still continues to increase in absolute numbers. What Marx did not foresee was the enormous growth in an advanced economy that would create employment, but not of the proletarian type.

COMPOSITION OF THE LABOR FORCE IN THE UNITED STATES

By Occupation Group, 1910-1950

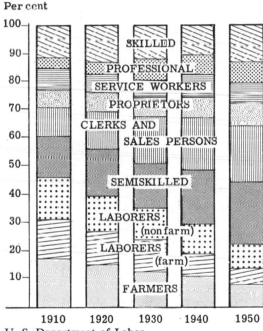

U. S. Department of Labor

In the United States, for example, the volume of industrial production and the number of persons employed in industry have increased tremendously since 1900, yet the proportion of the industrial working class in the total American population has consistently declined: we have seen in the last half century the development of a "salariat," men and women employed not in mines and steel plants (Marx's "proletariat"), but in the movie industry, radio and television, journalism, education, government, transportation, salesmanship, advertising, and the thousand and one new forms of service and entertainment directly flowing out of the worker's increase in leisure time over half a century.

In 1870, about 75 per cent of all workers were in industries producing physical goods. This percentage has gone down steadily over the years, and in 1955 only about 48 per cent of all workers were engaged in such industries. As the American economy becomes more productive, more and more people are engaged in "service industries" providing for the luxuries of life rather than for its bare necessities.

The accompanying charts illustrate the growth of the salariat and other changes in the composition of the American labor force in the years 1910-1950. Most striking are the proportionate doubling of clerical and sales persons from 10.2 per cent of the total labor force in 1910 to 20.2 in 1950, the sharp drop of the combined total of farm laborers and unskilled industrial laborers (Marx's "proletariat") from 29.2 per cent to 12.4 per cent, and the big increase of the proportion of semi-skilled and skilled workers from 26.4 per cent to 36.4 per cent. Politically, the latter is very important, because the skilled workers and foremen generally look upon themselves as middle-class, and tend to be more conservative in their political outlook. In 1956, 56 per cent of skilled workers voted Republican, but only 46 per cent of unskilled workers did so.

In line with the past trends of American economic development, the year 1955 was a milestone: for the first time in American history, or in that of any nation, the *number of persons engaged in the production of goods* was *smaller than the number of persons employed in the performance of services,* such as trade, finance, transportation, utilities, service industries, professions, and government.

If we assume that leisure time will continue to expand, that government activity is going to stay on a high plateau and probably will increase, that people will earn more and spend more, then it may be safely predicted that the changes in the American economy from 1950 to 1990 will be along similar lines as in the years 1910-1950. In that case, Marx's prediction about the proletarianization of the labor force will become even more untrue, since an increasingly larger proportion of the American labor force will be engaged in the performance of services rather than in the production of goods.

a philosophy of class hatred and war to remedy social injustices. Where democratic habits and institutions prevail, the underlying psychological tie in social relations is sympathy and affection; in such a climate, men and women are unwilling to accept a philosophy of hatred and violence, because it contradicts their daily experience of working things out by discussion and consent rather than by terror and intimidation.

Particularly in the United States, Marxism has proved itself a failure as far as wide popular appeal is concerned. In the last century the frontier seemed to many to offer utopia here and now, whereas the Marxian utopia lay in the distant future, separated from the present by a sea of blood. Also, Marxism has made little progress in the United States because it attacks not only the economic foundations of *capitalism*, but the very heart of American *democracy*.

In only two major countries did the ideas of Marx take root in the nineteenth century: Germany and Russia. Despite the façade of representative institutions, imperial Germany was in fact an autocracy that did not permit genuine government by the people. The Germans followed the philosophy of Hegel (although Marx claimed that he had turned Hegel upside down). Hegel had asserted that the *state* was an objective reality, and that its laws, like those of nature, were susceptible of being *understood*, but not *changed*, by man. Marx followed the cast of Hegel's thought by claiming that the laws of *society*, in respect to its nature and evolution, have the same scientific validity that Hegel had claimed for those of the state.

By contrast, the liberal philosophical tradition of the West rejects the Hegel-Marx conception that human reason can only understand the laws of the state and society, and affirms the possibility of rational control and creative change of social and political institutions. The experience of free government is the psychological background for an affirmative, activist philosophy, whereas the experience of autocratic government in Germany provided the psychological background for the determinism of Hegel and Marx. In an environment of social and political enslavement, man is prone to think of himself as small and helpless, and his emotional pattern will find philosophical expression in determinism. Such a philosophy assures him his own helplessness is not a personal misfortune, but a principle of order.

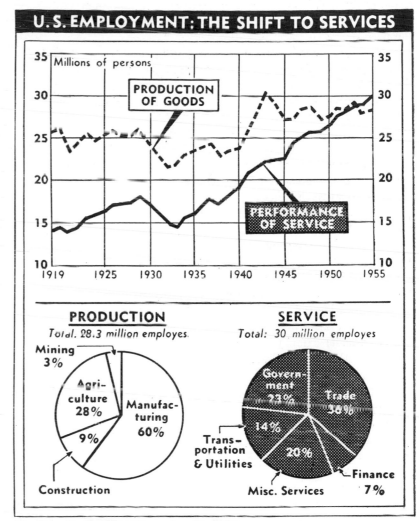

The New York Times (November 13, 1955)

Should the salariat continue to be the increasingly growing factor in the capitalist economy rather than the proletariat, then *time works against Marx,* as far as the social evolution of capitalism is concerned.

By contrast, where capitalism exists only in a rudimentary stage, as in the underdeveloped countries of Asia and Africa, the salariat is numerically and politically very weak, and communist infiltration stands a much better chance of success, as has actually happened in the past.

What is politically important in this development is that *the salaried person tends to identify himself with the middle and upper class rather than with the working class,* even if his income is below that of the worker. This is wholly contrary to Marx's expectations and predictions. Marx assumed—necessarily, from his interpretation of human action—that the transformation of the independent middle class into a dependent salaried class would automatically change the outlook of the old middle class from bourgeois to proletarian. Yet the new middle class of the salariat has generally refused to join the ranks of the organized working class.

This refusal has been particularly marked in societies with rigid class lines; but even in the United States, with its more fluid class lines, the salaried man (or woman) who earns $300 a month is generally politically more conservative than the wage earner who earns $100 a week or more. Because salary earners have failed to identify themselves psychologically with the working class, they have very largely remained outside the ranks of organized labor. In the United States, the labor movement has been able to organize the workers in industry and (to a lesser extent) in agriculture, but has found it very difficult to organize teachers, clerks, civil servants, and other groups of white-collar employees.

The political problems posed by the rise of the salariat are not confined to industrial development under capitalism; they also appear under communism. In its first phase of industrialization, Russia witnessed a tremendous growth of her industrial proletariat. But as the Soviet Union entered a second phase of industrialization, a new salariat began to develop, with a way of life of its own, and with its own ideas, ideas different from those of the working class. Because under communism the state has been so much more responsible for developing industry than under capitalism, the number of government workers and white-collar employees has increased proportionately faster than the number of factory workers.

Despite communist denials, class lines are beginning to crystallize in communist Russia and the other communist states, and one important line of differentiation is that between white-collar and factory worker, with little regard to differences of income. The influence

of the white-collar group ("intelligentsia" in Russia) is constantly rising at the expense of the working class, as can be seen in the changing social composition of Soviet political bodies, university students, and other key groups of social importance.

As long as the Soviet leaders adhere to Marxist-Leninist propaganda, they will find that time works against them, too, and that the slogans of Marxism-Leninism will not fit a society in which the white-collar class rather than the proletariat sets the style of life and thought. Thus a *class struggle* along orthodox lines is beginning to take shape *in communist societies* undergoing industrialization, and—as in capitalist countries—proletariat and salariat do not generally find themselves on the same side of the barricades.

The first explosions in the communist world took place in Czechoslovakia and Poland in the spring of 1953; they were followed by the major rebellion in Eastern Germany of June 17, 1953, the uprising of Polish workers in Poznan in June, 1956, the Hungarian Revolution of October-November, 1956, and the victory of "national communism" in Poland late in 1956.

The driving force of rebellion in all these instances was not the bourgeois middle class, as might have been expected from the prophecies of Marxism-Leninism, but the industrial workers, could no longer bear the ruthless exploitation by the communist in the party and government.

This kind of class war—proletariat against salariat— foreseen by Marx and Lenin, and communists today can it intelligently and effectively, because they must existence as incompatible with their dogma

LENIN'S CONTRIBUTION TO THE COMMUNISM

The nature and deeper meaning of quently be inferred from their appea of western Europe and the United lution as preached by Karl Marx liberal tradition in those count change. Although many soci Marx's indictments of cap

In nineteenth-century Russia, conditions for the acceptance of Marxian ideas were even more favorable than in imperial Germany. Whereas the latter paid homage to virtue by at least adopting the forms and formalities of representative institutions, Russian tsarism long recoiled even from such hypocrisy, on the ground that pretenses, if practiced long enough, might too easily turn into second nature.

Of all major states in Europe, Russia was easily first in illiteracy, economic backwardness, religious obscurantism, oppression of minorities, political despotism, and social inequality. Marx's prophecy, clothed in language of scientific magic, of the eventual liberation of man from bondage and oppression through revolutionary action made a strong impression on Russian radicals. *Das Kapital*, Marx's *magnum opus,* was translated into Russian before any other language; oddly enough, the tsarist censorship permitted the publication of the work on the ground that it would not be read by many because of its difficult style.

Among the Russian followers of Marx, Lenin (1870-1924) was both the leading theoretician and the most agile and effective practical politician.

Lenin's contribution to the theory of communism, perhaps the only one he made, is to be found in his pamphlet, *What Is To Be Done?* (1902).

Just as Hitler openly revealed his intentions to the world in *Mein Kampf,* without being believed until it was too late, Lenin has left in his writings, from *What Is To Be Done?* down to his death, an accurate blueprint of communist goals and the strategy and tactics to achieve them. Much discomfort and sorrow could have been spared the world if the basic ideas of Lenin had been more widely known and accepted at their face value.

Lenin's most important single contribution to the theory of Marxism is his concept of the *professional revolutionary.*

Marx, tinged by nineteenth-century respect for man's capacity to think for himself, had assumed that the working class would *spontaneously* develop its class-consciousness in the daily struggle for economic existence, and that its leadership would largely come from its own ranks. Lenin had much less confidence in man, even if he belonged to the select class, the proletariat. Communist activity, said

Lenin, is to be carried on along two lines. First, workers are to form labor organizations with primarily economic objectives, operating openly, legally, and as publicly as conditions allow.

Side by side with such organizations, there are to be small groups of professional revolutionaries, patterned after the army and the police, highly select and entirely secret. Lenin did not care whether the professional revolutionary was of proletarian origin or not, as long as he did his job well. The organizations of the professional revolutionaries must be highly centralized, Lenin went on, and must con-

"FELLOW-COMRADES AND UNDERCOVER AGENTS OF THE F.B.I. . . ."

stantly guide and supervise the open communist-led economic associations—the trade unions, the cooperatives, and the rest.

In particular, Lenin advised the professional revolutionaries to *infiltrate* and form cells in all existing social, political, educational, and economic bodies in society, be they schools, churches, labor unions, or political parties. Above all, Lenin advised professional revolutionaries to infiltrate the *armed forces,* the *police,* and the *government.*

Lenin also made it perfectly clear that communists should engage in *illegal* work even where legal communist parties are permitted.

Legal opportunities should be utilized to the fullest extent, in his opinion; he specifically advised communist activists to work through *front organizations,* constantly changing names and officers or organizations, but always keeping the ultimate objective in mind: revolutionary seizure of power.

In particular, the secret nucleus of professional revolutionaries is responsible for the recruitment and training of spies, saboteurs, and agents for all other activities relating to intelligence, foreign and domestic. When the name of Gerhart Eisler was first mentioned in the United States in 1947, his name was unknown, not only to the general public, but even to communists. Yet Eisler had been the secret head of the American communists for years, and he was in charge of the legal party activities as well as of the illegal activities. The official head of the party, William Z. Foster, was just a figurehead whose main function was to divert the attention of the public and the government from the real leadership and its activities.

When the Canadian spy ring was broken up in 1945, it was established that several secret communist spy rings, each independent of the others, operated in Canada, under the leadership of professional revolutionaries, many of whom had little connection with official, legal communist party activities.

From the testimony of former communist agents it is evident that one of the first things a recruit into the inner ring of communist leaders has to do is to break all connection with overt communist party or front groups, stop reading the party press, and lead the life of a solid, respectable bourgeois. There are bridges between the legal communist parties and the inner rings of spies and agents of the professional revolutionaries, since necessity often compels the choice of such agents from party ranks; ideally, however, the two sets of organizations are to be kept separate. Therefore what appears as the overt leadership of communist parties is but a front for bosses à la Eisler, men who are unknown to the public and even to the ostensible communist leaders in many cases, and who report directly to Moscow.

Outlawing the communist party is therefore no answer to the problem of how to deal with communism, because the hard core of communist leadership and activity is always underground, even when the law permits communist parties to operate above ground. And since there are always some links between the legal party and the inner nucleus of the professional revolutionaries, from a counter-espionage viewpoint a legally functioning party is an asset, small as it may be. It is for this reason that J. Edgar Hoover, director of the Federal Bureau of Investigation, opposed the outlawing of the Communist Party of the United States.

COMMUNIST DOCTRINE AND POLICY TODAY

Since Lenin's death in 1924, there has been no new addition or modification of basic Marxist-Leninist thought. Stalin, who ruled Russia from 1924 to his death in 1953, was stronger in practical administration and organizational ability than in theorizing. Most of Stalin's writings are but a rehash of Marx and Lenin, adapted to the momentary needs of his dictatorship. The core of the Stalinist summary of communist long-term strategy, also followed by his successors today, consists in the concept of the *four basic tensions* underlying our present-day world:

(1) The tension between capitalists and proletarians everywhere
(2) The tension between imperialist states and colonies
(3) The tension between rival imperialist states
(4) The tension between communist states and capitalist states

This conception of the four basic tensions, far from being a mere exercise in semantic classification, actually provides a clear blueprint for communist strategy and tactics. It is virtually impossible to open a newspaper without seeing some evidence of communist application of these concepts to practical issues and policies.

(1) The *tension between capitalists and proletarians* is the classical conception of Marxism, and goes back to Marx's contradiction between forces of production and relations of production. Capitalism today represents in communist propaganda the forces of production, the technological and scientific know-how, which cannot be fully utilized under the capitalist system of production for profit. The proletariat represents symbolically the relations of production, a new set of social institutions to be fully established after the overthrow of capitalism, allowing for the fullest use of all available knowledge and resources in a communist economic system, in which social institutions will aid, and not hamper, the productive process.

The great depression of 1929-1933 convinced the communists that capitalism is in a state of hopeless decay, and that the tension between actual production under capitalism and productive capacity under a communist organization of the economy must ultimately lead to a revolutionary solution. When after World War II a major economic crisis failed to materialize in the capitalist world, particularly in the United States, communists began to doctor facts and figures to prove that the prevailing prosperity was actually a depression, and that a really big depression was around the corner. Communist propagandists have been predicting a major depression for the capitalist world since 1946, and it stands to reason that eventually they may be right (very like the man who tenaciously predicted snow from July on, until he was finally proved right in December).

The main concern of communists with the tension between capitalists and workers is *political,* not economic.

Thus, in formulating a policy for a strike, a communist will ask himself one primary question: will it aid the cause of the communist revolution? The welfare of the particular group of workers involved is secondary to the over-all objective of serving communism.

When Russia was a friendly nonbelligerent on the side of Nazi Germany in 1939-1941, the communists fomented strikes in Britain and the United States, not to help British or American workers, but to paralyze production in Britain and the United States, the two main opponents of Nazi Germany. The moment Russia was drawn into World War II by the German attack on June 22, 1941, communists everywhere opposed strikes as treason, exhorted workers to work 60, 70, and 80 hours a week, and called everybody a fascist who sought to protect the rights of the workers against the demand for all-out production.

Some trade unions in Britain and the United States for a long time failed to understand that communist zeal and devotion to unions had little to do with genuine concern for the workers' welfare, but was primarily a vehicle to further communist objectives.

Unions have fought for over two generations against company unions; they now refuse to be dominated by a new type of company union boss—the communist union leader who represents the Soviet Union rather than the workers in his own country. As a result, there has been a thorough housecleaning of communists in most labor unions in this country and in Britain in the last few years.

In the Soviet Union itself, the nature of labor unions as company unions is most clearly evident: the official task of Soviet labor unions is not to defend the interests of the workers against their employer, the state, but to impose the decisions of the boss, the state, on the workers. Strikes are, of course, illegal.

(2) The *tension between imperialist states and colonies,* although mentioned by Marx, was more clearly elaborated by Lenin, who lived in an age of colonial rebellions. When communists speak of colonies, they refer not only to territories legally dependent upon another state, but also to small, weak states that are in fact dominated by stronger ones. From the communist viewpoint, most states in Latin America and the Middle East are colonial, although they are formally independent and sovereign. The communist strategy is always to help the colonial or weaker state against the western imperialist state, the main objective being to weaken the latter and thus create a vacuum of power in the backward area. All over the globe communists take up the cause of anti-imperialist struggle, as long as the imperialists are British, French, or American rather than Russian or Chinese.

Also, communists approach colonial tensions from a long-range viewpoint rather than in the light of the immediate interests of local communist parties. Thus, in Iran the ultranationalist dictatorship of Mossadegh was supported by Moscow until his downfall in 1953, despite his anticommunism, because he sought to oust Britain and the United States from any sphere of influence in that oil-rich country. In Argentina, the fascist dictatorship of General Perón was also endorsed by the Kremlin until his overthrow in 1955, because he was anti-British and anti-American.

Finally, in more recent years the Soviet Union has showered Colonel Nasser, the militarist dictator of Egypt, with arms and all forms of diplomatic support, although the communist party is outlawed in Egypt. This is a minor consideration to the Soviet government, as compared with the fact that Nasser is bent on wiping out any trace of western influence not only in Egypt but in the whole Near and Middle East.

The communist line in all these cases is simple: whatever hurts the influence or prestige of the western powers is good for world communism, although local communists may have to take this long-term view from prison cells. An ultranationalist, anticommunist, fascist-type regime in a backward or weak state is looked upon by Moscow as but a prelude to communization, provided American or British influence can be kept out of the picture. Communist support for anticommunist regimes in weak states makes perfect sense in the light of long-range communist objectives.

It would be unwise, however, to underestimate the weapon the communists have in their hand when they exploit the slogan of anti-imperialism for their purposes. In Asia and Africa, the two main areas of imperialist domination and spheres of influence, imperialism has been traditionally identified with the West (Britain, France, Holland, and the United States); although the western nations have been recently repenting and reforming, granting independence to their colonies or dependencies (Philippines, India, Burma, Pakistan, Ceylon, Indonesia, Tunisia, Morocco, Indochina, Ghana, and Malaya), such repentance and reform come at a late date in the eyes of impatient Asians or Africans. The communist propagandists harp on the sins of the past, and the colonial peoples have a longer memory of their sufferings than do those who have perpetrated them. Also, a major asset of communist anti-imperialist propaganda is the fact that western imperialism is a matter of experience, often bitter experience, to colonial peoples, whereas Russian or Chinese imperialism is unknown to them.

Paradoxically, as communist power spreads in Asia and other backward areas, it carries in itself a virus of immunization, because communist reality so patently belies communist words. Thus, many Indians were rudely jarred from their neutralist feelings about communism when they discovered one morning that Tibet, a state bordering on India, had been occupied by a communist army, and that the borders of India were henceforth under the direct surveillance of communist forces. On the issue of Korea, too, India's neutralist viewpoint was markedly shaken when Indian troops had direct contact with communists in administering the provisions of the armistice of 1953.

Finally, Russian brutality in suppressing the Hungarian Revolution in 1956 shocked many Asians into a rude awakening from neutralist pipe dreams. As the representative of Burma put it during the debate of the Russian intervention in Hungary at the United Nations in November, 1956: "Here, but for the grace of God, go we."

India and China now lead the struggle for the soul of Asia, and indirectly of all backward countries. China is following the Russian totalitarian system, whereas India is trying to combine political democracy with a program of rapid economic development.

If India succeeds, world communism will lose a decisive battle. If India bogs down in a quagmire of lassitude, corruption, and economic stagnation, the field may well be clear for communism in India, to sweep from there to the rest of Asia. In her first five-year plan, Red China spent 44 per cent of total investment on industrial development, and only 8 per cent on raising the supply of consumer goods, such as food, clothing, and housing. By contrast, in India's first five-year plan, 44 per cent of the total investment went into increased produc- tion of consumer goods, and only 14 per cent on increased industrial production. If this ratio should keep up for the next twenty or thirty years, India may well lose the economic race with China, although India is receiving billions in gifts, loans, and investments from the outside, mostly the United States, and China is not.

Politically, communism is still held in balance as long as India firmly adheres to democratic government. Yet in her foreign policy India has so far missed the chance of becoming the leader of the underdeveloped countries of the free world. During the Suez crisis of October-November, 1956, India was in the forefront of attacking Britain and France as aggressors, and she sided consistently with the Soviet bloc and the extremist members of the Asian-African group. Yet, when the issue of Russian aggression against Hungary came up at the same time, the first reaction of Prime Minister Nehru was that this aggression was essentially a civil war. It was only after a revulsion of public sentiment in India against this pro-Soviet attitude that the Indian government changed its tune—but only slightly. On November 9, 1956, the General Assembly of the United Nations passed a resolu- tion denouncing Russian intervention in Hungary, demanding that Soviet troops withdraw, and calling for free elections in Hungary. India was the only non-communist country to vote against the resolution.

Throughout the whole debate on Soviet intervention in Hungary at the United Nations in November and December of 1956, India was the most effective ally of the Soviet bloc, losing its potential leader- ship of non-communist Asian and African nations. By contrast, smaller Asian nations like the Philippines, Burma, and Ceylon took a vigorous stand against Soviet aggression, thus demonstrating that moral leadership in free Asia was moving away from India.

If India, with a population of 350 million, should ever go communist, the balance of world power would gradually, and irretrievably, shift to communism. In the general elections of 1952, the Indian Communist Party polled only 3.3 per cent of the popular vote; in the elections of 1957, this figure rose to an alarming high of 8.9 per cent, and the Communist Party was able to take over control of one state, Kerala, with a population of 14 million. Thus, Nehru's policy of coddling communism in world affairs was reflected in a substantial increase of communist strength in India itself.

Before China went communist, the impact of such a change was not understood in advance and too little was done to prevent it. With the example of China before them, the United States and Great Britain are awakening to the key position of India in the world struggle.

(3) The *tension between rival imperialist states* goes back to Marx's theory of the decay of capitalism. When the rate of profit falls because of large accumulation of capital relative to the labor force, the capitalist looks for profitable employment of capital outside of his own country, and finds such opportunities in backward countries, countries in which capital is very scarce and labor abundantly available. However, as time goes on, investment opportunities in backward areas constantly shrink, and capitalists then look to their governments for aid. According to the Marxist-communist doctrine the capitalist state is but the executive committee of the propertied classes, and therefore the flag willingly and eagerly follows trade. As capitalists from several countries collide in the same zone of influence and expansion, their governments become involved in a struggle for power.

War under capitalism is thus viewed by communists as a clash between rival imperialist forces motivated by the quest for economic expansion. World Wars I and II are interpreted by communists in this fashion, although if England was so anxious to preserve her commercial position in 1914, the communists have never explained why she did not go to war with the United States, which by 1914 had attained first place in industrial——and inevitably political and military——power. In 1939, American supremacy in industry, finance, and the resulting ability to wage war had become even more obvious, and communists again find it difficult to explain on Marxist grounds why

England and France chose to fight Germany rather than the United States.

Speaking on February 9, 1946, at a so-called "election" meeting in Moscow, Stalin reiterated the old communist argument that World War II was "the inevitable result of the development of world economic and political forces on the basis of modern monopoly capitalism." Yet at the same time Stalin deviated from orthodox communist dogma by conceding that World War II was from the very outset "an antifascist war, a war of liberation, one of the aims of which was also the restoration of democratic liberties." Stalin also called the war one between "freedom-loving nations" (Britain, France, the United States, the Soviet Union) and the Axis states (Germany, Japan, Italy), who were "out for world domination and the establishment of a fascist regime throughout the world."

Stalin was apparently unaware that the main issue could be either that of rival capitalist imperialist states, as viewed by a Marxist, or that of national liberty versus fascist enslavement, as viewed by a non-Marxist; in the latter case, it mattered little whether the victims of fascist aggression were capitalist or communist. However, Stalin never relapsed into that kind of deviation again; early in 1946, there was still hope for a temporary understanding between Russia and the West, and therefore communist dogmatism was less rigid than it usually is.

After 1946, as soon as the cold war between Russia and the West started, communist spokesmen fell back into the old dogma that war in the era of capitalism is always the result of clashing imperialistic interests. On September 28, 1952, Stalin emphasized before the 19th Congress of the Communist Party that the old theory of the *inevitability of war between capitalist countries* still held good and had to be followed by party members.

Whereas the British and American peoples look upon their mutual alliance as the strongest protection of peace and the most powerful coalition in any possible conflict, Stalin specifically stressed that Britain and France would some day enter into conflict with the United States, in order "to secure an independent position and, of course, high profits."

Although this assumption may seem unrealistic to noncommunists, communists not only believe in it but base their policy on it. Because they do not believe that capitalist states can work together peacefully and amicably, communists exploit existing tensions and create new tensions between capitalist states. Thus in Britain the main communist propaganda slogan is that America will fight to the last Englishman, whereas in the United States the communists ask why American boys should die for the preservation of the British Empire. In France, the communists have managed to exploit the issue of wine versus Coca-Cola as one of French national independence versus American imperialism; if the communists find themselves unable to promote military conflict between the capitalist nations, at least they are trying their best to create dissension and confusion.

The successful creation of NATO (North Atlantic Treaty Organization) has been a thorn in the flesh of world communism not only because of its military value against communist aggression, but also because the very existence of NATO belies the communist myth that capitalist states cannot collaborate for common objectives. Similarly, Soviet Russia suffered another major diplomatic defeat in 1955 when the rearmament of Western Germany, and her inclusion in NATO, were ratified in both Bonn and Paris. This was done despite Soviet promises and threats, following the customary totalitarian policy of "divide and conquer."

By contrast, the disunity between the United States and her French and British allies over the Suez issue and the whole problem of peace in the Middle East was one of the great successes of Soviet diplomacy, starting with the seizure of the Suez Canal by Dictator Nasser in July, 1956. The disunity between the United States and her Western European allies has enabled Russia to become firmly entrenched in the Middle East for the first time in her history.

(4) The *tension between communist and capitalist states* is increasingly recognized by communists to be the most important of all. Marx had never given much thought to the question of co-existence between capitalist and communist states. He thought in terms of conflict as the vehicle of social development, but his concept of conflict related to domestic class struggles. Being steeped in nineteenth-century economic optimism, Marx may have hoped that tensions between states would eventually be resolved through economic means. Lenin and Stalin, however, faced with the realities of governing the first communist state and spearheading what they considered to be a world revolution, gave a great deal of thought to the question of how communist and capitalist states can get along in one world.

As far back as 1924, when Russia was still on the defensive and struggling for her very existence, communist leaders developed a doctrine that was not taken seriously in the West, but that accurately anticipated future policies. In his *Foundations of Leninism* (1924), Stalin says that the world is divided into two hostile camps, "the world front of imperialism" and the "common front of the revolutionary movement in all countries." In particular, Stalin affirms that in the present stage of capitalism "wars cannot be averted," and he urges a *coalition between communist states in Europe and colonial revolutionaries in Asia,* such as the Soviet Union later practiced in China, Indochina, Malaya, and Korea.

In 1924, Stalin considered the Soviet Union as the "base for the overthrow of imperialism in all countries," and this idea of the *Soviet Union as the first phase of the inevitable communization of the world* has since then guided Soviet long-term strategy. In *Problems of Leninism* (1926) Stalin quoted with enthusiastic approval the following statement by Lenin: "We are living not merely in a state, but in a *system of states;* and it is inconceivable that the Soviet Republic should continue to exist for a long period side by side with imperialist states. *Ultimately one or the other must conquer."* Stalin also frequently quotes the Leninist statement that the Soviet Union should "attract to itself the oppressed classes of other countries, raising revolts in those countries against the capitalists, and in the event of necessity coming out even with armed force against the exploiting classes and their governments."

Occasionally Stalin seems to have contradicted the concept of inevitable war by admitting the possibility and even desirability of peaceful coexistence between communist and noncommunist states. Yet it must be recalled, if communist doctrine and policy are to be properly appraised, that such statements by Stalin were made—on not very many occasions—in interviews granted to foreign politicians and journalists, and were unquestionably intended as propaganda rather than as a serious statement of policy. By contrast, his doctrine of inevitable war between communism and capitalism was addressed to his home public, and is contained in his basic writings, writings printed in hundreds of millions of copies in the Soviet Union and far more easily accessible to the Soviet citizen than accounts in American papers of Stalin's talks with H. G. Wells, Roy Howard, Harold Stassen, and all the others who wanted to know of Stalin whether he believed in peace or not. They might as well have asked him whether he believed in loving one's mother.

With a slight dash of humor, Stalin held out one hope for the capitalist states. War is not inevitable, if the capitalist countries are willing to *surrender voluntarily* without resisting communization. Stalin wrote that communism may spread to so many countries that the remaining capitalist states will realize the hopelessness of resistance, and that "encirclement" by communist states will make voluntary surrender "expedient." Put another way, the alternative to enforced slavery is voluntary slavery.

Before World War II was over, Stalin betrayed every pledge he had made to establish democracy in eastern and southeastern Europe. With the help of the Red Army, communist regimes were set up in Rumania, Bulgaria, Hungary, Poland, and Eastern Germany. Leaders of proven democratic background and loyalty were imprisoned, exiled, or killed. In China and Indochina, communist revolutions were supported, with complete success in the former, and with partial success in the latter. In Greece, the communists started a civil war in December 1944, which ended in communist defeat after Yugoslavia broke with Moscow in the summer of 1948. In Malaya and the Philippines, communist guerilla forces fought for years against the established regimes, causing much bloodshed and devastation. In France and Italy, the communists tried to stage general strikes on several occasions, presumably with the ultimate intent of transforming industrial strife into civil war.

In the Balkans and eastern Europe, the communists argued that there had never been political democracy, and that the real choice lay between fascist totalitarianism and communist dictatorship. If such flimsy propaganda had any effect on noncommunists for some time, its value was completely destroyed in Czechoslovakia in February 1948. Although the Soviet Union used the Czechoslovakian Communist Party as its tool, here was the first case of the subjugation of a truly democratic nation to communist dictatorship by armed force, represented by the threat of the Red Army, standing on the borders of Czechoslovakia ready to intervene. Following Hitler's footsteps, Stalin repeated Hitler's technique of conquest. Just as Hitler's seizure of Prague was the beginning of his end, bringing about a rude and rapid awakening of the British and French governments and a determination on the part of those governments to resist further aggression, so the communist seizure of Prague in 1948 may someday be considered as the fatal blunder of world communism, the move from which its decline and downfall must be dated. For it was the communist seizure of Czechoslovakia that gave the prime impulse to the formation of the North Atlantic Treaty Organization, and that speeded up tremendously the rate of rearmament in the western nations, particularly in the United States.

Above all, the communist aggression in Czechoslovakia showed that the only argument the communists respected was force. It was partly because of the Czechoslovakian experience that the United States, joined by many other members of the United Nations, determined to resist armed communist aggression in Korea in 1950 by force.

After the death of Stalin in 1953, Nikita Khrushchev, First Secretary of the Communist Party of the Soviet Union, gradually emerged as Stalin's successor, the chief spokesman of the Soviet regime in domestic and foreign affairs. In a major address before the Twentieth Congress of the Soviet Communist Party on February 14, 1956, Khrushchev stated that Soviet foreign policy was guided by the following five principles: peaceful coexistence; nonaggression; noninterference in internal affairs of other nations; mutual respect for territorial integrity and sovereignty; and equality and mutual benefit. In addition, Khrushchev declared that communization of noncommunist nations need *not always* be carried out *by force,* particularly where this could be done by parliamentary majorities. Significantly, no country has ever gone communist as a result of free elections.

Khrushchev's acceptance of the principle of peaceful coexistence suggested to many that communism had abandoned its objective of world revolution and world conquest, and that post-Stalin communism would be different from Stalin's foreign policy. Some optimists in the West went even so far as to hail Khrushchev's address as a "dawn of liberalism" in the Soviet Union.

Yet only nine months later, in October and November of 1956, the dawn of Soviet liberalism turned into the nightmare of the Hungarian tragedy.

Immediately after the Hungarian Revolution was suppressed, Krushchev had this to say to a group of Western diplomats at a diplomatic reception in Moscow on November 18, 1956: "Whether you like it or not, history is on our side. *We will bury you.*"

On January 1, 1957, Khrushchev returned again to this issue. "The imperialists call us Stalinists," he said in Moscow. "Well, when it comes to fighting imperialism, *we are all Stalinists.*" Made at a large gathering of diplomats, this statement clearly indicated that Stalin's "hard line" of keeping and expanding Soviet power in the world by brute force would continue to guide Soviet policy under the new rulers as it did under Stalin.

SOCIAL-ECONOMIC CHANGES UNDER COMMUNISM

The first major attack in this century against the established social order occurred in Russia toward the end of World War I. The tsarist regime was overthrown in a bloodless revolution in March 1917, and it seemed as if Russia would have the opportunity to develop democratic institutions for the first time in her history.

The majority of the Russians wanted political liberty as well as fundamental social change. Inexperienced in the conduct of public affairs, however, and failing to understand the true nature and goals of communism, the new, democratic government of Alexander Kerensky allowed the Bolsheviks, led by Lenin and Trotsky, to subvert, and quickly destroy, the new democratic state.

Between March 1917 and November 1917, the Bolsheviks (the party was not known as the Communist Party until 1919) used three classical methods of gaining power, methods they were to repeat later in almost identical fashion in other countries.

First, they presented themselves in their propaganda as a people's party, dedicated to liberty, democracy, and social justice and opposed to all forms of reaction and social injustice. In an agrarian country like Russia, the communists played up, in particular, the need for agrarian land reform, and encouraged the seizure of land by the peasants even before they were in control of the government. A generation later the Chinese communists proclaimed themselves (and were believed by many to be) no more than "agrarian reformers," thus following the pattern of propaganda established by the Russian communists in 1917.

The second technique the Bolsheviks employed was to *infiltrate* other political parties as well as trade unions, soldiers' councils, and local government authorities. In particular, the communists managed to infiltrate, and gradually disrupt, the Social Revolutionaries, the largest party in Russia, dedicated to political democracy and social reform and especially concerned with the question of the peasants. This technique of infiltration was again employed by the communists during and after World War II, when they tried to take over socialist parties in a number of countries. Their most notable successes in that endeavor were in Italy and, to a lesser extent, in Czechoslovakia.

The third method used by the Bolsheviks in their revolution was *force*. In free elections in the summer and fall of 1917, the Bolsheviks polled about one-quarter of the total vote. Though this represented a far from negligible proportion, considering their fanaticism and frenzied activity, the Bolsheviks accepted the fact that in a free election they could not hope to win. In November 1917, therefore, the Bolsheviks seized the key positions of power in Moscow, and from there the revolution quickly spread all over Russia. Opposition to the communist revolution sprang up spontaneously in various parts of the country, and a civil war ensued that lasted until 1921.

The ravages of World War I, followed by the devastations of the civil war, made immediate social reform impracticable. Lenin was realistic enough to see that the Russian people would literally starve to death if communist principles were imposed at that time. As a result, he inaugurated in 1921 the New Economic Policy, which permitted limited private ownership; this policy's main objective was to maintain and increase production on the farms and in the workshops and factories, by retaining the old capitalist incentives of efficiency and profit. The application of the NEP for about seven years gave Russia a breathing spell, allowing the communist rulers to consolidate their power more effectively and giving the Russian people the temporary illusion that the bark of communism was worse than its bite.

But in 1928 Stalin decided that the time had come to put communist principles into practice, and he withdrew the temporary concessions earlier made by Lenin (who died in 1924). The First Five Year Plan, starting in 1928, aimed primarily at the rapid industrialization of Russia and secondarily at the collectivization of farming. In 1917 many peasants had sympathized with Bolshevism, not for reasons of theory or ideology, but because the Bolsheviks promised them the land they and their ancestors had tilled and coveted for centuries.

The reasons that motivated Stalin to force collectivization on the peasants were manifold. First, the communist rulers felt that agricultural production would be raised by mechanizing it, and that mechanization could be more easily effected in large-scale, collectivized farms than on small, individually owned ones. Second, individual ownership and operation of farms was a basic denial of a key principle of communism, namely that all means of production be transferred to public ownership. Collectivization would bring agriculture in line with industry, which was developed from the start on the basis of state ownership and operation. Third, the communist rulers saw in continued individual farm ownership a direct political and psychological threat to the acceptance of totalitarian political direction from the center.

The independent peasant had to be transformed into a dependent agricultural proletarian; as a member of a collective farm, the peasant was constantly working with others, talking to others, eating with others, and he could thus be more easily supervised and regimented.

Another reason behind collectivization was the need for labor for the newly developing industries in the cities; the required labor force could be obtained only by mechanizing agriculture and thus saving human labor. Finally, collectivization had an important military objective: in case of war, the collectives were to provide the nucleus for organized resistance behind the lines. In World War II, these military expectations were largely fulfilled: the Germans were never completely able to suppress Russian guerilla activities behind their lines.

The cost of fundamental social and economic change in Russia was heavy. In the process of collectivizing the farms in the years 1929-1933 between four and five million peasants lost their lives or were uprooted from their homes and deported to slave labor camps in Siberia or the Arctic. To show their resistance to collectivization, the peasants slaughtered as much livestock as they could, so that at the end of collectivization livestock had greatly decreased in numbers. The number of cattle in the Soviet Union was 67 million in 1928, 48 million in 1940, 57 million in 1953, and 67 million in 1955. Of the cattle, cows numbered 33 million in 1928, 23 million in 1940, 24 million in 1953, and 29 million in 1955. During the same period of 1928-1955, the Soviet population increased by 50 million, from 150 to 200 million. Fewer cows for more people means less milk, butter, and cheese per person.

In fact, Russia is one of the few countries in the world in which standards of food consumption today are lower than in 1913, before World War I. Between 1913 and 1955, Russian food production per head increased 8 per cent for grain, 40 per cent for potatoes, and 113 per cent for beets. By contrast, the production per head between 1913

Reprinted from *U. S. News & World Report,* an independent weekly news magazine published at Washington (July 3, 1953). Copyright (1953) United States News Publishing Corporation.

and 1955 declined by 8 per cent for eggs, 21 per cent for meat, and 27 per cent for milk. Advancing living standards usually show a shift from bread, potatoes, and beets to high-quality foods like milk, butter, meat, and eggs. The Russian pattern of food consumption between 1913 and 1955 shows unmistakable decline and impoverishment of the masses of the people.

By contrast with Soviet figures on livestock, there were 57 million cattle in the United States in 1928, and 97 million in 1955. Of the cattle, there were 22 million cows in the United States in 1928, and 35 million in 1955. As a result, per capita consumption of high-quality foods went up considerably in the United States in the period of 1928 to 1955: meat by 23 per cent, and eggs by 20 per cent. As to lower-quality foods: per capita consumption in the United States declined during 1928-1955 as follows: potatoes, by 35 per cent; wheat, by 32 per cent.

Looking at the farm picture as a whole, the contrast between Soviet and American agriculture is even more startling. In the United States, out of a total labor force of 65 million only about 6.5 million are in farming, or 1 out of 10. In the Soviet Union, out of a total labor force of 96 million, about 48 million are in farming, or one half. Yet the 6.5 million American farmers produce twice as much food as the 48 million Soviet farmers. In the United States, therefore, one person engaged in agriculture feeds himself and nine other workers on the highest standard in the world, not to speak of vast surpluses which are sold or given away to the rest of the world. In the Soviet Union, one worker engaged in farming can barely feed himself and one other worker—the staple diet is still largely made up of bread, potatoes, and beets, while there is a permanent scarcity of meat and dairy products. Before 1914, Russia was one of the world's leading exporters of farm products; now she is unable to feed her people on her own, and must import some foods, particularly meat, sugar, and dairy products.

Government-imposed low prices for farm products induced many Soviet peasants to grow as little as possible in the early years of collectivization; as a result, there was wide-spread famine in the early nineteen-thirties, particularly in the Ukraine, where peasant resistance was strengthened by the force of nationalism. After World War II, the Soviet government decided to go a step further, and collectivize the collective farms, thus creating new "agro-towns," in which the original scheme of destroying the individuality of the peasant was to be carried to its extreme conclusion. However, the peasants resisted again, and this time their resistance was more effective than in 1929-1933. Although thousands of collective farms were amalgamated into huge combines, the scheme as a whole was abandoned.

After the death of Stalin in 1953, the leaders of the Soviet Union, from Khrushchev downward, publicly admitted that the agrarian policy of Soviet communism had been a failure, and that Soviet agriculture was unable to feed the population in an adequate manner.

The failure of collectivization was also more or less tacitly admitted in the communized states of eastern and southeastern Europe, and from 1953 on a policy of emphasizing food production was pushed in the Iron Curtain countries. In 1952, when the Tito government in Yugoslavia allowed the peasants to decide whether they wanted to stay in farm collectives or return to individual farming, an overwhelming majority chose the latter course.

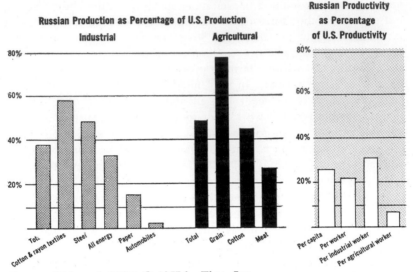

Fortune (February 1957) © 1957 by Time, Inc.

    Even after forcing steel production, the Soviets produce less than half as much steel as the U. S. Their total industrial output is less than 40 per cent of U. S. industrial output, and total energy production is only one-third of that of the U. S., or less than a quarter as much per worker. Although they produce more than half as much cotton and rayon textiles, their output of goods like paper is very low, and output of such consumer durables as cars is minuscule. Their farm output is only half U. S. farm output, and because there is little grain for animals, meat production is only a quarter of what it is in the U. S.

    Productivity, or output per man-hour, is the measure of the Soviet economy's inferiority to the U. S. The No. 1 Soviet goal today is to increase productivity much faster than it has been rising. Total output of the average Soviet worker is little more than a fifth of the average American worker's output, that of the Soviet agricultural worker very much less.

    After 30 years of farm collectivism, the Russian peasant is still deeply opposed to communism in agriculture. Peasant pressure has forced the government all along to allow the member of the collective to devote part of his time and a small plot of land to his own personal management; he may then sell the products of his own effort on the market at higher prices than are paid by the government (which enforces deliveries at artificially low prices bearing little relation to the natural forces of supply and demand).

Although the peasant's own piece of land amounts to only about 1 acre or so, it supplies him with half of his income, and these dwarf holdings—cultivated by personal incentive and initiative—supply a considerable proportion of farm products: about half of the milk, and a substantial amount of fruit, vegetables, and potatoes in the Soviet Union.

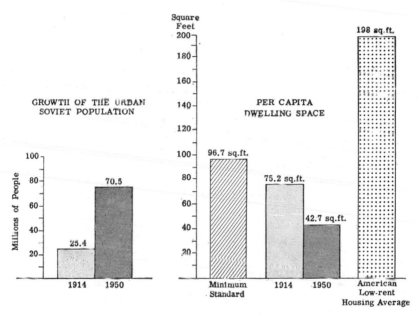

The Soviet rulers know that, as long as this remnant of private agriculture is permitted, the peasant will know from his daily experience that private family farming is more efficient than collectivized communist agriculture. Yet the Soviet rulers have so far not dared to abolish this private element in agriculture, because without it the people of Russia could not be fed at all.

In sum, it can be said that although the agrarian reforms of Soviet communism have failed to bring about higher living standards for the people, they have succeeded in two major objectives: freeing labor for the industrialization of the economy, and providing in the collective farms a nucleus of guerilla resistance in time of war.

Psychologically, the Russian peasant has not been transformed into a proletarian, as the communist rulers planned him to be. In the years after World War II thousands of Russian peasants who had been sent to Germany from German-occupied areas as forced labor for the Nazi war effort stayed on in Germany and other European

IF YOUR FAMILY OF FOUR LIVED
IN A CITY IN THE SOVIET UNION

(An Average Worker Earning 750 Rubles per Month)

Your family would have one room................ | ←—— 12. 7 ft.——→ / 161.2 sq. ft.

Your family would share your
four-room apartment with
eight other people............................

Your family would share one
faucet with eight other people..................

Your family would share
three electric plugs with
eight other people............................

countries, refusing to go back home after having seen life in the "decadent" West. Almost to a man, these peasants are opposed to collectivization, and hope to own their farms after communism is gone. They are not fanatical individualists, because they want to set up *cooperative* farm institutions, such as Canadian, Danish, and New Zealand farmers have developed.

There is a world of difference between collectivism and cooperation: the purpose of *collectivism* is to *destroy the individuality* of the farmer; the aim of *cooperation* is to *strengthen the individual farm*.

Interestingly enough, workers and professional people who have escaped from Russia have indicated in interviews that they wish not only to maintain public ownership in the key industries after communism is destroyed, but also to introduce private ownership in light industry, retailing, and some of the professions. These attitudes indicate the failure of completely dogmatizing the people in a generation of one-sided propaganda. Where economic activity—as in agriculture, light industry, and retailing—can be performed in the classical pattern of the individual owner-manager-worker, what little uncensored Russian opinion we have is opposed to the economic changes of communism. Only where—as in heavy industry and some public services—ownership, work, and management are technologically not feasible in one individual unit, public ownership seems to meet with approval.

In the field of industrialization, progress under Soviet communism has been immense, as was proved by Russia's ability to withstand the onslaught of Germany in World War II. Though Russia received some strategic supplies from the United States during the war, the bulk of the industrial production needed to defeat Germany came from Russian workshops and factories. Russian industrialization, from the First Five Year Plan on, was conceived primarily as a means of increasing, not the material welfare of the people, but the *power of the state*. For this reason, the government consistently emphasized *heavy industry,* as being especially vital to the production of armaments, and showed no great concern with the development of consumer goods industries.

The net result of economic change in Russia over a generation is not so much economic communism as a totalitarian state economy. In terms of sheer industrial power, Russia now ranks second in the world, preceded only by the United States. But this ranking is significant only in appraising the *power of the state to wage war* and not in reflecting the opportunity of the people to live the good life. Viewed from the latter angle, living standards in Russia are still way behind North America, most countries of Europe, Australia and New Zealand, and numerous other nations throughout the world.

Moreover, the price for this rapid industrialization has been steep.

Millions of Soviet subjects have been employed for years in slave labor camps to provide cheap (but inefficient) labor. The number of slave labor camp inmates is estimated to run from a conservatively low figure of five million to the more likely figure of seven to eight million. Another step in bringing back medieval serfdom to the Russian worker is the abolition of free mobility of Soviet workers since 1940. Just as in the Middle Ages the peasant was *glebae adscriptus* (attached to the soil), from which he could remove himself and his family only with the consent of the landlord, the Soviet worker, too, is attached to his job, and may not change it without

PROPORTION OF PRODUCER AND CONSUMER GOODS IN SOVIET INDUSTRIAL PRODUCTION

(Per cent)

Year	Total	Producer Goods	Consumer Goods
1913	100	33.3	66.7
1928	100	39.5	60.5
1932	100	53.4	46.6
1937	100	57.8	42.2
1940	100	61.2	38.8
1950	100	68.8	31.2
1955	100	70.6	29.4

U.S.S.R. Council of Ministers, Central Statistical Administration, *The U.S.S.R. Economy: A Statistical Abstract* (1956)

special permission of his employer, the state. In 1956, penal sanctions for absenteeism or quitting a job without permission were replaced by a new Soviet law providing instead for "disciplinary action and public censure" as remedies for such offenses.

Economic change in the Soviet Union has failed to solve the problem of social justice, for the sake of which the change was ostensibly undertaken in the first place.

During the first fifteen years of the Soviet regime, the attempt was made to limit inequalities of income to a moderate range of differential; from the middle of the nineteen thirties on, however, with the inauguration of the era of purges, the last vestiges of equalitarianism were wiped out, and an entirely new policy was brought into being. Wages based on performance rather than fixed hourly rates became the norm—a wage policy that labor unions in free nations had fought for two generations as a system of inhuman exploitation.

The old-fashioned capitalist appeal for higher production to be compensated by higher incomes was covered up with slogans like "socialist emulation," and workers were driven on to ever higher and higher production efforts by the policy of Stakhanovism, inspired by the alleged feats of a coal-miner named Stakhanov. Whereas the original communist concern had been with problems of distribution, Soviet policy has in practice concentrated on production. The incentive of higher income rather than service to the community has become the main appeal of Soviet social and economic policy, and the philosophy of equality has been derided as a "petty bourgeois prejudice." In line with this anti-equalitarian policy, personal income taxes are among the lowest in the world, and most of the revenue of the state derives from sales taxes and other indirect levies of the sort that proportionately hit the lower income groups hardest. Inheritance taxes, too, are lower than in representative capitalist countries, and are designed to stimulate personal effort and savings.

The group with the highest incomes is the same in Russia as in the United States: business managers and executives. Yet, whereas the income tax in the United States goes up to *91* per cent, the top tax rate in Russia for such high-paid business executives is only *13* per cent. Interestingly enough, the Soviet Union discriminates against some types of high incomes: thus, the top tax rate for artists and writers is 55 per cent, and for the clergy it goes up to 65 per cent.

According to official Soviet propaganda the problem of social classes has been solved in Soviet society, because from the Marxist viewpoint there can be no class inequality except on the basis of the private ownership of the means of production.

Yet Soviet reality tells a different story. There are at least *four distinguishable classes.* In the first group—numbering a few hundred thousand families, perhaps as many as a million—there are the top government officials, party leaders, military officers, industrial executives, scientists, artists, and writers. The second group is made up of the intermediary ranks of civilian and military officials, collective farm managers, and some of the more affluent skilled workers and technicians in industry—this group forms the middle classes of Soviet society and numbers about two to three million families. The third class is made up of the bulk of the population, the mass of workers and peasants, numbering over forty million families. The fourth class includes the millions of slave laborers and other disadvantaged persons who, for political or other reasons, are placed outside the confines of ordinary society.

What is remarkable about social stratification in communist

How Incomes Vary in U.S.S.R.'s "Classless" Society

Some sample weekly wages in rubles:
(Official exchange rate: 4 rubles to $1.
Actual value of ruble: about 12 to $1.)

Kindergarten teacher	104
Woman street cleaner	115
Sales girl	115
Unskilled worker	138
Secretary	185
Chauffeur	185
Taxi driver (including tips)	254
Construction worker (including bonus)	254
Experienced high-school teacher	300
Experienced doctor	323
Skilled mechanic	346
Factory foreman	392
Young engineer (including bonus)	392
Skilled instrument maker	462
Experienced engineer (including bonus)	577
Head buyer in large plant (including bonus)	738
Department-store manager	808
Professor	1,385
Dean of college	2,077
Manager of large plant (including bonus)	2,769

Reprinted from *U. S. News & World Report,* an independent weekly news magazine published at Washington (July 8, 1955). Copyright (1955) United States News Publishing Corporation.

countries is that the *income spread between the different classes has been steadily widening,* while it has been continuously narrowed in the democratic nations of the West through taxation and other measures. Moreover, within the bulk of the population—the working class—the *difference between wages of skilled and unskilled workers* has been constantly on the increase in the Soviet Union, whereas in democratic nations this differential has been systematically reduced, largely owing to the pressure of free labor unions.

Before World War II, American skilled workers generally earned about twice as much as unskilled workers: at present they earn only

about one third more. By contrast, the Soviet skilled worker earns
2-4 times as much as the unskilled worker. The differential between
skilled and unskilled worker is thus 6-12 times greater in the
Soviet Union than in the United States.

The following table on the comparative pay scales in the Soviet and
United States armies speaks for itself.

COMPARATIVE PAY SCALES IN THE SOVIET AND AMERICAN ARMIES
(Base Pay = Private's Pay = 1)

Rank	Soviet Army	U.S. Army
Private	1	1
Private First Class	1.5	1.2
Corporal	3	1.4
Sergeant	4.3	1.8
Master Sergeant	9	2.4
Second Lieutenant	16	2.6
First Lieutenant	19	3.1
Captain	24.3	3.8
Major	30	4.6
Colonel	45	6.9
Brigadier General	None	9.3
Major General	68	11.2
Lieutenant General	81	11.2
General	96	11.2
Marshal (General of the Army)	114.3	15.2

Commentary.

The growing inequality between and within classes in communist states is one of the most explosive sources of unrest and revolt. The East German workers who rebelled in 1953, the Polish
and Hungarian workers who rebelled in 1956 objected less to the
ideology of communism than to the brutal economic exploitation
to which they were exposed, an exploitation that meant austerity
for the masses of the people and affluence for a small privileged
clique of party bosses and government officials. The reality of communist economics thus taught the workers that the mere transfer of
property from private to public ownership did not in itself bring
about a new society built on justice and equality.

As Aristotle said over two thousand years ago, the main question is not *who* owns property, but *how* property is used.

In our own day, the experience of communist economic change teaches again that the principal issue is not whether the government owns the means of production, but *who owns the government.*

The economic implications of arbitrary government were fully demonstrated in recent years by the decision of the Soviet government in 1957 to postpone for 20-40 years repayment of interest and principal on 260 billion rubles ($65 billion at the official rate of exchange) lent by citizens to the government in the form of bonds. In theory, the buying of such bonds was voluntary; in practice, workers and collective farmers had to buy bonds amounting to 6-8 per cent of their annual income. The bond drives started in 1927. When the bonds matured in 1937, redemption was postponed for 10 years. In 1947, there was still no redemption, but old bonds had to be exchanged at the rate of five old bonds for one new one, to mature in 20 years. In 1957, the Soviet government announced the freeze of all payments—on interest and principal—for another 20-40 years. What started out as forced saving finally turned out to be forced taxation, since few Russians have the illusion that the government will redeem the bonds in the years 1977-1997, having broken its pledges so often before. Since the purchase of bonds was based on a roughly equal rate for all citizens (6-8 per cent of the annual income), it bore down more heavily on the lower than on the higher income groups, in line with the general Soviet philosophy of regressive taxation.

The virtual repudiation of the national debt by the Soviet government in 1957 is bound to discourage saving, and will make it completely impossible for Soviet citizens to plan for the future, thus making them even more dependent on whatever the state chooses to hand out to them. The hoarding of cash, too, is a risky business in the Soviet Union. In 1947, the government decreed that money outside of banks, that is, held by individuals, was to be exchanged at the rate of one new ruble for ten old rubles; those who had saved in this fashion—so popular in economically backward countries—lost 90 per cent of their savings. Thus, cash savings were expropriated in 1947, and bond savings in 1957.

Having no confidence in either money or government bonds, the

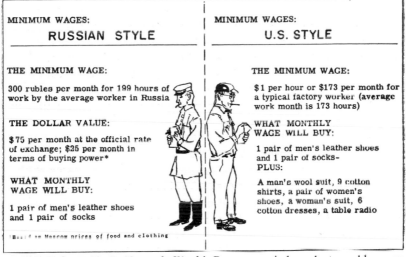

MINIMUM WAGES: RUSSIAN STYLE	MINIMUM WAGES: U.S. STYLE
THE MINIMUM WAGE:	**THE MINIMUM WAGE:**
300 rubles per month for 199 hours of work by the average worker in Russia	$1 per hour or $173 per month for a typical factory worker (average work month is 173 hours)
THE DOLLAR VALUE:	**WHAT MONTHLY WAGE WILL BUY:**
$75 per month at the official rate of exchange; $25 per month in terms of buying power*	1 pair of men's leather shoes and 1 pair of socks— PLUS:
WHAT MONTHLY WAGE WILL BUY:	A man's wool suit, 9 cotton shirts, a pair of women's shoes, a woman's suit, 6 cotton dresses, a table radio
1 pair of men's leather shoes and 1 pair of socks	
*Based on Moscow prices of food and clothing	

Reprinted from *U. S. News & World Report,* an independent weekly news magazine published at Washington (September 21, 1956). Copyright (1956) United States News Publishing Corporation.

Soviet citizen is in a real dilemma if he seeks to provide for the future by thrift or investment. The only safe thing left is the American dollar, which circulates in a flourishing black market, being sold at a rate 4-10 times higher than the official rate of exchange. However, the supply of American dollars as a form of saving is limited to a few large cities, and only a tiny fraction of the Soviet population, even in the major cities, has access to the supply of dollars in the illegal black market.

The theory that under communism the interests of government and people are identical is still orthodox doctrine in the Soviet Union, but two or three other communist states are gradually accepting a more realistic view. The leader of Red China, Mao, created a furor in the communist world, particularly in Moscow, by conceding in his historic address of February 27, 1957, that "certain contradictions do exist between the Government and the masses," and he singled out the contradictions "between democracy and centralism, between those in leadership and the led, and contradictions arising from the bureaucratic practices of certain state functionaries in their relations with the masses." Translated from involved Chinese into Basic English, Mao conceded that governmental oppression and social inequality may, and do, exist under communism. While Mao's new version of communism did not mean wholesale acceptance of Titoism, or out-and-out anti-Moscow national communism, it was significant that national communists throughout the world, and particularly in Poland and Yugoslavia (where they are in control), hailed Mao's revision of the Moscow line as a milestone of communist theory.

Mao's point about the contradictions between the rulers and the ruled under communism was expressed even more forcefully by a leading Yugoslav communist, Vladimir Dedijer. He describes the Soviet system as *totalitarian state capitalism,* "in which the exploitation of man by man is the fact of life." (*New York Times,* May 25, 1957).

Sources of Strength in Communism

Among communism's sources of strength, the most important is probably the enormous *widening of the base from which the elite is recruited.* Before World War I, the Russian elite—in government, the army, business, science, and the arts—was drawn from a relatively small social group of upper-class and upper-middle-class background. There was a tremendous gap between the small governing classes of Russia, in intimate contact with western Europe, and the vast inchoate masses of peasants. The communist revolution, particularly in its first impetus, swept away distinctions of class, sex, or nationality and opened up a new world of opportunity for people who had hitherto been excluded from opportunity of any sort. Until 1940 university education was free of charge and most students received scholarships toward their maintenance. Industrialization, perhaps the most dynamic key in creating new opportunities (in science and government as well as in industry), formed a *new managerial class,* recruited on a very wide basis, for which there was no precedent.

A quick glance at the social background of the top leaders of the Soviet Union today gives us a fair idea of the Soviet leadership as a whole:

Leader	Occupation of father
Bulganin	white collar worker
Gromyko	artisan
Khrushchev	coal miner
Kosygin	poor worker
Mikoyan	worker
Shvernik	poor worker
Voroshilov	railroad worker
Zhukov	poor peasant

These top leaders are typical representatives of the men who run Russia's industry, government, and armed forces. Those westerners who have dealt with them agree that they are able and confident, full of drive and energy. In the United States, these men would be corporation executives, political and military leaders, and top government officials—the very same jobs they hold in the Soviet Union. Because their ideas and aims seem irreconcilable with western ideas and objectives, many have been blinded to their high technical and executive ability.

The competition for leadership positions in the Soviet Union is more ruthless than in the democratic world, the premium for success greater, and the penalty for failure harsher. The successful manager who overfulfills his production quota is rapidly promoted, and his rewards are—in relation to the rest of the population— more ample than in the free world. By contrasts, the manager who fails in his production job is not only likely to be fired, but may even face imprisonment or execution, because technical or economic failure is easily interpreted by his superiors as deliberate sabotage. This exclusive, and harsh, emphasis on performance may seem ruthless, but it works, if results are the only things that count.

In World War I, Russia sustained more losses from lack of medical facilities, faulty supplies, slow transportation, and other shortcomings of a technological nature than from direct combat casualties. In World War II, most of the generals who outmaneuvered and defeated the German General Staff were sons of serfs, workers, and small peasants; there is no doubt that in World War II Russia was able to draw on more of her people's talent than in World War I.

The less a position in the elite is directly tied up with politics, the more recognition can be given to talent and merit. As long as a leading surgeon, chemist, mathematician, engineer, or industrial executive keeps his mouth shut (politically speaking), and opens it only for the purpose of expressing his loyalty to the regime, he will generally (but not always) be left alone. The more a position in the ruling group is tinged with politics, the more criteria besides merit and talent become relevant and frequently decisive.

Rapid *industrialization* is the second main source of communist strength, in Russia as well as in other communized states. Before World War I, Russia was an overwhelmingly agricultural country; Russian industrial power was very low, ranking behind the United States, Britain, Germany, France, Japan, and Austria-Hungary. After World War II, Russia moved up to second place, preceded only by the United States. Industrialization in all communist states is concentrated on heavy industry, the base of military power.

In absolute figures, industry in Russia and the communist states still lags considerably behind the United States and her allies. But what is alarming is the rapid *rate of industrial growth* in the communist states, which considerably exceeds that of many western nations. Even if it be argued that the communist states have now the initial advantage of backward countries undergoing rapid industrialization, and that their present rate of expansion cannot be indefinitely maintained, the western nations will have to step up their own productivity and rate of industrial growth if the present balance of industrial power, still heavily in favor of the noncommunist states, is not to be lost.

If the free nations are to win the industrial race with communism, they will have to give more attention in their industrial programs to saving and productivity, and less to immediate consumption and "ice-cream" investments.

In terms of output per head, the Australian economist Colin Clark has estimated that a man-hour worked in communist Russia is exchangeable for about one-eighth of the goods and services that a man-hour worked in the United States can buy. Since the Russian standard is 46 hours per week as compared with 40 hours in the United States, and since more women work, the standard of living is higher than one-eighth. In terms of productivity—the basis for determining the living standards of a nation—Russia still ranks on a par with backward countries, such as Hungary, Rumania, Turkey, or Brazil. Below Russia are India, with half the level of

TWO DAYS' WORK FOR A POUND OF TEA

The Soviet industrial worker must work longer to buy a given quantity of food than his opposite number in any country in western Europe. The food-buying power of the average Italian worker (even without his family allowance) is about 45 per cent higher than the Moscow worker's; the Norwegian's 300 per cent higher. The comparisons below (computed by the U.S. Labor Department) show minutes of work time required to buy various foods.

Food (Per pound)	U.S. (Sept. '51)	France (Oct. '51)	Italy (Sept. '51)	Moscow (April '52)
			(Minutes)	
Bread	6	9	13	14
Beef (avg.)	31	126	128	132
Fish	18	33	65	135
Butter	30	135	162	270
Milk (qt.)	8	16	20	42
Eggs (doz.)	32	118	126	187
Potatoes	2	3	5	9
Apples	4	19	—	89
Coffee	32	175	250	531
Tea	49	—	—	960
Sugar	4	21	37	110

Fortune (February 1953) © 1953 by Time, Inc.

Russian productivity; China, with one-fourth of Russian productivity; and most of the other underdeveloped countries in Asia, Africa, and Latin America.

Since Russia's hope of communist expansion in the near future lies in underdeveloped areas, it is of greater importance that her industrial productivity is superior to that of China or India than that it is inferior to that of the United States or Britain.

In Asia, communist industrialization has perhaps been the single most valuable propaganda asset of Soviet Russia; backward Asian countries compare their condition with that of neighboring or near-by Russia rather than with that of Britain or the United States, whose background is so different from their own.

Industrialization means saving on a large scale, that is, the withdrawal of resources from consumption and their employment in producing capital goods. In the early phase of industrialization in the West, the formation of capital was facilitated by long work days, low wages, and the use of the machinery of the state against recal-

	NOW	TREND	OUTLOOK FOR 1970
TOTAL ANNUAL PRODUCTION	West*—$690 billion Soviet—$155 billion	West's production growing about twice as fast	West will be even further ahead
AGRICULTURAL PRODUCTION	West—abundance Soviet—food shortage	Expansion rapid in West, slow in Soviet	Western diet will be increasingly better
POPULATION	West—441 million Soviet—304 million	West's population has been increasing faster	West will hold numerical edge
LABOR FORCE	West—192 million Soviet—about 160 million	West's working-age population growing faster	West will still be ahead
OUTPUT PER WORKER	Many times larger in the West	Efficiency increasing faster in West	Western superiority will be greater
RAW MATERIALS	West better supplied in most materials	Variable, reserves of most materials adequate	Neither side will feel serious pinch
ANNUAL STEEL PRODUCTION	West—165 million tons Soviet—50 million tons	Western production going up faster	West will have a bigger lead
ANNUAL COAL PRODUCTION	West—926 million tons Soviet—361 million tons	Soviet production rising faster	West's lead will still be huge
ANNUAL ELECTRIC-POWER PRODUCTION	West—815 billion kilowatt-hours; Soviet—193 billion	Soviet expanding at greater rate	West will still have far more
ANNUAL PETROLEUM PRODUCTION	West—323 million tons Soviet—68 million tons	West finding more oil reserves	West's advantage will be greater
TRANSPORTATION FACILITIES	West far ahead of Soviet bloc in all types	West still gaining on Soviet bloc	West will be even better off

*This figure also includes Canada

Reprinted from *U. S. News & World Report,* an independent weekly news magazine published at Washington (March 1, 1957). Copyright (1957) United States News Publishing Corporation.

citrant workers. In the twentieth century, however, rapid industrialization can be carried out in a free society only if its members have enough self-discipline to consume little and to save much. Where national cohesion and individual self-discipline are high (as in Norway or Britain), a high level of saving (and capital investment) can be attained without resort to coercion. It is doubtful, however, whether there are many nations in which such standards of public conduct prevail.

In countries not strong in self-discipline, where the preference for the maintenance of democratic institutions is stronger than the desire for rapid industrialization, as in France and Italy, economic stagnation is the inevitable result. Conversely, a country where rapid industrialization takes precedence over the maintenance of free institutions is likely to resort to fascism or communism, these being the only institutional systems that allow of sufficient coercion to bring about the forced savings that are required for the production of capital goods.

The classical pattern of industrialization in Britain, France, and the United States in the eighteenth and nineteenth centuries cannot easily be copied. By an accident of history, industrialization in those countries occurred at a time when they had developed sufficient self-government to mitigate its worst excesses and abuses. In Germany, industrialization in the nineteenth century was largely directed from above, and much of the current economic development in Latin America is state-directed.

Technical progress has made it even more difficult to keep the state out. In the eighteenth and nineteenth centuries, when technology was still relatively primitive, plants were small, and initial capital investments were relatively low. In the twentieth century, industrialization means huge initial capital investments, so huge that they can be provided only by foreign investors or the state. If foreign investors are unwilling to invest, or are excluded by political regulation, the state is left as the only big investor.

Finally, whereas the classical patterns of British, French, and American industrialization created strong middle classes independent of the state, *industrialization in politically backward societies has the opposite tendency of strengthening the state,* since the whole program is planned, executed, and supervised by public officials. Paradoxically, therefore, to the extent that Point IV assists the industrialization of backward areas by lending capital and know-how to *government* agencies, it strengthens *collectivism* rather than individualism, even if the receiving government is explicitly anti-communist.

Finally, the most direct and dangerous source of communist

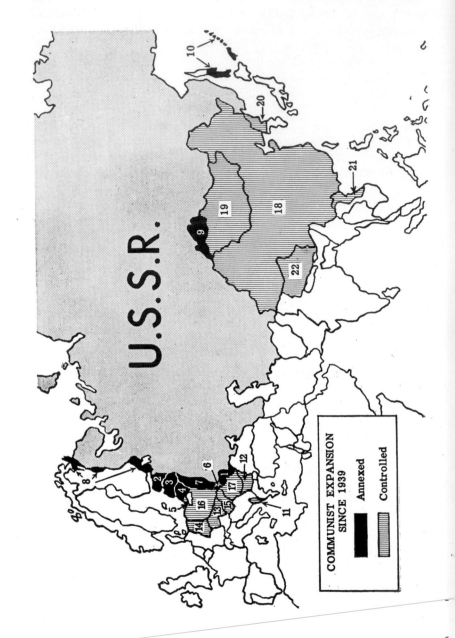

EXPANSION OF THE COMMUNIST COLONIAL EMPIRE
SINCE 1939

USSR ANNEXED	Year	Area (square miles)	Population
1. PART OF RUMANIA	1940	19,400	3,700,000
2. ESTONIA	1940	18,300	1,200,000
3. LATVIA	1940	25,400	2,100,000
4. LITHUANIA	1940	23,000	3,000,000
5. PART OF EAST PRUSSIA	1945	5,400	1,200,000
6. EASTERN CZECHOSLOVAKIA	1945	4,900	730,000
7. EASTERN POLAND	1945	69,900	11,800,000
8. PART OF FINLAND	1940	17,600	450,000
9. TANNU TUVA	1944	64,000	65,000
10. JAPANESE POSSESSIONS	1945	17,800	433,000
SOVIET SATELLITES			
11. ALBANIA	1946	10,700	1,300,000
12. BULGARIA	1946	42,800	7,300,000
13. CZECHOSLOVAKIA	1948	49,300	14,000,000
14. EASTERN GERMANY (INCLUDING SOVIET SECTOR OF BERLIN)	1949	41,500	18,500,000
15. HUNGARY	1947	36,000	10,000,000
16. POLAND	1947	121,100	26,500,000
17. RUMANIA	1948	91,600	17,000,000
18. COMMUNIST CHINA (NOT INCL. TIBET)	1949	3,281,000	582,000,000
19. OUTER MONGOLIA	1945	626,000	1,000,000
COMMUNIST CHINA'S COLONIAL EMPIRE			
20. NORTH KOREA (WITH COMMUNIST CHINA)	1948	48,500	9,000,000
21. NORTH VIETNAM	1951	72,000	12,000,000
22. TIBET	1951	469,000	1,200,000

strength lies in *military power*. Since the outbreak of World War II in September 1939, the Soviet Union has acquired an area larger than all the New England and Middle Atlantic states, and a population of about 25 million.

On June 27, 1930, Stalin had declared in his Report to the Sixteenth Congress of the Communist Party "We do not want a single foot of foreign territory," but he cynically belied those words when the Red Army was strong enough to impose its will on enemies as well as on friends (such as Czechoslovakia). In addition to these outright annexations, Russia has also communized, or helped to communize, Poland, Czechoslovakia, Hungary, Rumania, Eastern Germany, Northern Vietnam, Outer Mongolia, North Korea, and China —about 700 million people in all. Since Russia's population now exceeds 200 million, over one-third of the human race has thus been brought under the sway of communism within one generation.

Never before in history has imperialistic expansion acquired so much in so short a time.

SOURCES OF WEAKNESS IN COMMUNISM

The first source of weakness in communism is the stress on *conformity*. The most distinguishing quality of a leader is his courage to be different, to have new ideas, to be in a minority, even in solitude. Yet as time goes on, the leader in communist regimes is increasingly being replaced by the bureaucrat, the yes-man. The era of the purges in Russia in the middle nineteen thirties was the conflict between the leaders who had made the Revolution and the bureaucrats who administered it. Conformist as prerevolutionary Russia was, it was a paradise of diversity compared with the communist regime; Lenin, Trotsky, and Stalin were all products of precommunist Russia. Malenkov, Stalin's immediate successor, was the first Big Brother in Russia who was a product of communism. It is interesting to note that he did not possess the qualities of a leader. In 1955, he was removed as Prime Minister, and in 1957 he was "purged" by Khrushchev, and exiled to Central Asia.

The growing conformity has even invaded *science,* thus creating one of the potentially most dangerous weaknesses in world communism. Under Lenin, orthodoxy was required in social and political thought, but science and the arts were left pretty much alone. Under Stalin, as under his successors, the party line applied to the physical sciences as much as to social science.

Thus, in the field of biology, Lysenko attacked all accepted biological knowledge by claiming that acquired characters can be inherited. When many biologists in the Soviet Union revolted against this theory, which is contradictory to all known and controllable facts, Lysenko addressed the Lenin Academy of Agricultural Sciences on July 31, 1948 on "The Situation in the Science of Biology." After damning traditional scientific biology, Lysenko made this statement: "The question is asked in one of the notes handed to me what is the attitude of the Central Committee of the Communist Party to my report. I answer: The Central Committee of the Party examined my report and approved it."

Thus, a question of utmost scientific importance was settled by the fiat of the Central Committee of the Communist Party rather than by the experimental method of the decadent capitalist scientists. How Lysenko's charlatanism will affect Soviet agriculture over the years is anyone's guess; humans can be made to submit to fraud, but nature is more resilient. In any event, for some time to come Lysenko is likely to play a leading part in Russian biology. Vavilov, the leading Russian geneticist and the outstanding opponent of Lysenko, was arrested in 1941 and exiled to Siberia, where he eventually died.

After Stalin's death, Lysenko was attacked in several Soviet journals, and his influence declined for a while. But in 1957, the tide turned again in favor of Lysenko. Discussing (on April 10, 1957) the controversy between Lysenko and his opponents, Khrushchev authoritatively stated before a scientific gathering as follows: "If you asked me for which scientist I would vote, I would say without hesitation—for Lysenko." Since Khrushchev's one vote carries a great deal of weight in Soviet scientific circles, Lysenko's prestige was thus officially restored.

In the field of physics, the communists have fully reached the nazi level. Just as the nazis promoted a Nordic physics or mathematics, to be freed from Jewish or other non-German influences, the communists have introduced their own party line into the natural sciences. Einstein was attacked by the nazis for his Jewish physics; the communists have attacked him for expressing bourgeois, idealistic concepts incompatible with truly proletarian dialectics. Western physicists like Niels Bohr and Heisenberg have been attacked for harboring a "narrow, reactionary outlook similar to Nazism," and have been admonished to tread the "path indicated by Lenin and Stalin" along with communist or fellow-traveling scientists like Langevin and Joliot-Curie in France or Blackett and Haldane in Britain, all of whom have been cited by official communist spokesmen for special merit.

The fate of psychoanalysis under communism is another case in point. Until 1930, psychoanalysis was tolerated in the Soviet Union, having attracted considerable attention in Russia long before the Revolution. After 1930, psychoanalysis gradually fell into disfavor, and in 1936 the Communist Party officially decided that psychoanalysis was incompatible with Marxism-Leninism-Stalinism. After having been branded by the nazis as false because of its Jewish origin, psychoanalysis was condemned by communists as a web of false bourgeois concepts, and was finally assailed as an "ideological instrument of American imperialism"!

In the field of pure and applied philosophy, the communists have done much housecleaning, too. Their opposition to more conservative thinkers was to be expected, but eventually they took on "progressive thinkers" also. John Dewey, for example, has been roundly condemned for his pragmatic philosophy, which patient communist research has revealed to be yet another cleverly disguised instrument of American imperialism.

Stalin felt as much at home with music as with the other muses. In January 1948 the Central Committee of the Communist Party of the Soviet Union decreed that all music must henceforth be popular, simple, easy to digest, and tuneful; at the same time the committee condemned the "formalism" of the best known composers in Russia, such as Shostakovich and Prokofiev. The attack was also directed against instrumental music in general and chamber music in particular, which, the composers were told, "the people did not care for," and the production of more vocal music urged instead. In some instances, the communists not only have attacked modern art as "formalistic," "remote from the people," and "bourgeois"—the usual epithets—but have imitated the nazis faithfully enough to charge some works of art with being "cosmopolitan."

In literature, the communists have no use for the classical theme "boy meets girl." Instead, officially approved communist art (called "socialist realism") revolves around a new theme: "Boy and girl meet machine; production goes up; and all three live happily ever after."

For nearly thirty years, until 1956, Dostoevsky's novels were practically unobtainable in Russia, because his primary concern with *individual* guilt and responsibility proved to the Soviet rulers that he was reactionary in his thinking and dangerous to the regime.

Returning from a trip to the Soviet Union, Truman Capote, the American writer, reported in the *New York Times* (March 4, 1956) that a young Russian writer asked him who Freud, Proust, and Kafka were—he had never heard of them! By contrast, as soon as "national communism" under Gomulka was firmly established in Poland, Polish translations early in 1957 of George Orwell's *1984* and Arthur Koestler's *Darkness at Noon,* the two greatest novels on communist totalitarianism, were instantaneous and sensational successes.

One of the most hopeful aspects about communist indoctrination and thought-control is that they have proved much less effective than was believed until quite recently. Thus, the remarkable thing about the Hungarian Revolution of 1956 was the predominant role of young people in the fight for freedom. Most of the fighters were in their teens or early twenties—all the products of communist monopoly in education and mass communication. Starting out as a rebellion against the Russian type of communism, the fight soon turned against any brand of communism, and for freedom and democracy. Years of communist indoctrination, supported by political terror and torture, proved a complete fiasco, and for five days—from October 29, 1956, to November 3, 1956—Hungary was free, and it was hard to find communists.

In Russia, too, forty years of communist indoctrination have not proved as successful as the Soviet leaders and the outside world thought. After Khrushchev's anti-Stalin speech before the Twentieth Congress of the Communist Party of the Soviet Union on February 25, 1956, there was a breath of fresh air, for a few months at least, and young people began to show strange feelings and interests. University students pinned foreign broadcast texts to bulletin boards, raised unorthodox questions in party-sponsored meetings, and otherwise made such a nuisance of themselves that the Communist Party of Moscow had to admit that "some sections of the student body have been subjected to the influence of unhealthy tendencies, and have occasionally come under the influence of ideas alien to the spirit of their motherland." (*Manchester Guardian Weekly,* January

3, 1957) In Leningrad, too, the *Pravda* became alarmed by the unrest among students, and demanded disciplinary action against the "politically illiterate demagogues" among the students, or those who spoke too freely, and showed the "influence of unhealthy tendencies" toward freedom of expression.

Despite Soviet anti-foreign, and particularly anti-American, hate propaganda over four decades, Soviet youth shows of late an insatiable hunger for foreign styles, fashions, and music, "particularly anything and everything American." (*The New York Times,* February 3, 1957) Jazz, which had been forbidden for many years as the music of decadent American capitalism, became the rage of Soviet youth, as soon as the ban was lifted in 1956. Louis Armstrong, Stan Kenton, Glenn Miller, and Erroll Garner are among the jazz idols of the Soviet hit parade. Frank Sinatra has had a devastating effect on the Soviet female contingent, from bobby-soxers to stately matrons, and Doris Day, Rosemary Clooney, and Patti Page have conquered the hearts of the male segment of Soviet youth. The pathetic craving of Soviet youngsters for western "culture" is most dramatically evidenced by Elvis Presley, the secret weapon of the United States in the struggle with austere communism: cut in Russia on discarded hospital x-ray plates, Presley records sell for as much as 50 rubles ($12.50 at the official rate of exchange).

The craze for American music, particularly jazz, went so far that Soviet leaders felt it necessary to call a halt, and to propose a return to Stalinist standards and tastes in music, as in other fields. Dmitri Shepilov, top Communist Party propagandist (and former editor of *Pravda* and Minister of Foreign Affairs) warned Soviet composers on April 3, 1957, not to imitate "decadent western composers" and particularly American music, which he described as follows: "All this nervous and insane boogie woogie and rock 'n' roll are the wild orgies of cavemen. They are devoid of any elements of beauty and melody. They represent an uncontrolled release of base passions, a burst of the lowest feelings and sexual urges."

The craving of Soviet youth for foreign, particularly American, ways of feeling and acting is partly due to their pent-up curiosity after having been cut off from the outside world for so long. Partly, and perhaps more importantly, it is due to something deeper—a sense of dullness and frustration produced by Soviet conditions of living. Over and over, Soviet youth express their feeling to foreign

"TONIGHT AT TEN—VOICE OF AMERICA—ROSEMARY CLOONEY—
PASS IT ON."

visitors in these words: "It is so boring here. Life is so dull." (*The New York Times,* February 3, 1957)

If the lack of freedom will not eventually make Soviet youth rebellious, the dullness and austerity of Soviet life perhaps will.

Thought control can have tremendous practical effects in the long run, and even in the short run, as the nazis found out. In World War II the nazis lost the race for the atomic bomb because some of the most brilliant German physicists, forced to leave Germany, chose to do their atomic research in Britain and the United States. It is possible that communist states, too, by imposing a party line on agricultural biology, physics, and medicine, will in the long run greatly weaken their scientific proficiency, one of the crucial elements of industrial and military strength.

For the time being, it would be dangerous to assume that communist ideology has already done in the military sciences what it did in genetics. The Soviet hydrogen bomb, the Soviet giant jet bomber, and other military achievements suggest that Soviet military science remains at a high level.

The *main weakness of communism,* however, is the *discrepancy between ideal and reality.* Its leaders proclaim lofty ideals for the renewal of mankind and yet use inhuman means, age-old instruments of oppressive despotism. One of the deepest insights of the liberal way of life is that *means and ends cannot be too sharply separated* from each other, and that the nature of the means employed in realizing an end will determine the character of the end itself. Communism acts in total disregard of this axiom, and purports to build a new fellowship of love and fraternity with the knout and the slave labor camp.

One of the most powerful original messages of communism was its protest against social inequality and privilege based on class and caste. Yet in communist Russia a class system is being created that exceeds by far the class system Marx sought to supersede. In addition, communism has created the caste of political commissars, men who do not feel themselves accountable to man or God, men for whom the execution squad is the final method of persuasion.

Finally, the gap between promise and performance can be clearly seen with regard to the *freedom of nations.* The communist promise is international brotherhood and equality of all nations. In the Soviet Union itself, a fervent cult of the Great Russians has been built up in recent years; outside of the Soviet Union, the Russians have carried on a foreign policy that is openly and cynically imperialistic. Tito's crime in 1948 was not abandoning communism for capitalism, but the much worse offense of trying to regain national liberty and independence for the peoples of Yugoslavia from Moscow. Titoism is, by communist admission, a disease rampant throughout the communist world. No communist state or party is free from it. Titoism, or "national communism," reflects a people's natural desire to be free from foreign domination, an issue over which many empires have come to grief in the past.

Revolts Against Soviet Communism

After Tito's rebellious break with Moscow in 1948, the next major explosion took place on June 16 and 17, 1953, in East Germany. Food conditions had steadily deteriorated under Soviet exploitation and East German communist mismanagement, and there was less food than during World War II. Even bread and potatoes, the staple diet of communist economic planning, were scarce.

EAST BERLIN 1953

Wide World Photos, Inc.

The spark which fired the smouldering resentment of the people was a government announcement on May 28, 1953, that workers' wages would be cut further unless they produced at least 10 per cent more than in the past. On June 16, building workers on Stalin Avenue in East Berlin started a spontaneous strike, and marched toward government headquarters. The strike spread quickly throughout East Germany on that day and the next, and in many communities the workers were in command of the situation, occupying police offices, liberating political prisoners, and setting government and communist party buildings on fire. Many members of the police either took a wait-and-see attitude, or even went over to the rebels. Before long, the rebels demanded, in addition to more tolerable living conditions, free elections, free labor unions, and the end of Soviet domination.

Hesitating at first to intervene directly, the Soviet forces quickly realized that the communist regime would soon be overthrown completely, and thousands of Soviet tanks moved into the major strongholds of rebellion, suppressing it in a few days. Several hundred Germans died in the uprising, hundreds were wounded, and about 50,000 were imprisoned.

Exactly three years later, on June 28, 1956, the Polish uprising in Poznan took place. On that day, thousands of workers of the Stalin Steel Works went on strike early in the morning, and moved toward the center of the city, chanting "bread, bread, bread," singing Polish national songs, carrying the old Polish national flags, and refusing to disperse despite the tank formations quickly brought into the city by the communist authorities. Before long, the striking workers occupied the communist party headquarters, the radio station, and set the city prison on fire after freeing the prisoners. In the ensuing battle with army and police, a battle that lasted for several days, about 200 Poles lost their lives, thousands were wounded, and many more thousands arrested.

Militarily, the rebellion was successfully repressed, but politically it unleashed a chain of events which is still in the making. On October 19, 1956, the Central Committee of the Polish Communist Party met in Warsaw, and it was rumored that big changes were contemplated. The Soviet Government dispatched Khrushchev, Molotov, Mikoyan, Kaganovich, Marshal Koniev, and a staff of

POZNAN 1956

United Press Photo

generals to Warsaw to pressure the Polish communist party into
continued subservience to Moscow.

On the following day, it was announced that Wladyslaw Gomulka
had been elected First Secretary of the Polish Communist Party.
This announcement came as a bombshell, because Gomulka was
known as the leader of Titoism or "national communism" in Poland,
and had spent several years in prison for that crime.

On October 21, 1956, it was further announced that Marshal
Rokossovsky was not reelected a member of the new Central Committee of the Polish Communist Party. Rokossovsky, a Russian
officer, had been the head of the Polish armed forces and Minister of
Defense since 1949, and for all practical purposes the real ruler of
the country.

For a moment, the Russians considered full-scale occupation of the country and the reestablishment of Stalinism by force. But the Poles stood their ground, and the top Soviet leaders as well as Marshal Rokossovsky returned to Moscow. Poland had won, for the time being, its struggle for some degree of national independence, although its government continued to be communist-dominated.

One of the first steps of the new leadership was to release Cardinal Wyszinski, the symbol of Catholic resistance to communism, from prison, and to permit again religious instruction in public schools.

The peasants were given the choice of leaving the collective farms, and 90 per cent made use of that new-won liberty without much waiting. But even the remaining 10 per cent of collective farms did not continue in the old ways, but were transformed into cooperatives. In the field of industry, too, Gomulka admitted that Poland was near economic ruin, and that in coal-mining, for example, Polish miners were producing one-third less per man-hour than in the capitalist Poland of 1938.

Since the triumph of Gomulka in October of 1956, Poland has steadily, though cautiously, moved away from Stalinist totalitarianism to a mixture—as yet unsettled in its final proportions—of authoritarianism in government and relative liberty in thought, religion, and literature. The Polish people, who have always considered themselves the last outpost of Western civilization on the European Continent, the cultural boundary between Europe and Asia, are desperately looking to the West for encouragement and inspiration.

In foreign policy, the new Polish government has treaded softly, because "Poland's neighbors are not Australian shepherds," as Poles are being reminded by their leaders. Poland is still a member of the Warsaw Pact, the Moscow-sponsored military counterpart to NATO, including Russia and the East European communist-run states. She realizes that she can no more offend Russia openly and directly than can Finland, which also, though democratic and independent, must refrain from any foreign policy that could be construed as anti-Soviet by the Kremlin.

Yet in 1957 the Polish government took the—for a communist country—bold step of sending a mission to the United States to obtain economic and financial aid. In granting such aid, the first instalment of which was 95 million dollars, the United States took a calculated risk, since Poland might revert to Stalinism some day, and since such aid allows the Soviet Union to divert resources from Poland to more aggressive purposes. Should Poland continue on her path of independence from Moscow, American aid might strengthen her ties with the West, and show the Polish people who is exploiting them, and who is helping them in an hour of need.

For the time being, totalitarianism of the Stalinist type is dead in Poland. During the Hungarian Revolution of October-November, 1956, the Polish public and newspapers openly sympathized with the Hungarians, and dismissed the Russian version—that the rebels were fascists, not democrats; capitalists, not workers—as fabricated fraud and falsehood. The newspapers and magazines have attacked Soviet communism of the Stalinist type as a web of lies in idea and action, and have been systematically attacked in return by Soviet writers and political leaders for such daring heresies. Moreover, any country that allows, or encourages, the publication of books like Orwell's *1984* and Koestler's *Darkness of Noon* is deeply hostile to totalitarianism as a way of life.

What happened in Poland in October 1956 was nothing short of a revolution. So far we have witnessed only the first act of that drama, so fateful for the future of Soviet communism. The present situation is only a transitional stage—to what? Either to more democracy and fuller national independence, or to a renewed Russian attempt to crush the present system, and reestablish Stalinist-Khrushchevite communism by tanks and mass murder.

The events in Poland immediately raised hope and passion in Hungary. On October 23, 1956, university students, soon to be joined by thousands of industrial workers, held a mass meeting in Parliament Square. Expressing their sympathy for the Polish fight for freedom and independence, they put forward a series of demands, including among others: the evacuation of Russian troops from Hungary, free elections; free labor unions and the right to strike; revision of workers' wages and a complete reorganization of the economy; the immediate release of political prisoners and the return of Hungarians deported to the Soviet Union; removal of the statue of Stalin; and, finally, reorganization of the compulsory system of farm collectives.

When the political police fired on the demonstrators, a peaceful meeting quickly turned into revolt, spreading like wildfire throughout the whole nation. On the one side were the Hungarian political police and the Russian tank forces, and on the other, the united Hungarian people, including most of the soldiers, officers, and regular police. The workers of Hungary declared a general strike, one of the principal and most effective weapons of the revolution. In six days of bloody fighting, the revolution triumphed. The factories were taken over by workers' councils, and governmental authority was exercised by spontaneously set up bodies of representatives of workers, peasants, soldiers, and youth organizations.

By October 29, 1956, the revolution had completely triumphed. The Communist Party had disintegrated and virtually disappeared. The old democratic parties were reestablished, and a free press published again. Political prisoners were set free, the most notable being Cardinal Mindszenty, jailed and tortured since 1948. Whereas at the beginning of the revolution, on October 23, a Gomulka-type solution of national communism combined with diplomatic dependence on Russia would have been acceptable, the utter defeat of the Russian forces and the Hungarian political police made such a solution impossible. On November 1, 1956, the Hungarian Premier, Imre Nagy, a former "Titoite" communist, announced the withdrawal of Hungary from the Warsaw Pact, declared Hungary's neutrality, asked for guarantees of Hungarian independence by the Big Four (United States, Russia, Britain, and France), and promised free elections and the return to a democratic party system. What the Hungarian people now wanted was more than the Polish solution; nothing short of complete political liberty and national independence would do.

This period of freedom, the first Hungary had known for many years, lasted for exactly five days, until November 3. On the next day, 200,000 Russian troops and 5,000 tanks moved into Hungary to suppress the revolution by large-scale warfare. Fighting throughout the country lasted for over a week, followed by minor acts of resistance throughout November and December of 1956. Without aid from the outside world, there was no hope of military victory for the Hungarians. Prime Minister Nagy was kidnapped by the Russians on the first day of their entrance into Budapest on November 4, 1956, and the Russians installed Janos Kadar as their puppet ruler. Since then Hungary has been occupied and ruled by the Russian army, with no pretence of Hungarian sovereignty or independence.

The cost of the revolution was high; 35,000 Hungarians were

killed, and several times as many wounded; over 200,000 left their homes and families, either to seek refuge throughout the free world (over 30,000 came to the United States), or to be deported by the thousands to Siberia. Most Hungarian cities were utterly devastated.

A joint dispatch by the correspondents of the Associated Press, the United Press, and Reuters (the leading British news agency) had this to say about the effect of Russian "liberation" on Budapest: "The destruction of the city surpasses the most morbid imagination. During a walk of a mile along the outer ring of Pest, these correspondents saw not one habitable house. Every building on either side of the great avenue was wrecked, shattered, burned, or roofless." (*The New York Times*, November 13, 1956) Taking the country as a whole, the physical destruction was far greater than during all of World War II, when Hungary was an active battleground for many months between major powers.

Since the French Revolution of 1789, there has been no democratic revolution in the world comparable to the Hungarian Revolution in its glory, tragedy, and impact. As time goes on, history may show that the heroic fight of the Hungarian people for freedom was the beginning of the inevitable doom of communism.

Despite their military defeat by Soviet tanks, the Hungarians learned several lessons which neither they nor the rest of the world will soon forget.

First, the spectacle of rebelling workers trampling and burning the red flag as the symbol of oppression destroyed the myth, once and for all, that Soviet communism represents the cause of the workers. Throughout the whole Hungarian Revolution, the Hungarian Workers' Council, and local workers' councils across the nation, were the center of anti-Soviet and anticommunist activity. After the revolution was suppressed, the workers' councils were the last revolutionary bodies to offer resistance, until they, too, were dissolved by Soviet force.

Communism as military imperialism will continue to threaten the world so long as the Soviet Union has millions of men under arms, tens of thousands of planes and tanks, and the ultimate weapons of destruction—the atom and hydrogen bombs. But communism as a myth, as a messianic promise of justice and liberty, is dead.

Second, the Hungarian people learned that communism, far from being a "people's democracy" (as the Soviet-controlled regimes of

Eastern Europe like to call themselves), depends on tanks and bayonets for its survival, and does not dare to face the people in free elections.

Third, the Hungarian Revolution proved that Moscow-sponsored regimes of Eastern Europe are not national governments, but stooges

COMRADESHIP IN HUNGARY
Reprinted by permission of the artist. © Low (all countries)

of the Kremlin. Without the 200,000 Russian troops and 5,000 tanks, the Hungarian Revolution would have decisively triumphed, and there was very little resistance on the part of the few native communists. A popular joke in Hungary summed up this feeling as follows: "Except for 9,000,000 fascist and counter-revolutionary capitalists, factory owners, industrialists, bankers, financiers, landlords, counts, and cardinals, the Hungarian workers and peasants remained completely loyal to the people's democratic regime, and all six of them formed the Kadar Government."

Fourth, the Hungarian Revolution taught the Russians that they can henceforth no longer rely on the satellite armies, because during the revolution the Hungarian regular army and police went over to the rebels *en masse*. In fact, in isolated cases even Russian soldiers went over, and some deserted across the Austrian border.

Fifth, the Hungarian Revolution revealed the inefficacy of communist indoctrination. The revolution was touched off by university students—the product of communist education and indoctrination.

Pavlov, the great Russian physiologist of the nineteenth century, discovered in his experiments with dogs the phenomenon of "conditioned reflexes" through continued repetition of the same stimuli. The communists have tried to apply Pavlovian techniques to humans, in order to transform man into a conditioned reflex machine, behaving automatically and unthinkingly in accordance with a predetermined pattern inculcated in him by his masters.

The evidence of the Hungarian Revolution, particularly as supplied by the resistance of youngsters in their teens and early twenties, suggests that—despite Pavlov and communist indoctrination—there is still a difference between man and dog.

Sixth, the reaction of the Hungarian people to the release of Cardinal Mindszenty by the revolutionaries (he was forced to seek asylum in the American Legation in Budapest shortly after the reentry of Russian troops) proved that the antireligious propaganda of the communist rulers had been a failure. In fact, such persecution had made many Hungarians more loyal to, or at least more respectful of, church and religion.

Seventh, the Hungarian Revolution gave the death-blow to the theory, obsessively clung to by the free world, that revolution in a totalitarian police state is impossible. According to this theory, revolution was possible in the eighteenth or nineteenth century, because the government did not then possess the powerful weapons of suppression available to it in this century. The Hungarian Revolution has proved that the mind of man is still king, as it has always been, and that totalitarian despotism of the twentieth century cannot rely exclusively on terror and torture any more than despotism could in the past.

Finally, the Hungarian Revolution provided a conclusive answer as to the variety of Soviet reactions to deviations of satellites from the Moscow line. Why did the Soviet Union tolerate the changes in Yugoslavia and Poland tending toward "national communism" independent of Moscow, whereas it suppressed by military force the uprisings in East Germany, Poznan, and Hungary? Specifically, why did it allow, at almost the same time in the fall of 1956, the changes in Poland, the most important of the satellites, while it ruthlessly suppressed the changes in Hungary, a much less important satellite?

The answer to these questions may be found in this consideration: in both Yugoslavia and Poland, the changes were brought about *from the top*. They were palace revolutions within the top leadership of the Yugoslav and Polish Communist parties, whereas the movements in East Germany, Poznan, and Hungary stemmed *from below*. The Soviet people themselves are used to palace revolutions within the communist leadership; by allowing Titoism and Gomulkaism, the Soviet leaders demonstrate to the Soviet people that changes in a communist state can only come from the top. Had the Soviet Union given in to the popular pressure and uprisings in East Germany, Poznan, and Hungary, such examples might have set a dangerous and provocative precedent for possible changes in the Soviet Union itself. By tolerating Tito and Gomulka and saving them from true popular democracy, the Soviet leaders think of their own necks.

Thus, in his historic anti-Stalin speech of February 25, 1956, before the Twentieth Party Congress, the most sensational address by a communist party leader in the whole history of communism, Khrushchev conceded that Stalin was an insane despot who had committed mass murder, extorted confessions by torture, weakened Soviet industry and agriculture by purges, practically destroyed the fighting force of the Soviet army in the mass killings of its leaders in the 1930's, deported whole nations, nearly lost the war through military and diplomatic blunders, and that he was a coward at heart. Yet the theme of Khrushchev's accusations against Stalin was not Stalin, the oppressor of the Russian people, but Stalin, *the oppressor of the Communist Party*. The charge was that "many thousands of honest and innocent communists died" as a result of his monstrous and despotic rule. Khrushchev did not have a word of criticism against the Soviet system itself; in his analysis, the crimes of the Stalinist period were due to one man, and one man only.

On the constructive side, Khrushchev promised, not more popular democracy, but *changes from the top:* henceforth the "cult of person-ality" would no longer be tolerated, and Russia would be ruled by a group of despots instead of by just one, as under Stalin. Later in the same year, Khrushchev and his associates decided that "liberalization" had gone too far, and that a harder line, domestically and internation-ally, must be followed again. In both cases, the present Soviet leader-ship thus made it clear to its own people that changes in Soviet life could come only from the top, and that no popular pressure or inter-

© 1955 The New Yorker Magazine, Inc.

"I'VE BEEN AWAY. WHO'S INSIDE?"

ference would be tolerated. This same philosophy underlies the actions of the Soviet leadership in dealing with the communist satellites in Eastern Europe.

In line with Khrushchev's theory of change from the top only, a major shake-up in the Soviet leadership occurred in July, 1957. Five of the eleven members of the Presidium of the Central Com-mittee of the Communist Party—Molotov, Malenkov, Kaganovich, Pervukhin, and Saburov—and Shepilov, the former Foreign Minister and editor of *Pravda,* were summarily purged, expelled from their top jobs in government, and accused of "anti-Party activities." This was the most important purge and governmental change in twenty years, yet the news was first broadcast to foreign countries before the Soviet public was permitted to learn what had happened. Ironically, Khrushchev used his attacks against the Stalinist "cult of personality" to establish himself by this ruthless purge as the undisputed master of the Soviet Government and the Communist Party.

THE ISSUE OF COMMUNISM

The communists, following Lenin and Stalin, assert that the issue which divides the world, and for which there is no peaceful solution, is the clash between individual, capitalist enterprise and public, collective ownership of the means of production.

This communist analysis of the world situation is concurred with, oddly enough, in capitalist countries by some extreme conservatives, men who claim to be the most uncompromising foes of communism. Such men constantly acknowledge the validity of the communist party line by asserting that the preservation of free enterprise is the supreme goal of the free world, and that the main threat of communism lies in its opposition to private enterprise.

Yet to accept this communist-conservative interpretation of the present world struggle is to fall into an erroneous analysis of the facts and an even more disastrous formulation of policy. The progressive socialization of basic industries in Britain and the Scandinavian countries has proved that varying forms of industrial ownership and organization do not in themselves constitute a source of conflict. The staunchest allies of the United States are Britain and Norway in Europe, Australia and New Zealand in the Pacific, and Israel in the Near East—nations with the strongest socialist movements in the world, and nations, moreover, that have gone a long way toward the socialization of the basic industries. The Anglo-American alliance after World War II, culminating in the North Atlantic Treaty Organization, is the closest association of the United States and Britain ever formed in time of peace, and on the British side it was initiated and carried through by the socialist Labor government.

Socialists in Britain, as in other countries, understand that their disagreement with certain aspects of American capitalism, or even with capitalism in general, is a minor issue compared with their disagreements with communist totalitarianism.

What makes communism an issue of peace or war is not its opposition to capitalism, but its determination to impose its philosophy by force of arms. *The proper division of the world therefore is not between communism and capitalism, but between nations that prepare for aggressive conquest and nations that honestly and sincerely wish to maintain peace.*

The internal economic system—be it capitalism, socialism, a mixed economy, or communism—is of no necessary relevance to the main issue of world peace and the right of nations to be free.

Similar to the error of confusing communism with anticapitalism is the equally common error of confusing it with *antidemocracy.* However understandable the emotional and intellectual revulsion of free men from communist despotism and cruelty, they must not lose sight of the fact that communist antidemocracy is no more the main issue than communist anticapitalism. Numerous antidemocratic regimes throughout the world are gladly accepted by the free nations as allies in the struggle against communism, just as they were welcomed earlier in the struggle against fascism. Most Latin American states are governed by antidemocratic (or, at least, nondemocratic) regimes. Portugal has had for over twenty-five years a restrained, gentlemanly sort of one-man dictatorship; if the main division of the world were between democracy and autocracy, Portugal (as many another nation) would be a weak candidate for the democratic side, yet she is helping to resist imperialist aggression.

From a practical viewpoint, the identification of communism with antidemocracy and anticapitalism plays right into the hands of the communists, since both capitalism and democracy (as understood, for example, in the United States) are not typical, but rather exceptional, in the world at large. If western policy were to limit admission to the alliance of the free nations to a select group of a few countries happily matching the economic and political institutions of Britain or the United States, the resulting group of states would be hopelessly inadequate in meeting the threat of communism.

From the viewpoint of international ethics and common sense, the main interest one country has in another is the latter's willingness to preserve the peace. Only when autocracy is accompanied by aggres-

sive imperialistic designs does it become a danger to the world. And
then what is dangerous in it is its aggressiveness, not its autocracy, and
the two should not be confused.

Yugoslavia is a case in point. In 1948, she broke with Moscow,
while retaining both the political dictatorship of the Communist
Party and the economic system of communist collectivism. But in
her *foreign policy* Yugoslavia effected a fundamental change. Instead of being tied to the communist bloc of aggression dominated
by the Kremlin, Yugoslavia asserted her right to be an independent
nation, and she resisted communist threats heroically, as she had
resisted nazi imperialism in 1941 and throughout World War II.
The free nations are not committing any act of hypocrisy by supporting Yugoslavia in her struggle for independence against Soviet
subversion and aggression. Whether Yugoslavia believes in capitalism or democracy is an important question, to be sure, but the
number one question is whether Yugoslavia is willing to fight with the
aggressors, or against them.

The case of Spain is similar. In 1939, the Franco regime was set up
as an admittedly antidemocratic, authoritarian government, with
strong sympathies for the fascist systems of Mussolini and Hitler. Yet
despite such doctrinal sympathies, Spain refrained during World War
II from entering the conflict on the side of Italy and Germany, thus
enabling the British and American navies to win the Battle of the
Atlantic with less cost and sacrifice than would otherwise have been
the case.

After World War II, the Franco regime has gradually mellowed
politically, toning down its authoritarian tendencies, although still
being far removed from a liberal democracy. Since 1953, the United
States has been building, with the cooperation of the Spanish government, vast naval and air installations on Spanish soil, and the impact
of this American aid, combined with the direct personal influence of
thousands of American civilians and military, has been in the direction of bringing Spain closer to the western democracies.

As in the case of Yugoslavia, no one can seriously maintain that
Spain is a democracy. Yet even more important to the free world is
the fact that Spain is willing to play her part in the struggle against
communist imperialism, and can be counted upon to be a much more
reliable ally in that struggle than many other states, such as Yugoslavia or some Asian nations.

If the free nations draw the line sharply between themselves and the communist world conspiracy, the issue can be presented in the age-old terms of human liberty versus serfdom and slavery. Thus expressed, the issue will be clear wherever men and women prize liberty, and communist propaganda will fail in its attempt to picture the world struggle as one between Wall Street and the peoples of the world. If the free world would thus commit itself to the fight for human liberty against communist aggression as the main issue of the present crisis, there is little doubt of the ultimate outcome of the struggle.

FOR FURTHER READING

Almond, Gabriel A., *The Appeals of Communism* (Princeton University Press, 1954)

Bauer, Raymond A., and others, *How the Soviet System Works* (Harvard University Press, 1956)

Beke, Laszlo, *A Student's Diary: Budapest, Oct. 16-Nov. 1, 1956* (Viking, 1957)

Belov, Fedor, *The History of a Soviet Collective Farm* (Praeger, 1955)

Berlin, Isaiah, *Karl Marx* (Oxford University Press, 1948)

Brant, Stefan, *The East German Rising* (Praeger, 1957)

Burnham, James, *The Web of Subversion* (John Day, 1954)

Campesino, El, *Life and Death in Soviet Russia* (Lion Books, 1953)

Counts, George S., *The Challenge of Soviet Education* (McGraw-Hill, 1957)

Crankshaw, Edward, *Russia Without Stalin* (Viking, 1956)

Cronyn, George W., *A Primer on Communism: 200 Questions and Answers* (Dutton, 1957)

Crossman, Richard, *The God That Failed* (Bantam Books, 1952)

Dallin, David J., *The Changing World of Soviet Russia* (Yale University Press, 1956)

————, *Soviet Espionage* (Yale University Press, 1955)

Djilas, Milovan, *The New Class: An Analysis of the Communist System* (Praeger, 1957)

Dudintsev, Vladimir, *Not by Bread Alone* (Dutton, 1957)

Ebenstein, William, *Great Political Thinkers*, 2nd ed. (Rinehart, 1956), ch. 23

————, *Political Thought in Perspective* (McGraw-Hill, 1957), chaps. 24, 25

Evans, Joseph E., *Through Soviet Windows* (Dow Jones, 1957)

Fryer, Peter, *Hungarian Tragedy* (Dennis Dobson, 1956)

Guins, George C., *Communism on the Decline* (Philosophical Library, 1956)

Hazard, John N., *The Soviet System of Government* (University of Chicago Press, 1957)

Heller, Andor, *No More Comrades* (Regnery, 1957)

Hildebrandt, Rainer, *The Explosion: The Uprising Behind the Iron Curtain* (Little, Brown, 1955)

Hodgkinson, Harry, *Double Talk: The Language of Communism* (George Allen and Unwin, 1955)

Hunt, R. N. Carew, *The Theory and Practice of Communism* (Macmillan, 1950)

Koestler, Arthur, *Darkness at Noon* (Mentor Books, 1948)

Lasky, Melvin J. (ed.), *The Hungarian Revolution* (Praeger, 1957)

Masaryk, T. G., *The Spirit of Russia,* 2nd ed. (Macmillan, 1955)

McVicker, Charles P., *Titoism: Pattern for International Communism* (St. Martin's Press, 1957)

Metaxas, Alexandre, *Russia Against the Kremlin* (World, 1957)

Michener, James A., *The Bridge at Andau* (Random House, 1957)

Mikes, George, *The Hungarian Revolution* (André Deutsch, 1957)

Possony, Stefan T., *A Century of Conflict: Communist Techniques of World Revolution* (Regnery, 1953)

Princeton University Conference, *The Challenge of Soviet Industrial Growth* (Princeton University Conference, 1957)

Roberts, Henry L., *Russia and America* (Mentor Books, 1956)

Russian Institute, Columbia University, *The Anti-Stalin Campaign and International Communism* (Columbia University Press, 1956)

Scholmer, Joseph, *Vorkuta* (Weidenfeld and Nicolson, 1954)

Schwartz, Harry, *Russia's Soviet Economy,* 2nd ed. (Prentice-Hall, 1954)

Schwarz, Solomon M., *Labor in the Soviet Union* (Praeger, 1951)

Seton-Watson, Hugh, *From Lenin to Malenkov* (Praeger, 1953)

Stipp, John L. (ed.), *Soviet Russia Today* (Harper, 1956)

Wilson, Edmund, *To the Finland Station* (Anchor Books, 1953)

Wolfe, Bertram D., *Khrushchev and Stalin's Ghost* (Praeger, 1956)

Zinner, Paul E. (ed.), *National Communism and Popular Revolt in Eastern Europe* (Columbia University Press, 1956)

2

TOTALITARIAN FASCISM

SOCIAL BACKGROUND OF FASCISM

Communism was the first major twentieth-century totalitarian revolt against the western, liberal way of life; *fascism* was the second. Stripped to its essentials, fascism is the totalitarian organization of government and society by a single-party dictatorship, intensely nationalist, racialist, militarist, and imperialist. In Europe, Italy (1922) was the first to go fascist, followed by Germany (1933). In Asia, Japan went fascist in the nineteen thirties, gradually evolving totalitarian institutions out of its own native heritage. In the Western Hemisphere, a semi-constitutional government of a landed oligarchy was destroyed in Argentina in 1943 in a revolt of dissatisfied officers, and a fascist dictatorship was subsequently built up under the leadership of Colonel (later General) Perón, lasting until its overthrow in 1955.

Clearly, then, whereas communism is the form of totalitarianism typically linked with poor and underdeveloped nations (Russia in Europe, China in Asia), fascism is the form of totalitarianism that typically grows in wealthier and technologically more advanced nations (Germany in Europe, Japan in Asia). In the Americas, Guatemala, one of the poorest and most backward nations, for years encouraged the growth of communism, until the pro-communist regime of President Arbenz was overthrown in June 1954; fascism,

85

on the other hand, saw its most intense development in Argentina, the wealthiest of the twenty Latin American republics.

Whereas communism is very largely the product of predemocratic and preindustrial societies, fascism is *postdemocratic* and *postindustrial:* fascism is impossible in countries with no democratic experience at all. In such societies, dictatorship may be based on the army, the bureaucracy, or the personal prestige of the dictator, but it will lack the element of mass enthusiasm and *mass support* (not necessarily majority support) characteristic of fascism. Moreover, although no fascist system can arise in a country without a little democratic experience (as in Germany or Japan), there is not much likelihood of fascist success in countries that have experienced democracy over a long period, for example, Switzerland, Scandinavia, Holland, England, or the United States.

Paradoxically, experience has proved that in general the more violent and terroristic fascist movements are, the more popular support they tend to have. Thus fascism in Germany was both the most brutal and the most popular; in Italy fascism was less popular and less brutal. Such fascist dictatorships based on mass support are not to be confused with traditional dictatorships such as existed in Europe in several countries during the nineteen thirties, particularly in the Balkans and Eastern Europe. The present authoritarian dictatorships in Spain and Portugal, too, are essentially traditional, relatively moderate, and rest on the established forces of the bureaucracy and army.

In Latin America, too, there are numerous dictatorships, but they are not fascist (with the exception of Argentina from 1943 to 1955), because they typically rest on the personal magic of one man, usually a general. Relying as he must on the good will of his army, the Latin American dictator has no need for, and rarely has, the mass support that characterizes fascism. Popular political movements hardly enter the picture.

The second condition essential to the growth of fascism is a considerable degree of industrial development. There are at least two principal points of contact between fascism and relatively advanced industrialization. First, fascist terror and propaganda require a good deal of technological organization and know-how. Second, as a system of *permanent mobilization for war,* fascism cannot hope to succeed without considerable industrial skills and resources.

It may be argued that the connection between fascism and modern industry goes even deeper. Every industrial society brings about social and economic tensions. Such tensions can be dealt with in one of two ways: the liberal way or the totalitarian way. The liberal society recognizes the variety of economic interests and their necessary conflict (such as between labor and management, agriculture and industry, skilled and unskilled workers), and seeks to reconcile such conflicts by the experimental method of peaceful, gradual adjustment. The totalitarian fascist state either denies that there are divergent social interests (abhorring as it does the notion of variety, especially in the form of departures from state-imposed uniformity), or, if it half-heartedly concedes the existence of divergent social interests, it resolves such differences by force.

The difference between communism and fascism on this point may be briefly (and with some oversimplification) formulated in this way: communism is the totalitarian way of *industrializing a backward society;* fascism is the totalitarian method of *solving conflicts within an industrially more advanced society.*

In its social background, fascism has particularly appealed to two groups: first, a numerically small group of *industrialists* and *landowners* who are willing to finance fascist movements in the hope of thereby getting rid of free labor unions. Industrialists are not, as a class, any more fascist-minded than other social groups; in countries with strong liberal and democratic traditions, for example, industrialists are no better and no worse than other people as far as their faith in the democratic process is concerned. But where democracy is weak, as in Germany, Italy, or Japan, it takes only a few wealthy industrialists and landowners to supply fascist movements with ample funds. In *I Paid Hitler* (1941), Fritz Thyssen, one of Germany's wealthiest steel manufacturers, has given a typical account of the support, running into many millions of dollars, that the nazis received in the nineteen twenties and early thirties from German big business and finance.

Where the pressure of public opinion is strongly democratic and liberal, individual industrialists who are inclined toward fascism will find that supporting fascist groups is bad business; but where democratic traditions are weak, leaders of big business like Thyssen and Krupp in Germany, or the Mitsui trust in Japan, will find it possible to side openly with the cause of fascism.

The second main source of fascist support—and numerically by far the most important—comes from the *lower middle classes,* mostly in the salaried group. Many persons in this class dread the prospect of joining (or rejoining) the proletariat, and look to fascism for a salvation of their status and prestige. The salaried employee feels jealous of Big Business, into whose higher echelons he would like to rise, and fearful of Labor, into whose proletarian world he would hate to descend. Fascism very cleverly utilizes these jealousies and fears of the "salariat" by propagandizing simultaneously against Big Business and Big Labor. Although such propaganda is neither logically nor politically consistent, its very inconsistency both reflects the confusion of, and appeals to, the salaried class, uncertain as that class is where to turn politically.

Paradoxically, organized labor frequently contributes to this uncertainty and demoralization of the salariat without meaning to do so. For psychological reasons, white collar workers are generally unwilling to organize into unions. As a result, the *incomes of workers,* particularly those organized in unions, *have tended to improve much faster than the incomes of salaried employees.* As the gap between the economic status of workers and that of salaried persons widens, the latter become more and more resentful of losing what they consider their rightful place in society, and may turn to fascism, which promises to keep unions and other "upstart" organizations under control. The leaders of organized labor may point out that the weak economic position of salaried persons is their own fault, and that such persons are in error in refusing to organize and bring pressure upon their employers; such arguing points, however, though they may be logically valid, are psychologically ineffective. In times of prosperity the divergence between labor and the salaried class may not be too upsetting politically, but in times of crisis and depression the smallest class antagonisms may turn into political dynamite.

Another important social group that has shown itself particularly vulnerable to fascist propaganda is the *military.* Even in a strong and well established democracy, professional military people tend to overestimate the virtues of discipline and unity; where democracy is weak, this professional bias of the military becomes a political menace. Thus, in the early stages of nazism in Germany, the military class of the nation either openly supported Hitler or at best maintained an attitude of benevolent neutrality. The top military leaders

of Germany knew that a high proportion of nazi bosses were criminals and unscrupulous psychopaths, yet they supported the nazi
movement as a step toward the militarization of the German people.
In Italy, too, fascism in its early stages received considerable support from army circles, and in Japan fascism developed with the active
and enthusiastic support of the army, which had every reason to be
the main pillar of a regime committed to imperialist expansion. In
Argentina, semi-constitutional government was overthrown in 1943 in
a revolt of the "younger officers," under Perón, who set up his own
brand of fascism, named "peronismo" after him.

Although fascism is not a direct or necessary result of *economic
depression,* as Marxist-communist theory suggests, there *is* a relation
between the two. In times of depression, fear and frustration undermine faith in the democratic process, and where the faith in rational
methods weakens, fascism is the potential gainer. The small businessman blames Big Business for his troubles; Big Business puts the blame
on the unreasonableness of the labor unions; labor feels that the only
way out is to soak the rich; the farmers feel that they are not getting
enough for farm products and that they are made to pay too high
prices for manufactured goods; city people envy the security of the
farmers ("always something to eat and a roof over your head");
and—worst of all—there is the large mass of unemployed people.

What democratic nations have failed to understand sufficiently is
that the worst feature of unemployment is not economic suffering
(which can be mitigated by adequate relief), but the feeling of being
useless, unwanted, outside of the respectable ranks of society. It is
among these spiritually homeless that fascism makes serious inroads
during a depression: by putting an unemployed person into a uniform
a fascist movement makes him feel that he "belongs," and by telling
him that he is a member of a superior race or nation such a movement
restores some of his self-respect.

This sense of not belonging is, in a way, characteristic of life in
modern industrial society in general. Industrialization and urbaniza-
tion have debunked and frequently destroyed traditional values,
without always providing adequate substitute values in their place.
The disorientation and confusion resulting from these effects of
industrialization provide the social and psychological background of
fascism, with its attempt to restore the old, preindustrial way of life
in a modern nation.

It can thus be seen that the Marxist interpretation of fascism in terms of class (identifying fascism with capitalism in decay) is not borne out by the facts. *Fascism cuts across all social groups:* wealthy industrialists and landowners support it for one reason, the lower middle classes for another, psychopaths and criminals for another still—and finally there are the many nationalists and chauvinists in every country who prove themselves vulnerable to every promise of conquest and empire. In terms of explicit programs, fascist movements must make the most contradictory promises to satisfy all their adherents; such contradictions are one main weakness of fascism. Yet in terms of implicit psychological background, fascism looks within all social groups for the great common denominators, *frustration, resentment,* and *insecurity.* These psychological attitudes can easily be turned into hatred and aggression, against both internal and external "enemies."

Because these social and psychological attitudes are not the monopoly of any one social class, fascism manages to appeal to large masses of people in some countries. When Adolf Hitler joined the nazi party in 1919, he was Member No. 7. Yet within fourteen years nazism became the greatest mass movement in German history, including in its ranks members of all groups of German society, from hobos to members of the imperial family and the royal houses of the German states. By 1932, the nazi vote had mounted to 14 million, and in March 1933, 17 million Germans (almost half the total vote) voted for nazism, not to speak of several more millions who voted for nationalist and militarist parties that were nazi in all but name. It is obvious that 17 million voters cannot consist exclusively of wealthy bankers and industrialists, and that only a party with a national, rather than class, appeal can obtain such high votes. In no other country has fascism ever been as widely popular as in Germany, but there has been no fascist regime anywhere without some popular support.

PSYCHOLOGICAL ROOTS OF TOTALITARIANISM

In countries like Germany and Japan, the clue to the understanding of fascist tendencies lies in broad social forces and traditions. In those countries, the authoritarian tradition is the predominant one, and democracy is still a very frail plant. As a result, a German or

Japanese with fascist tendencies is no outcast, and may be considered perfectly well adjusted to his society. Even when his society explicitly condemns fascism, as it is likely to do each time it loses a war, much in the implicit habits and customs of German and Japanese life tends toward the authoritarian way of life, and from authoritarianism to fascism there is only a step. In democratic societies such as Britain or the United States, on the other hand, the appeal of fascism can be more fruitfully judged from the angle of individual psychology. Empirical studies in the United States have shown that 10 per cent of Americans are strongly authoritarian, and about 20 per cent partly authoritarian (T. W. Adorno and others, *The Authoritarian Personality*, 1950).

The traditional analysis of political dictatorship has been centered on the motivations of dictatorial leaders, driven by lust for power and sadistic cravings for domination. The followers and subjects of a dictatorship are viewed exclusively as "victims," who just happen to fall into the misfortune of oppressive rule. Every insurance company knows that some persons are more "accident-prone" than others, and every policeman knows that some persons are more likely to attract criminals than others.

Similarly, it is not too far-fetched to suggest that some people (and some nations) are more "dictatorship-prone" than others. Plato knew enough psychology—over two thousand years before Freud—to suggest in his *Republic* that constitutions grow not "from stone to stone," but "from those characters of the men in the cities which preponderate and draw the rest of the city after them." The very existence of an authoritarian mass movement like fascism depends on the *desire* of many persons *to submit and obey*.

Rational democrats may not understand why anyone should prefer to obey rather than take the responsibility of making decisions for himself—they take it for granted that men *should* make their own decisions rather than have their actions dictated by others. But this democratic stereotype overlooks what are the *comforts of irresponsibility* to many persons. Children love the feeling of being sheltered and secure behind the benevolent power and authority of their parents. The mark of the mature adult is his willingness and capacity to stand on his own feet, to take responsibility and be independent of others. Yet relatively few persons ever attain this sort of maturity; the process of growing up, as every adolescent knows, is painful, and many rebel against being driven out of the Garden of Eden into the cold world, where they must struggle for themselves without the omnipotence and omniscience of parental love and security. In all human beings there is a *latent tendency toward dependence* based on the parent-child relationship, although some manage to develop self-reliant adulthood more than others. The totalitarian system, whether communist or fascist, appeals to people who, for whatever personal reasons, look for the father-child relationship, for security in dependence.

What are some of the empirically ascertainable traits that characterize the authoritarian personality, particularly the personality attracted to the fascist type of authoritarianism? First, a tendency to conform compulsively to orthodox ideals and practices; emotional rigidity and limited imagination; excessive concern with problems of status and strength; strong loyalty to one's own group ("in-group") coupled with vehement dislike of outsiders ("out-group"); and stress on discipline and obedience, rather than freedom and spontaneity, in human relations (education, sex, family, religion, industry, government). The "herd-minded" (or "ethnocentric") element in the fascist personality is perhaps the single most important one, although no one element in itself conclusively defines a personality as authoritarian.

The key role of the *family* in the formation of basic attitudes seems to be brought out by all the clinical and theoretical studies we have; but the family is not, after all, an isolated and independent agent. Rather it reflects the predominant social goals and values, and constitutes, to the child, the cultural and psychological representative of society at large.

No person is ever completely authoritarian or completely democratic, just as no human being is ever an utter devil or a perfect angel. In each case it is a question of quantity and degree, although differences of quantity eventually become differences of quality. Although there has been no major fascist mass movement in the United States so far, it is a matter of record that some Americans looked upon German and Italian fascism in the nineteen thirties as the "wave of the future" (as it was called in a book of that title), and that others sympathized with Argentine fascism in the nineteen forties and fifties.

Dependence and submission in a totalitarian society—fascist or communist—give a person the security for which he hungers, but deny him self-expression and self-assertion, which are as deeply embedded in human nature as the desire for security. Thus denied, these drives turn into repressed hostility and aggression, for the expression of which fascism provides two channels, one for the ruling class, one for the ruled. Within the apparatus of the dictatorial party and government, there is the pattern of the cyclist: crouching before the superior above, pressing down on the subordinate below. Only the leader need not crouch before anyone—he only presses down. Below the top leader—"Big Brother," as Orwell called him in *1984*, the classic fictional portrait of totalitarianism—although each member of the party and government hierarchy must kowtow to someone above him, in return he may tread on those below him.

Persons outside the ruling class, however, have no one to command; they can only obey. How can they express their hostility and aggressiveness? Since the vast majority of the people in a totalitarian state form the group of those who can only take, but not issue, commands, this is a serious problem for every dictatorship. Although officially the dictator claims that he is universally beloved, he knows that there is much repressed hatred and hostility directed (or capable of being directed) toward him and his regime.

The answer of totalitarian dictatorships is to *direct this latent hostility of the people against real or imaginary enemies.* For the communist, the enemy may be the bourgeois, Trotskyites, Titoites, or Wall Street. Hitler first chose the Jews as the target of German aggression; once given a direction for their savagery, the Germans were not satisfied until they had sent six million Jews from central and eastern Europe to the gas chambers. Later new enemies took the place of the Jews: Britain, the United States, Churchill, Roosevelt, Bolshevism, the churches. Finally, when they felt that the end was close, Hitler and his cohorts unleashed their vengeance on the Germans themselves; if they had to go down, the German people had to be destroyed with them. In a more recent fascist regime, peronist Argentina, American imperialism and international finance were the chief targets of fascist hate propaganda.

If men cannot be masters of their own lives, fascism promises mastery over other peoples; and if fascism cannot deliver the triumphs it promises, the hatred of the people may turn against their leaders, as it did against Mussolini, who was tried before a partisan committee in northern Italy in April 1945, executed, and

then publicly hung from a lamp-post in Milan. Having taught his
people violence and hatred, he reaped himself what he had sown.

The psychological interpretation of totalitarianism—fascist or
communist—is of particular value where the prevailing cultural pattern is not authoritarian, where it takes some personal quirk to break
with the democratic pattern of the environment. Thus, in societies
like Britain or the United States, the psychological analysis of people
who have embraced communism or fascism is of great value; because
there emerges from such an analysis a definite pattern of personality
factors that is typical in many American fascists or communists.

Yet it would be futile to explain the strength of fascism in Germany or Japan, or of communism in China or Italy, by means of
personal psychology. It may be argued that an American or Englishman who embraces communism or fascism is not well adjusted, comes
from a broken home, or has had an unhappy childhood, but the same
can hardly be said of 17 million Germans who voted for Hitler in
1933, or of the many millions of Frenchmen and Italians who have
persistently voted communist since the end of World War II. Where
totalitarianism assumes the proportions of a mass movement, the
main avenue of analysis must be that of the great social, economic,
and cultural forces and traditions of a nation.

Whereas the cure for an American fascist or communist may be
the psychoanalyst's couch, the cure for five million Frenchmen who
vote communist is more take-home pay every Saturday, and a more
decent life all round. Similarly, the origins of fascist totalitarianism
in Germany, Japan, and Argentina lie deeper in the collective lives
of those nations than can be revealed from a study of individual
personalities. There was plenty that was wrong in Hitler's personality
as viewed through non-German eyes, but to the 17 million Germans
who identified themselves with him in the election of March 1933 he
must have been an admirably adjusted personality indeed.

ELEMENTS OF FASCIST DOCTRINE AND POLICY

Although fascism, like communism, is a movement that exists
everywhere, it has no such authoritative statement of principles as
communism has; moreover, there is no one country, at present,
directing a fascist world conspiracy. During the nazi regime (1933-

1945), Germany was the most powerful of the fascist states then in existence, and world fascism was very largely directed, financed, and inspired by German brains and money. Since the defeat of the fascist Axis (Germany, Japan, Italy) in World War II, however, there has been no really major fascist state; Argentina never possessed anything like the world-wide influence that nazi Germany had until 1945.

The absence of a universally recognized authoritative statement of fascist principles is not total. Hitler has left in *Mein Kampf* (1925-1927) a trustworthy guide to his thought, and Mussolini's *The Doctrine of Fascism* (1932), a moderate statement of fascist principles, expresses the Italian brand of fascism. The latter has served as a model for most other fascist movements in the world because it is more universal in outlook; nazism, a specifically German brand of fascism, has proved for that reason less suitable for export.

Although there is no *Fascist Manifesto* with undisputed authority among fascists, it is not too difficult to state the principal elements of the fascist outlook:

(1) Distrust of reason
(2) Denial of basic human equality
(3) Code of behavior based on lies and violence
(4) Government by elite
(5) Totalitarianism
(6) Racialism and imperialism
(7) Opposition to international law and order

(1) The *distrust of reason* is perhaps the most significant trait of fascism. The rational tradition of the West stems from Greece, and is one of the three basic components (the other two being Jewish monotheism and Christian love) that have given the West its characteristic culture and outlook. Fascism rejects this Greek root of western civilization and is frankly *antirationalist,* distrusting reason in human affairs and stressing the irrational, sentimental, uncontrollable elements of man. Psychologically, fascism is *fanatical* rather than reflective, *dogmatic* rather than open-minded; as a result each fascist regime has its "taboo" issues (such as race, empire, the leader), and it is the nature of a taboo issue that it must be accepted on faith and cannot be critically discussed. During the fascist regime in Italy (1922-1945), Mussolini's picture was shown in every classroom in the country over the caption "Mussolini is always right."

The communist states have the taboo issue of Marxism-Leninism, a set of final truths that must not be questioned. In addition, there are the more passing taboo subjects as defined by the top party leaders, such as Khrushchev in Russia, Mao in Red China, or Tito in Yugoslavia.

As a matter of basic principle, democracy recognizes no taboo issue: there is no subject that cannot be questioned or challenged, not even the validity of democracy itself. In practice, of course, democracies do not always live up to that ideal. Thus, it is argued by some that in the United States the question of the validity of democracy is on its way to becoming a taboo issue, especially since the Supreme Court's 1951 decision upholding the constitutionality of the Smith Act of 1940 (under which the advocacy of the duty, desirability, necessity, or propriety of revolution is a criminal offense).

The individual, too, may have taboo issues, "dark corners" in his heart or mind that must not be pulled out and subjected to rational examination. The mentally healthy individual has few, or (ideally) no, taboo issues, because he is able to face reality as it is, and does not insist on living in a dream world in defiance of reality. Psychologically, the existence of taboo issues in the individual or in a group, party, or nation is due to a sense of insecurity or guilt, or both.

Under conditions of stress and strain, the individual as well as the collective group may take refuge in the temporary shelter of the taboo, postponing the facing of reality, but unable to shut it out forever. Since totalitarian regimes permanently operate in a state of high tension and crisis, the taboo is part and parcel of their normal environment. Democracies succumb to the temptation of the taboo, and its false security, only in periods of exceptional strain; it is significant that the Supreme Court's decision on the Smith Act took place in 1951, at the height of the Korean war.

(2) The *denial of basic human equality* is a common denominator of fascist (as well as communist) movements and states. True enough, democratic societies do not always live up to the ideal of human equality, but they are subject to attacks of conscience if they fail, and they at least accept equality as the long-term goal of public policy. By contrast, fascist societies not only accept the *fact* of human inequality, but go further and affirm inequality as an *ideal*.

The concept of human equality goes back to the three roots of western civilization. The Jewish idea of one God led to the idea of one mankind, since all men as children of God are brothers among themselves. The Christian notion of the inalienability and indestructibility of the human soul led to the ideal of basic *moral* equality of all men. Finally, the Greek-Stoic concept of reason led to the oneness of mankind on the basis of reason as the most truly human bond that all men have in common.

Fascism rejects this Jewish-Christian-Stoic concept of equality as soft and nonsensical, and opposes to it the concept of inequality, which can most simply be spelled out in the contrast of superiority and inferiority Thus, in the fascist code, men are superior to women, soldiers to civilians, party members to non-party members, one's own nation to others, the strong to the weak, and (perhaps most important in the fascist outlook) the victors in war to the vanquished. The chief criteria of equality in the western tradition are man's mind and soul, whereas the fascist affirmation of inequality is based ultimately on *strength*.

(3) The fascist—like the communist—code of behavior stresses *violence and lies* in all human relations, within and between nations. From the democratic viewpoint, politics is the mechanism through which social conflicts of interest are peacefully adjusted. By contrast, the fascist view is that politics is characterized by the *friend-enemy relation*. Politics begins and ends, in this fascist way of thinking, with the possibility of an enemy—and his *total annihilation*. The democratic antithesis to the friend is the *opponent*, and in democratic nations the opponent of today is considered the potential government of tomorrow (the opposition in the British Parliament is officially called "Her Majesty's Loyal Opposition," and the leader of the Opposition receives a special salary to do his job well). The fascist knows only enemies, not opponents, and since enemies represent evil incarnate, total annihilation is the only solution. This doctrine applies to domestic as well as to foreign enemies: thus, the nazis first set up concentration camps and gas chambers for German citizens, and later used the same facilities on non-Germans.

Contrary to common opinion, *concentration camps* and *slave labor camps* are not incidental phenomena in totalitarian systems like fascism and communism, but are of their very core. It is in the concentration and slave labor camps that totalitarian regimes seek to destroy the legal and moral person in man, and to deprive him of the last residue of individuality. The technique of "brain-washing" used by fascists and communists deliberately seeks to break man's mind to the point where he will publicly confess to crimes he did not commit and perhaps could not have committed. After a period of brain-washing, the victim no longer has a mind of his own; he merely plays back, like a record, what is expected of him.

By institutionalizing organized mass murder in concentration and slave labor camps, totalitarian regimes demonstrate to the entire population what is in store for anyone in disfavor with the men in power, and at the same time they provide the shock troops of the regime with a peacetime outlet for savagery and fanaticism. Imme-diate death is often considered too humane a penalty by such regimes; moreover, the slow death of concentration or slave labor camps has a greater demonstration value than the clean, old-fashioned method of the execution squad or the gallows.

(4) *Government by elite* is a principle that fascists everywhere frankly oppose to the "democratic fallacy" that people are capable of governing themselves. The concept that only a small minority of the population, qualified by birth, education, or social standing, is capable of understanding what is best for the whole community, and of putting it into practice, is not an invention of twentieth-century fascism. Plato, one of the founders of western political philosophy, strongly believed that only one class—the "philosopher-kings"—are fit to rule society. The contrary belief—that the people as a whole are capable of self-rule—is of relatively recent origin, and has suc-cessfully worked only in limited areas of the globe.

The fascist idea of government by a self-appointed elite (a fascist government usually *shoots* itself into power) is undemocratic.

Such a government does not always lack popular approval—strange as it may seem to the democrat, who expects everybody to behave as he does, people have throughout history frequently ap-proved of autocratic governments. Approval alone, however, is no evidence of democracy: what makes a government *democratic* is that it always *depends* on popular *consent, given in free elections.* In fascist regimes, even when the government enjoys popular ap-proval, it is carried on *independently of popular consent,* without free elections, a free press, or a freely functioning opposition.

The fascist *leadership principle* expresses the extreme form of the elite concept. It fully reflects the irrational nature of fascist politics: the leader is considered infallible, endowed with mystical gifts and insights. In a conflict between popular opinion and the fascist leader, the will of the latter prevails: the leader represents the public interest, the way all people would think if they knew what was best for the whole community (what Rousseau called the "General Will"), whereas the people express only individual whims and desires not necessarily in harmony with the public good (Rousseau's "Will of All").

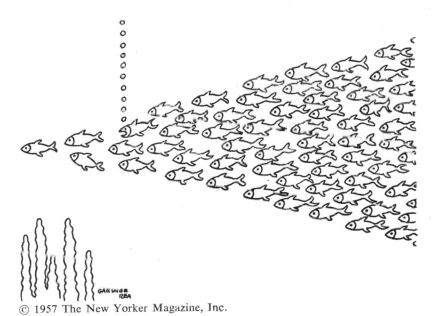

"GOD KNOWS WHAT WE'D DO IF ANYTHING SHOULD EVER HAPPEN TO HIM!"

The emphasis on leadership is contrary to the fascist enforcement of orthodoxy and conformity. Hitler, Mussolini, and Perón were formed in nonfascist societies with considerable free competition. So far it has been impossible to appraise the leadership qualities of a generation born and bred under fascism. The German, Italian, and Argentine brands of fascism did not last long enough (1933-45 in Germany; 1922-45 in Italy; and 1943-55 in Argentina) to supply conclusive evidence on the matter.

(5) *Totalitarianism* in all human relations characterizes fascism

as a *way of life* rather than as a mere system of government. There are many dictatorships, particularly in Latin America, in which the authoritarian principle is applied only in government. If the people do not make any trouble politically, and do not interfere with the rule of the dictator and his henchmen, they can lead their own lives pretty freely. Education, religion, business, and agriculture are not touched very much by the political dictatorship. By contrast, fascism is *totalitarian:* it employs authority and violence in *all* kinds of social relations, whether political or not.

With regard to women, the largest discriminated-against minority of the world, fascism is antifeminist. Women should stay in their place, said the nazis, and their concern should be the famous three K's—*Kinder, Küche, Kirche.* Since women are unable to bear arms, they are automatically second-class citizens, according to the fascist view, and are excluded from leadership positions in government or party. They have the right to vote, but since this right in fascist countries means only the right to be enthusiastic about the leader and his party, it is not much of a practical asset. Within the family, the father is "the leader," and both his wife and his children get a strong taste of domestic authoritarian government, which has more effect on their everyday lives than the operations of the remote political government in the capital. In the extreme case of modern fascism, nazi Germany, the contempt for women was finally demonstrated in the official ridicule of the institution of marriage as a false Jewish-Christian prejudice, and German women were encouraged to produce children for the fatherland outside of wedlock.

Fascist countries also make a point of refusing to employ women extensively in schools. From the fascist viewpoint, schools are to teach discipline and obedience, specifically to prepare the boys for military service and the girls for related domestic activities. In a program of such importance, fascist educators feel women teachers have no place.

Thus it can be seen that fascist totalitarianism, unlike the old-fashioned dictatorships of Latin America, is *totalitarian in its objective:* to control all phases of human life, political or not, from the cradle to the grave. It begins the control even before the cradle, by pushing definite population policies, and has been known to reach into the grave, so to speak, to decide whether a dead person should have a burial at all, and if so in what form.

But fascism is also *totalitarian in its means;* it will use any form of coercion, from verbal threats to mass murder, in obtaining its ends. By contrast, the classical authoritarian dictatorship was, and is, more restrained in its means, and resorts to murder only on a limited scale. Thus, whenever a Latin American dictator is ousted, he is usually permitted by his opponents to assemble his family and peacefully depart to a foreign country.

(6) *Racialism and imperialism* express the two basic fascist principles of inequality and violence as applied to the society of nations. Within the nation, fascist doctrine holds, the elite is superior to the rest and may impose its will upon them by force. Similarly, between nations the *elite nation* is superior to the others and entitled to rule them. German fascism went furthest in its racialist and imperialist policies. A straight line led from the theories of the superiority of the German-Nordic "race" to the mass murder of millions of people. The German objective of world domination included the elimination of some nations through genocide, and the enslavement of the rest. After the expected defeat of Britain and Russia, the United States was to be next on the list. The Japanese race theories found their practical imperialist expression in the concept of "co-prosperity," under which Japan would prosper by exploiting Asia and the Pacific.

Italian fascism was for a long time (from 1922 to 1938) remarkably free from exaggerated race theories; early Italian propaganda in this general field concentrated on the idea of reviving the old Roman empire. In 1938, however, Mussolini discovered that the Italians were a pure and superior race, and he became more closely tied to Hitler Germany.

In Argentina, the Perón government strongly emphasized the mission and destiny of Argentina, and accompanied this doctrine of Argentine superiority with a deliberate policy of imperialism. Peronist imperialism, probably out of respect for the tremendous power of the United States in the Western Hemisphere, which makes any fascist territorial ventures highly dangerous, limited itself to economic, political, and ideological expansion; but Argentina built up a vast armament industry, and her neighbors could not help wondering against whom this Argentine war potential was to be used. Only the overthrow of the Perón dictatorship in 1955 removed these fears of Argentine imperialism.

Racialism and imperialism are not an exclusive monopoly of

fascism. Although communist theory rejects both, Russian communism is strongly imperialistic, and after World War II a Great Russian cult was built up, differing only in degree from the Great Russian superiority concept as it was officially held in pre-Bolshevik Russia.

In the democracies, too, there is a tradition of racialism; in the United States, for example, racial discrimination has seriously corroded the vitality of democratic ideals. Called (by the Swedish social scientist Gunnar Myrdal) "the American dilemma," the race issue in the United States may ultimately decide the fate of the democratic way of life at home and abroad.

The communists have concentrated much of their propaganda in Asia and Africa on British imperialism and American racialism; both points have proved effective in many of the underdeveloped countries, and if the communists have frequently failed to make converts out of such propaganda, they have at least succeeded in paralyzing Anglo-American influence by fostering a position of neutralism, as in India and Latin America. The neutralist Indian is so haunted by the phantom of yesterday's British imperialism that he is unable to see the reality of today's communist imperialism.

(7) *Opposition to international law and order* is the logical outcome of the fascist belief in inequality, violence, racialism, imperialism, and war. Whereas nonfascists (with the exception of out-and-out nonresisting pacifists) accept war as a tragic fact, which should be abolished, fascists raise war to the level of an *ideal,* because, as Mussolini put it, "war alone brings up to their highest tension all human energies and puts the stamp of nobility upon the peoples who have the courage to meet it."

Any type of international organization assumes some form of *government by consent,* which is directly contradictory to the fascist principle of *government by force.* Also, equality of states before the law of nations is a basic principle of international order. The fascist concept of the elite leads, as we have seen, to the leadership of one nation over the society of nations as it does to the leadership of one man within the nation's government. Fascist states therefore shy away from international organizations in which they are expected to abide by majority decisions, and in which government is carried on by methods of discussion rather than by force.

The fascist regimes of Italy and Germany had no use for the League of Nations, Germany withdrawing at a very early date in 1933, and Italy in 1937. In the United Nations, peronist Argentina consistently played a lone wolf role. In the Organization of American States, she did all she could to prevent effective cooperation between the United States and the Latin American republics.

Diplomatically, fascist states shy away from general multilateral agreements; they prefer *bilateral agreements,* particularly with states they plan to overrun. Whenever Hitler offered a pact of friendship and nonaggression to a small state, the world received the clue to the next victim of nazi aggression. Japan and Italy followed the same technique under their fascist regimes, and Argentina under Perón would also rather deal with (and thus control) individual neighbors than enter into multilateral agreements over the execution of which the Argentine government had no exclusive control.

The Soviet Union, too, has employed this technique of dominating other states through bilateral agreements. It has tied the communist satellite states to the Kremlin through such agreements; and it has successfully prevented noncommunist Finland from joining any multilateral agreements like the North Atlantic Treaty Organization. As for Turkey, Russia has failed to cajole her into submission, cloaked in the language of bilateral friendship and nonaggression, only because Turkey can quickly call on outside aid to meet Russian aggression.

In sum, it can be seen that the fascist theory and practice of international politics are not so different from those of communism. Both accept force and war as the vehicles of resolving differences.

For the communist, the concept of *class* plays the dominant role in the struggle, whereas fascism sees in *race* and *nation* the key concepts in the dynamics of change.

In practice, both communism and fascism lead to the same thing in international relations, although their theoretical starting-points differ. When Germany and Russia finally clashed in 1941, the reason was not ideological but practical: they could not agree on the division of the spoils. Since Russia was not satisfied with German proposals for dividing up the world, Germany attacked Russia as an obstacle on its path to world dominion.

FASCIST ECONOMICS: THE CORPORATE STATE

The corporate state applies fascist principles of organization and control to the economy. The fascist economy is subdivided in state-controlled associations of capital and labor, and each association has a monopoly in its trade or occupation. *The one-party state is the ultimate arbiter of conflicts between capital and labor.*

The philosophy of the corporate state rests on two assumptions. First, man (except for the small ruling elite) should not be politically articulate as a *citizen,* but only as a worker, entrepreneur, farmer, doctor, or lawyer; general political problems are assumed to be too complicated for the mass of the people, who are only expected to understand issues that bear directly on their vocational or professional work. Second, members of the small ruling elite are supposed to understand broad problems that affect the whole society, and they alone are therefore qualified to govern the community. This conception is Platonic in origin, and in modern times antidemocratic thinkers like Burke and Hegel have supported it against the claims of the democratic theory.

The democratic conception rejects this corporate approach to economic and political organization for several reasons. In the first place, *it is not always easy to separate economic from political aspects.* Tariffs seem to be a purely economic issue, yet they directly affect political and diplomatic relations with other states. Immigration seems at first sight to be an economic problem, yet delicate psychological and diplomatic issues are involved in it. Economic aid to other nations, as the United States has learned in the last fifteen years, has profound military and political aspects as well as economic effects. To take another illustration: the morale and economic efficiency of British coal miners not only determine the volume of fuel that can be put into industrial use, but also vitally affect Britain's position as a world power. The fascist assumption, therefore, that every citizen should be heard only in economic issues (and then only to the extent that he has a day-to-day familiarity with them) falls down on the very difficulty of separating economic from political issues.

Second, the democratic theory holds that only the man who

wears the shoe knows where it pinches; the *mystic knowledge and insight of the ruling elite are no substitute for the experience of the ruled*—or, as Aristotle put it, the guest is a better judge of the meal than the cook. Fascists insist that the cook not only ought to be the final judge of his product, but also should impose his judgment on the guests, by force if necessary.

Finally, the democratic theory rejects the fascist assumption that members of one particular class are superior in *judgment* to the rest of the people, and are therefore the nation's natural rulers. Formal education can supply knowledge only, not judgment. Judgment is not something that can be learned in fascist schools for leaders; it is the result of character, intelligence, experience, and personal philosophy. Formal training and education in leadership, party doctrine, public administration, history, and politics do not necessarily add up to true leadership. Jesus did not obtain a Ph.D. in religion, Socrates did not attend a school of education, Lincoln did not major in political science, and Churchill never went to college at all.

The kind of wisdom and moral courage that make up the essence of leadership may be greatly aided by formal education, but the two should not be confused. The democratic theory thus rejects the assumption of fascist doctrine that only a small elite has insight into the public good. From the democratic viewpoint, only God has a perfect understanding of Truth with a capital *T*, and when it comes to men, every man is capable of seeing truth with a small *t*, or at least part of it.

What the one-party state with the secret police and concentration camps is to the political side of fascist regimes, corporatism is to fascism's social and economic aspects. Just as in the political sphere fascism replaces the pivotal concept of individual liberty with unlimited state authority, so in the economic sphere it rejects the conception of a free welfare economy—be it capitalist, socialist, or middle-of-the-road. The objective of the corporate state is the *power of the state* rather than the welfare of the individual. More specifically, the ultimate objective of the corporate organization of the economy is the preparation of a *permanent war economy*, because aggressive imperialism is the ultimate aim of fascist foreign policy.

The corporate state has drawn its ideological inspiration from several sources. *Syndicalism,* one such source, was fairly strong in

Italy, Spain, and France early in the twentieth century. A mixture of revolutionary, semi-anarchist, and socialist elements, syndicalism opposed the capitalist state as unjust and undemocratic, and sought to conquer it by organizing syndicates, or unions of workers, who would eventually take over the state by the device of a general strike. In this syndicalist conception, it is not the individual or the state, or the whole working class as such, that occupies the central position in the social scene, but the syndicate, the union of a particular industry, to which every worker in that industry belongs as a producer. There is little consistent political theory in syndicalism, since its emphasis is on the economic organization of society.

The second root of the corporate state is *nationalism*. It is nationalism that has given to the theory and practice of the corporate state the doctrinal insistence on the supremacy of the state and nation over the group and individual. Nationalism has also imbued the syndicalist elements of the corporate state with the inflexible authoritarianism and unflinching imperialism characteristic of nationalist ideas and inspirations.

In 1919, forces led by the Italian poet Gabriele d'Annunzio conquered the City of Fiume in a surprise attack, and d'Annunzio issued a constitution containing the basic principles later to be followed in Italy and other fascist states. The people of the city were to be organized on the principle of functional activity. Employers, merchants, and workers were to strive in a common effort for the development of production, and class war was not to be tolerated.

The Italian fascist regime, installed in 1922, copied d'Annunzio's scheme, and set up a corporate state that was to show to the Italians and the world that fascism was not mere reaction, directed against liberal capitalism and socialism, but a new creative principle of social and economic organization. The economy was divided into syndicates of workers, employers, and the professions. Only one syndicate was recognized in each branch of business or industry, and although membership in a syndicate was not obligatory, the payment of dues was. The officials of the syndicates were either fascist politicians or persons of reliable loyalty to the fascist regime. In effect, these associations of workers and employers were nothing but instruments of state policy, with no will or life of their own. Since each syndicate had a monopoly of organization in its field, state control was made that much easier.

To make this method of control more nearly complete, the fascist government established *corporations*, which were administrative agencies in a given industry designed to unite and control the associations of *workers and employers* in that industry. According to law, the syndicates were autonomous; in fact, however, they were run by the state. The corporation, supreme instrument of fascist economic organization, made no pretense of autonomy, being as it was nothing but an *administrative agency of the state* and in no way different from the prisons and the other tools of fascist government by force and propaganda.

Despite the same name, the fascist corporation is, of course, not to be confused with the business corporation in the United States. They have nothing whatever in common. The fascist corporation is a government agency, whereas the American business corporation is a company of limited liability, owned by private citizens, and engaged in business.

In the final analysis, the much advertised corporate state was no new principle of social and economic organization, but merely a sign of the fact that in the totalitarian system of fascism economic relations, like all other aspects of society, could not be left to the free interplay of the competitive liberal society. In his speech of November 14, 1933, Mussolini stated that the essential bases of the corporate state were a *single party,* a *totalitarian government,* and an atmosphere of *strong ideal tension.* The fascist party provided the first two essentials of the corporate state, and the strong ideal tension was brought about by the ceaseless propaganda of expansionist imperialism.

The first real test for the corporate state in Italy, the best developed historical example so far, came with that country's entry into World War II in June 1940. Fascist Italy revealed itself to be wholly unequal to the task of fighting a first-class war, not only from the military and political viewpoint, but also for the standpoint of economic efficiency. For twenty years, the corporate state had sacrificed the welfare and happiness of a poor people to the dream of a powerful empire and the megalomania of a would-be conqueror of continents. Yet when the first real test of battle came, Italian fascism failed on the economic front even more than on the military front. The economic legacy of the corporate state was not wealth and empire, but the loss of the colonies, poverty, and destitution.

After the execution of Mussolini in the spring of 1945, the Italian people destroyed whatever vestiges were left of the corporate state and embarked upon a new chapter of economic rehabilitation, based on a mixture of economic liberalism and political democracy. In the last analysis, much of the economic ruination of Italy wrought by fascist corporatism was ultimately paid for by the American tax-payer, as the United States poured billions of dollars into Italy after World War II to help her stand on her own feet again.

In the Western Hemisphere, Colonel Perón, speaking for the fascist regime in Argentina just after the successful coup of June 1943, declared his admiration for the fundamental conceptions of the corporate state at the very moment when Italian fascism, the model and inspiration of Argentine fascism, had reduced Italy to ashes and ruins. To Argentina as to other nations, the corporate state under Perón brought inflation and meatless days—meatless days in a country that formerly had been the largest exporter of meat in the world. Above all, corporatism in Argentina (called "justicialismo") meant the end of free labor unions and their replacement by govern-ment-sponsored puppets. The employing class, too, was put under the control of the government. Finally, the peronist regime followed the corporate systems of other fascist states by dedicating the economy to the hasty development of heavy industry and the manu-facture of armaments. Thus, "justicialismo," which set out to defend justice against both capitalism and socialism, ended up as the servant of an imperialistic dictator and his political machine, until both were overthrown in 1955.

PERONISM: THE CASE OF ARGENTINA

The defeat of the Axis in World War II has by no means removed the threat of fascism forever. In terms of military security, to be sure, the chief danger now confronting the free nations is the danger of communist aggression; there has been no major threat of fascist aggression after the defeat of the great fascist powers, Germany and Japan. As an attitude of mind, however, and as a reflection of social and political authoritarianism, fascism has shown that it can survive temporary defeats; only a few years after fascist regimes led Germany and Italy to disaster and humiliation, neo-fascist organizations in both countries brazenly resumed operations.

The case of Argentina is more complex, and it proves that the Western Hemisphere is not immune from the virus of fascism. In 1943, a group of discontented younger officers overthrew the existing democratic regime, which was far from being perfect, but which nevertheless was democratic. The officers were under the leadership of Colonel Juan Perón, who in several years in Italy as a military attaché had become a fervent admirer of Mussolini and of fascist ideas. As soon as the peronist clique took over, Argentine foreign policy became openly hostile to the democratic nations in World War II, and friendly to the fascist powers. On March 27, 1945, when the war was practically over, Argentina, in order to be admitted to the San Francisco Conference under the terms of the Yalta agreement, declared war on Japan, as well as on Germany "in view of the character of the latter as an ally of Japan." Thus the pro-fascist and pro-nazi sentiment of the peronist regime was manifested in the wording, as well as the timing, of its declaration of war.

Perón at first stayed in the background, but then took over the ministries of war and labor. The war ministry gave him control over the armed forces, with which he could supplement the deep affection in which the people allegedly held him. Control over labor removed, as in other fascist states, any threat of organized mass action. The radio was completely subordinated to the government, and the opposition was deprived of access to it. In the newspaper field, Perón leveled his sights at *La Prensa,* one of the five or six great newspapers in the world, with an old and revered tradition of independence. First the peronist government tried to cajole and harass *La Prensa* into submission by administrative subterfuges rather than by open action. When all pressures and threats failed, Perón seized *La Prensa* early in 1951 and converted it to the pro-government, fascist line. *La Prensa's* owner, Dr. Ezequiel Paz, obliged to flee to the United States to save himself from prison, was the most famous Argentine refugee; but he was just one of the many who sought asylum in the other American republics and in France and England.

In most of its policies, the peronist regime followed the techniques and aims of Hitler and Mussolini. Yet in one respect—and a very important one—Perón showed intelligence considerably superior to that of his models and masters. Without exception, all the other fascist dictators—like all communist dictatorships—abolished political parties other than the ruling party; and since there could be no regular elections without opposition candidates, fascist elections became plebiscites, in which the voters were presented with a major issue and asked to vote "Yes" or "No." The votes in fascist elections were usually announced to be somewhere in the neighborhood of 99.6 per cent in favor of the dictator.

It is at this point that Perón improved on Hitler and Mussolini. Perón apparently had too much of a sense of humor to announce to the world that 99.6 per cent of his people insisted on his leadership. He was satisfied with considerably less. Thus in the presidential elections of 1946 Perón was elected by a majority of only 55 per cent, a figure that gave the election the appearance of having been fought under conditions of free campaigning. Nothing was further from the facts. Thus, early in 1944 all political parties were abolished, a measure that hurt the opposition parties more than the government; it was only shortly before the elections, in late February of 1946, that political parties were reconstituted. Much of the election campaign was conducted in a state of siege, a favorite measure in Latin American dictatorships, under which the government can legally suspend all rights of individual civil liberty. The opposition parties and their leaders were subjected to physical terror from a mob that operated under government protection. In many cases, the police itself used violence against anti-peronists, and there were numerous murders in the campaign.

In 1949, Perón had the Argentine Constitution of 1853 changed because under it immediate re-election of the President was illegal. A modest man, Perón claimed he did not wish to run for the presidency again, but as a patriotic Argentine he finally gave in to the mounting pressure from all sides and allowed himself to be drafted. The election of November 1951 gave Perón a victory of over 60 per cent, still way below the 99.6 per cent victories of the other fascist dictators.

In the 1951 election, terror against opposition parties was practiced even more openly than in 1946. Hundreds of candidates were jailed during the campaign, for no worse crime than daring to run against the existing regime, and conditions were so chaotic that two presidential candidates were out of the race even before the campaign was over. The socialists withdrew from the campaign altogether when it became apparent that the whole thing was a farce. Their candidate for the presidency had been imprisoned, as were hundreds of leaders of other parties, six weeks before the election. In typically fascist fashion, the government declared that it had discovered a subversive plot, and a state of siege was once again proclaimed, so that ruthless terror could be legally employed. In the congressional elections of April 25, 1954, the peronist slate obtained two-thirds of the popular vote. Every radio station was compelled to broadcast Perón's speeches, and the opposition was unable to get any radio time for its candidates. This monopoly of the government was supplemented by many other forms of discrimination, and occasional terror, against the opposition. It was remarkable in the election of 1954, as in 1946 and 1951, that so many Argentines still dared to vote against the peronist regime.

Late in 1954 Perón started his campaign against the Roman Catholic Church, which was the beginning of his undoing. After persisting in that campaign for several months, he was excommunicated by the Vatican on June 16, 1955. On that same day, the Argentine air force and parts of the army staged an armed uprising, but it failed. Three months later, provincial units rebelled again, and this time Perón's fate was sealed when the entire navy went over to the rebels. Only four days after the outbreak of the revolution, on September 19, 1955, Perón quietly slipped away in a Paraguayan gunboat, fleeing eventually to Panama. Since there was virtually no resistance to the revolutionary forces, Perón had to flee in a hurry.

What he left behind came as a shock to the Argentine public. Many were aware that agriculture and industry were in a mess, that public finances were in chaos, and that graft was wide-spread, that Perón's nearest relatives were among the leading grafters, and that honesty and integrity had just about disappeared from public life. But few people knew much about Perón the man, as distinct from Perón the dictator.

In his several homes were found stacks of Argentine currency, running into millions of dollars; boxes of gold money and valuables made of gold and silver; fabulous jewels of his late wife, Eva Perón; and foreign bank books. It was estimated that his bank deposits in foreign banks must be worth many millions of dollars. Since Perón had always posed as an anticapitalist and friend of the poor, the extent of his private wealth and grafting came as a shock to many of his followers. Finally, his houses contained collections of pornographic literature and intimate correspondence with young girls, revealing him as a lecher of the first order. As a result, hatred of the dictator became reinforced by ridicule.

Perón's own evidence—which he had no time to destroy because of his eagerness to escape the law—thus condemned him in the eyes of the Argentine people more than any public trial staged by the new Government could have done. Frontal attack may injure a dictator, but ridicule is bound to kill him.

Since Perón's downfall, Argentina has steadily progressed toward democratic government and a sane economy. Although direct experience with fascism has an immunizing effect, the transitional phase of recovery and recuperation may take some time. Also, Argentina's relations with the democratic nations, particularly with the United States, have greatly improved since the elimination of peronism. During that dictatorship, opposition to the democratic cause became identified with hostility to the United States; now that the dictatorship is gone, Argentina's dedication to democratic government makes friendly relations with the United States possible. Also, American business feels encouraged again to invest in, and trade with, Argentina, since peronist economic policies, based on extreme nationalism and little respect for agreements, proved a source of anxiety and fear to foreign businessmen.

Like fascism elsewhere, fascism in Argentina would never have come into power if the democratic forces of the nation had been more alert to subversion. This was not the first time that Argentina ruled by a dictatorial regime, but this was her first experience with fascism. Authoritarian political dictatorships have come and gone in Latin America, but the peronist regime was the first example in the Western Hemisphere of a full-fledged fascist state, totalitarian in objectives, and totalitarian in means.

Is Fascism Still a Threat?

Is fascism still a threat in the leading democratic nations? The tendency now is to say emphatically "No." On balance, this may be the right answer, but to say that fascism is unlikely to take over the government of the United States, for example, is not to say it may not be a serious menace. To the extent that an *anti-intellectual* tendency exists in this or any other democracy, it undermines the faith in rational processes; whereas such a tendency need not lead straight to fascism, it prepares the mentality without which there can be no effective fascist movement. *Racialism,* to the extent that it still exists, is another source that feeds the fascist potential in the United States, as in other democracies. Democracy as known before no longer exists in South Africa, for example: racialism and democracy just do not mix. The racialism that started out in South Africa to be directed solely against the Negroes later turned against the Indians, and finally took in the whole English-speaking part — nearly one-half—of the white population. Conversely, to the extent that there has been progress in race relations in the United States— and the progress in the last twenty years has been truly inspiring— the chances of fascism in the United States have decreased.

The *cold war* with world communism has been another contributing factor in the revival of fascism. Because fascism and democracy are both opposed to communism, some democrats have wrongly concluded that democracy and fascism are natural allies in the struggle against communism, overlooking this important distinction: the quarrel between communism and fascism results from the inability of burglars to agree over the division of the loot, whereas the quarrel between communism and democracy is that between the burglar and the law. And the same quarrel exists between fascism and democracy.

Possibly the most dangerous softening up of democratic resistance to fascism is the destruction of democratic habits and institutions, not by outside attacks, but within the citadel of democracy itself. If there is any fascist threat to democracy today—and there is—it no longer comes from Berlin, Rome, and Tokyo. It derives its parasitic strength from the inertness and apathy of the citizens of a democracy, because without such civic diseases there can be no support for demagogues and fearmongers who seek to aggrandize themselves at the expense of the whole body politic.

Is should be kept in mind that the practical alternative is not between 100 per cent virtue and 100 per cent sin, but always between mixtures with varying proportions of ingredients. The danger in a democracy like the United States is not outright fascism on the German, Italian, or Argentine patterns, but the insidious and unnoticed slow corroding of democratic habits and institutions by pre-fascist and pro-fascist attitudes. Huey Long, who as governor of Louisiana in the early nineteen thirties set up the nearest thing to a fascist dictatorship in the United States, once jokingly said that if fascism ever came to the United States it would be under the slogan of 100 per cent Americanism.

Long was right: the open, self-confessed fascist will not get a sympathetic hearing in the United States, because the verbal symbols of fascism are identified too profoundly with evil in the American mind; the fascist fellow-traveler, the crypto-fascist, the proto-fascist, the pre-fascist, and the pro-fascist are more dangerous than the plain unhyphenated fascist. By declaring himself publicly what he is, the fascist can no longer work under the mantle of respectability. A politician with fascist leanings who denies that he is a fascist, and who emphasizes his patriotism, can do much more harm than the open fascist, because he is still permitted to work within the institutional framework of public life. The danger of not recognizing this pre-fascist attitude is that, should it become full-fledged fascism (as it well might in an economic depression or in some other disaster of the sort that periodically shake men's faith in democracy), recognition of it as a threat may come too late for those whose earlier diagnosis of the disease was too charitable.

For Further Reading

Adorno, T. W., and others, *The Authoritarian Personality* (Harper, 1950)

Alexander, Robert J., *The Perón Era* (Columbia University Press, 1951)

Baumont, Maurice, and others, *The Third Reich* (Praeger, 1955)

Blanksten, George I., *Perón's Argentina* (University of Chicago Press, 1953)

Ebenstein, William, *Fascist Italy* (American Book Company, 1939)

————, *The German Record* (Rinehart, 1945)

————, *The Nazi State* (Rinehart, 1943)

Friedrich, Carl J., and Z. K. Brzezinski, *Totalitarian Dictatorships and Autocracy* (Harvard University Press, 1956)

Fromm, Erich, *Escape from Freedom* (Rinehart, 1941)

Lippmann, Walter, *The Good Society* (Little, Brown, 1937)

Orwell, George, *1984* (Signet Books, 1950)

Rauschning, Hermann, *The Revolution of Nihilism* (Alliance, 1939)

Russell of Liverpool, Lord, *The Scourge of the Swastika* (Ballantine Books, 1956)

Schapiro, J. Salwyn, *Liberalism and the Challenge of Fascism* (McGraw-Hill, 1949)

Vermeil, Edmond, *Germany in the Twentieth Century* (Praeger, 1956)

Warren, Robert Penn, *All the King's Men* (Modern Library, 1953)

Wheeler-Bennett, J. W., *The Nemesis of Power* (St. Martin's Press, 1953)

Whitaker, Arthur P., *Argentine Upheaval* (Praeger, 1956)

PART TWO

the democratic way of life

DEMOCRATIC CAPITALISM ♦ 3

DEMOCRATIC SOCIALISM ♦ 4

3

DEMOCRATIC CAPITALISM

Two Conceptions of Democracy

In 1948, George Bernard Shaw proposed that, in order to eradicate misunderstanding and confusion about the meaning of democracy, the leading scholars and thinkers of the world be convened, and the issue be settled once and for all. Unfortunately, the root of the trouble lies deeper. Disagreements about the concept of democracy are not semantic, but reflect differences of a more fundamental nature.

When a representative of the United States, Britain, or France talks about democracy, he frequently means the very opposite of what a Russian or Chinese communist has in mind when he uses the same term. Thus at the end of World War II, when the United States, Britain, France, and the Soviet Union occupied Germany, one of their chief objectives was the "democratization" of Germany. At first all four powers wholeheartedly agreed on the objective, but it soon became evident that the Russian concept was entirely different from the Anglo-American-French understanding of democracy.

The western powers took the view that bringing democracy to Germany meant free elections; a free press; freedom of political association; freedom of religion, thought, and speech; equality before the law; the right to oppose the government; the right to choose one's job; the right to form free trade unions; the right to move freely within one's country, go abroad temporarily, or emigrate permanently; and—in a general way—the right of every person to develop his mental and moral faculties to the fullest possible extent.

Above all, *freedom from fear* is basic in the western concept of democracy. No society can be called free unless its citizens feel safe from unwarranted intrusion into their affairs by governmental authorities.

This aspect of democracy has been most aptly described in this

Tarantel (West Berlin)

"I'LL TELL YOU WHY THE MINISTER OF JUSTICE HASN'T PARDONED YOU. I'M THE MINISTER."

way: in a free country, a knock at the door early in the morning means the milkman is here; in a totalitarian country, the same knock might mean the secret police are here, come to snatch a man from his home and family and to jail, exile, or execute him without trial or due process.

The communist conception of "democratizing" Germany was entirely different from the western. In the first place, when the communist speaks of democracy, he has in mind, not government *of* the people, nor government *by* the people, but, as a leading Soviet philosopher puts it, "whether this or that policy is carried out in the interests of the people, in the interests of its overwhelming majority, or in the interests of its minority" (G. F. Aleksandrov, *The Pattern of Soviet Democracy*, 1948).

Which doctrine reveals whether government is carried out *in the interests of the people?* Marxism-Leninism-Stalinism. Who interprets this doctrine correctly? The Communist Party. Who in the Communist Party determines the party line? The Presidium, a group of a dozen men or so. Who in the Presidium determines its general policy? The communist dictator, Khrushchev in Russia, Mao in China, and whoever controls the army, the party, and the secret police in the lesser communist states.

In the elections of Western Germany in 1953, only 2.2 per cent of the vote was for the Communist Party. Yet from the communist viewpoint, Western Germany is a dictatorship, because the *interests* of its population are not determined by the one party that knows what is best for the Germans, the Communist Party. In particular, as long as capitalism exists in Germany there can be no democracy there, the communists say, because capitalism is by definition a dictatorship of the wealthy over the poor, even though a majority of the latter may vote in its favor. From the communist viewpoint, Western Germany today could be called a democracy only if the Communist Party, supported by 2.2 per cent of the popular vote, ruled Germany, because only the Communist Party could rule in the interests of the German people.

It is for this reason that the communists call the essentials of democracy—freedom of speech, press, and association, equality before the law, and all the other fundamental democratic rights and liberties —*formal* democracy, as compared with the *real* democracy of communism, in which the means of production are owned by the state. In this communist conception, the traditional democratic freedoms assume a new meaning. Freedom of the press? By all means, provided the newspapers function "in conformity with the interests of the toilers" (Article 125 of the Constitution of the Soviet Union). Freedom of speech? Completely and unqualifiedly, provided the speaker's words support the communist cause.

The Soviet Union therefore looks upon Eastern Germany as a true democracy, because the means of production have been transferred to public ownership and management. The fact that a communist one-party dictatorship rules Eastern Germany, the fact that a network of concentration and slave labor camps has been set up through the area, is irrelevant to the communist proof of democracy.

DEMOCRACY AS A WAY OF LIFE

From the above illustration, the principal characteristics of the western concept of democracy as a way of life clearly emerge:

(1) Rational empiricism
(2) Emphasis on the individual
(3) Instrumental nature of the state
(4) Voluntarism
(5) The law behind the law
(6) Emphasis on means
(7) Discussion and consent in human relations
(8) Basic equality of all human beings

(1) *Rational empiricism* is perhaps the most important single element in the free way of life. It is based on confidence in reason, and in the applicability of reason, not only to physical nature, but also to human relations. Dogmatists—such as communists or fascists—*know* what the truth is; for communists the concept of class is the ultimate in truth, whereas to fascists race and nation are the last repositories of truth. Since the dogmatist is so sure that he knows, he need not inquire further; his aim is to strengthen what he knows already, and he brands whoever questions his knowledge guilty of intellectual subversion. The psychological and historical relation between dogmatism in philosophy and authoritarianism in politics is clear: absolute certainty of knowledge leads to fanatical enthusiasm in sentiment, which in turn leads to intolerant repression in government.

By contrast, empiricism, first fully developed by John Locke (1632-1704), is based on the idea that *all our knowledge derives from experience*. In this conception, truth (with a small *t*) is tentative, changing, and subject to constant checking and verification.

Since the history of both physical science and social thought is full of truths that turned out to be wholly or partly untrue, the rational empiricist refuses to believe—as the dogmatist believes—that mankind has in any field finally arrived at the end of its quest for truth and knowledge. The rational empiricist views truth, in the study of nature as much as of man, as an endless process, and considers the knowledge or truth of today no more than a *probability*, to be changed if new facts are brought to light. Bertrand Russell, one of the most outstanding representatives of this liberal outlook, says in his *Philosophy and Politics* (1946) that the genuine liberal says not "This is true," but "I am inclined to think that under present circumstances this opinion is probably the best."

In science, opinions cannot be accepted as true simply on the basis of authority; they must be verified by rational methods of observation. Because the scientist is aware of the incompleteness and temporariness of his data, he bears no grudge against the person who disagrees with him, but expects that the stronger evidence will ultimately prevail. Because he knows he may be wrong, the scientist does not consider his opponent as an enemy or traitor, a moral derelict to be liquidated or otherwise silenced. In a sense, *liberal democracy seeks to apply this rational, empirical outlook to the field of politics.*

The democratic process, like the scientific process, prescribes *how* truth is to be ascertained, not *what* specific truth is going to be discovered. The Constitution of the United States does not primarily determine, as a dogma would, what laws of Congress are good or bad, but rather prescribes what methods are to be used in making, executing, and interpreting the laws. Just as the scientist seeks to discover all available evidence that bears upon a problem before he decides upon the probable solution to that problem, the democratic procedure requires that *all opinions be heard* before a decision is made. Since in a democracy no one can claim infallible *a priori* knowledge of the true answer to a social problem, the only way to find out is to get all the ascertainable evidence.

The English Parliament started out as a High Court, and to this day parliamentary procedure in all democracies follows the judicial method of gathering and weighing all available facts and opinions before the legislative judgment is rendered.

As in science, too, the democratic method in politics can never promise, nor deliver, final truths. Whereas dogmatists and totalitarians are never satisfied with anything that is not the final answer, rational empiricists and democrats tackle smaller issues that settle nothing definitively. The communist, in approaching the problem of economic organization, sees only the dilemma of complete capitalism versus complete collectivism. The democrat does not set out to abolish hell or bring heaven overnight; he is more interested in free school lunches or in increasing the income tax by two per cent than in providing the final answer to the problem of poverty and suffering.

Because the rational empiricist knows that his viewpoint cannot be perfect, he does not feel that criticizing it is a sign of moral delinquency on the part of the critic; in fact, he is anxious to have it criticized so that it can be improved. The dogmatist, by contrast, knows that his truth is final and perfect, and criticizing it is therefore a grave intellectual error at the very least, if not downright moral subversion.

It is probably no coincidence that rational empiricism and democracy have developed more or less simultaneously in England, France, and the United States. In England, for example, John Locke, the founder of empiricism, is still the most persuasive exponent of political liberalism. In the United States empiricism has been the dominant school of thought, culminating in John Dewey (1859-1952), whose application of rational empiricism to philosophy and politics has been a lasting contribution to the American liberal heritage.

(2) The *emphasis on the individual* sharply separates liberal democracy from both fascist and communist totalitarianism. In fascism, the emphasis is on nation, state, race, and empire. In communism, the emphasis is on the concept of class. By contrast, liberal democracy stresses the *individual* as the center of all doctrine and policy. In the eyes of the liberal democrat, no social or political institution, be it a local boy-scout group, a party precinct, or the state, has a purpose of its own other than to serve and aid the individual in living a fuller life.

In the totalitarian doctrine, the state is the master, the individual the servant. Hegel, the intellectual ancestor of both fascism and communism, says in his *Philosophy of Law* (1821) that the individual finds his liberty in obeying the state, and the fullest realization of his liberty in dying for the state. Only when the individual dies for the state does he lose the last trace of any personal whimsicality and uniqueness and become completely a part of the state.

By contrast, Locke sees the indestructible essence of man in resisting, rather than in blindly obeying, the state. The liberal principles of life, liberty, and the pursuit of happiness are thus the exact opposite of the authoritarian concept of citizenship as duty, discipline, and death for the state.

Thomas Jefferson, one of the greatest liberal individualists of all time, once remarked (in a letter to Colonel William Stephen Smith, dated November 13, 1787) that "the tree of liberty must be refreshed from time to time with the blood of patriots and tyrants." The Declaration of Independence, too, states that life, liberty, and the pursuit of happiness are among the inalienable rights of man, and that "whenever any form of government becomes destructive of these ends, it is the right of the people to alter or to abolish it, and to Institute new government, laying its foundations on such principles, and organizing its powers in such form as to them shall seem most likely to effect their safety and happiness."

The historical roots of individualism are three: first, the Jewish concept of one God leads to the idea that all men, as children of God, are brothers to each other. Second, the Christian doctrine of the indestructibility of the human soul maintains that whatever social, economic, and political inequalities may exist, all men possess a spiritual equality and uniqueness that no earthly power can override. Third, in the Stoic view, the one principle of action that governs all things is *to be at one with oneself*, to know oneself, and to act in conformity with one's rational principles and purposes. The true self of man, according to the Stoics, is not his flesh or bones, but the faculty that uses them, his *reason*, the part of man that more than anything else characterizes him as human.

At no time, of course, has this individualism been fully accepted, and the counterforces of totalitarianism always threaten it. At the present time, in particular, the threat of all-destructive atom and hydrogen bomb war leads to a strengthening of anti-individualist attitudes, stressing the idea of "let's close ranks" rather than "let each man decide what is right or wrong and act accordingly."

(3) The *instrumental theory of the state* views the state as a mechanism, to be used for ends higher than itself. Both Plato and Aristotle, the founders of Western political theory, conceived of the state as an organic entity, with a life and purposes of its own, superior to the purposes of the individual. Plato and Aristotle thought of the state as the *highest moral good*, the source of moral values and spiritual enrichment for the individual.

From the Jewish-Christian viewpoint of religion, the instrumentalist theory of the state maintains that the highest values in man's life relate to God, and that no earthly law can claim to supersede God's. The function of the state is to maintain peace and order, so that men can pursue their activities devoted to higher ends. From the rational-humanist viewpoint, the instrumentalist theory of the state affirms that the ability of the individual to use his reason in discovering what is right and wrong is the ultimate test of political authority, and that the state therefore cannot turn evil into good or wrong into right solely because it possesses the means of physical coercion.

The liberal doctrine stresses society far more than the state; in the classical liberal doctrine—and to a considerable extent today— *society is considered basically self-sufficient, and the state is to step in only when the voluntary efforts of society fail.*

The instrumentalist theory of the state thus relegates the state to a supplementary position. As long as individuals can get along without the state, the liberal bias is against the state, even if the state could do the same thing a little better.

In the totalitarian state, the assumption is always in favor of the state, because it is credited with omniscience and omnipotence. Thus the totalitarian state organizes and controls, not only the sensitive areas of the economy, education, and religion, but even chessplayers and Sunday afternoon hikers, because the state does not wish to leave any activity to the free discretion of its citizens.

(4) By contrast, the democratic theory sees in the principle of *voluntarism* the very lifeblood of a free society. Fellowship can most deeply be experienced in small, voluntary groups. Such groups were first formed in seventeenth-century England on a religious basis, and to this day the English-speaking world abounds with thousands and thousands of religious sects that are small in size and entirely voluntary in nature.

Later, the principle of voluntary association was applied in the field of politics (parties), education (private schools), and economics (labor unions and employer's associations). In charity, the Red Cross and local community chests testify to the fact that there is still a strong sentiment for retaining voluntary activity. Even in England, with its national health and social security program covering every person from the cradle to the grave, there has been a reassertion of the importance of voluntary organization in social welfare, supplementing the governmental programs.

(5) The concept of *the law behind the law* flows directly from the *federal* view of state and society in classical liberalism. Society is conceived as an aggregate of diverse voluntary associations, and the state itself is looked upon as an essentially voluntary body, because its authority is derived from the consent of the governed. Whenever authority is organized on a federal basis, there has to be a higher law defining the relationships of the parts among each other and of each part to the whole.

Classical liberalism, therefore, has always adhered to the idea that the relations between state and society, between government and individual, are ultimately defined by a law higher than that of the state. In fact, classical liberal thought in Britain and the United States assumes that the *law is not the product of the state, but precedes it.* The right to life, liberty, property, and the pursuit of happiness is not a gift of the state to the individual, but precedes the state. The function of the state in relation to man's basic rights is to protect and define such rights, not to create them.

In the United States, in particular, the concept of the law behind the law has never been challenged as the foundation of American political thought and experience. The Declaration of Independence specifically recognizes it, and the Constitution has also recognized that no legislative body can make laws without due process, or laws that otherwise violate basic principles of reason. The very existence of the United States is, of course, due to the insistence that above the law then ruling—the law of imperial Britain—there was a higher law, to which the revolting colonists pledged allegiance.

Opponents of democratic government have charged that this concept of a higher law, making government dependent upon the consent of the governed, opens the door to rebellion and anarchy. In his *Two Treatises of Government* (1690), John Locke answers this charge with three counter-arguments. First, Locke concedes that the democratic theory of government admits of the possibility of rebellion, but he denies that it does so more than any other theory. When the people are made miserable, they will rebel under any form of government, let the governors be "sacred and divine, descended or authorized from heaven, give them out for whom or what you please, the same will happen." Second, Locke says, men do not rebel "upon every little mismanagement in public affairs," or "for light and transient causes," as the Declaration of Independence puts it. Third, and here Locke moves from the defensive to the offensive, government by consent coupled with the right of the people to rebel is "the best fence against rebellion."

Locke could only guess in 1690 whether his arguments would be proved by experience, because in 1690 democracy was still a thing of the future. Yet experience has proved him perspicacious. The British and American systems of government, based on the Lockean-Jeffersonian admission of the people's right to rebel against oppression, have proved themselves the stablest and most successful political systems the world has ever seen, and the same may be said of countries (smaller in size but equally great in the glory of freedom) like Holland, Switzerland, and the Scandinavian nations. By contrast, where the "higher law" has been rejected in the name of law and order, the political results have been blood purges, conspiracies, plots and counterplots, and violent swings from one extreme to another—the political record, specifically, of communist and fascist dictatorships.

(6) The *emphasis on means* in democratic life is based on the realization that ends lead no existence apart from means, but are continually shaped by them. The totalitarian makes a clear-cut distinction between means and ends. In his dogmatic way of thinking he is absolutely certain of what the ends are, and possessing this certainty, he pays little attention to the nature of the means. Thus, the communists believe in universal brotherhood and cooperation as their officially professed end, yet they fail to realize that the means employed in bringing about communism—secret police, slave labor camps, thought control, denunciations, repression of dissent—increase hatred and misery rather than diminish it.

One of the main difficulties in separating means from ends is the fact that *in most practical situations a means is simultaneously an end.* Thus, education is for some an end in itself; for others, it is but a means to an end—to a degree, for example. Yet, a degree may again be only a means—the end being a happier, fuller life, or a better job. Again, a better job is not necessarily an end in itself; it is likely to be a means to some higher end, such as expressing a sense of craftsmanship or serving society.

The central position of means in free societies is well entrenched in their living experience. Magna Carta, Habeas Corpus, and jury trial, to mention but a few roots of liberty in the English-speaking world, are originally all *procedural devices,* means, and the history of liberty may aptly be described as a history of procedure. In representative assemblies, too, it is not the legislative product that distinguishes a democratic body from a nondemocratic one, but the difference of procedure. In the one case, procedure aims at the fullest and fairest guarantee of the right of the minority to be heard; in the other, procedure aims at silencing minorities and bringing about the loudest possible volume of cheers for the dictator.

At present, the danger in democratic societies lies in the possible waning of this awareness that differences over means are the heart of the difference between democracy and totalitarianism. In fighting a totalitarian system like fascism or communism there is a natural tendency to imitate their means, and because the tendency is natural, special efforts must be made to guard against it. In defending democracy, some persons are willing to use means that are bound to destroy the very thing they seek to defend.

(7) *Discussion and consent* are the means by which a democratic society typically settles divergent viewpoints and interests. It is the democratic view that, since no one possesses absolute truth, both sides to an argument may make a contribution to the best possible answer, and that the only way to get that answer is to marshal all the available evidence.

The *independent voter* in a democracy typifies the person who profoundly reflects this unwillingness to support any one political party without previous careful reflection. In a totalitarian state, there are no independent voters, only followers or enemies of the prevailing manner of thought. In a free society, the independent voter starts from the assumption that neither party is always right or always wrong; like the man from Missouri, he wants to be shown before he makes up his mind. In the 1952 elections in the United States, the Republican Party, for example, selected General Eisenhower over Senator Taft as its presidential candidate, mainly for his wider appeal to the independent voter.

In the theory of the democratic society, governments derive "their just powers from the consent of the governed" (Declaration of Independence), because the state has no reason for existence other than to serve the people. If the state becomes oppressive and unmindful of the rights of the people, then the democratic theory, as was pointed out earlier, upholds not only the right, but the duty to revolt against such government.

However, this right to rebel can be claimed only where the methods of discussion and consent are blocked by tyrannical despotism; where the channels of discussion are open, as in a democratic state and society, no democrat would claim the right of rebellion against the state.

The communist who today claims the right to revolution as a general democratic privilege utterly distorts this concept for his own purposes. From the democratic viewpoint, *the democrat has the moral right, and duty, to rebel against the totalitarian system, but the totalitarian possesses no such right against the democratic system.*

(8) The *basic equality of all human beings* is a point of democratic doctrine and policy that is frequently misunderstood. No democrat has ever said that all men are identical, but only that in *basic* respects they are equal. The very uniqueness of each and every person creates a kind of equality that is important in the democratic outlook. From the religious viewpoint of the Jewish-Christian tradition, all men are equal before God; God's challenge to every human being is the same, although men's response to it varies enormously. From the rationalist-humanistic viewpoint, all men share, over and above differences of race, sex, religion, nationality, and class, one common trait: the ability to reason. In this sense, all men are citizens of the world, rather than of a particular, distinctive group, and their basic equality derives from what they have in common rather than from what separates them.

The Declaration of Independence makes it perfectly plain that all men are created *equal,* in the sense that they have certain unalienable *rights,* such as life, liberty, and the pursuit of happiness. The equality that men receive at birth, according to democratic theory, is thus not in the nature of an outright gift or grant, but a loan, as it were, an *opportunity,* a *challenge.* The Jeffersonian phrase "pursuit of happiness" admirably expresses the thought that man does not have the right to happiness, in the sense that the state or his family or friends owe him happiness, but only in the sense that he has the right to *pursue* happiness, unhindered by unreasonable obstacles.

However, equality does not mean, as Plato charged it meant, "dispensing a kind of equality to equals and unequals alike." The contrary is true, of the ideal democracy at least. In practice it is not easy to ascertain when equals are still equal, and when they become unequal. Thus, to take an illustration: the most common interpretation of democratic equality is "equality of opportunity." Yet a grave difficulty arises immediately: if all men were endowed with the same talents and abilities, and were born into the same homes, and received the same schooling, giving all an equal opportunity would be a fair solution. Yet people differ in native talent, and even more in background and education.

Legislative action cannot equalize the I.Q. of the population, and there will always be differences of ability, drive, and motivation, but laws can make equality of opportunity more real by trying to equalize conditions before the race starts: increased inheritance taxes lessen the impact of inherited wealth, progressive income taxes favor the lower-income groups, and free education (from nursery school to university) benefits the indigent more than the affluent. In other words, equality of opportunity, if it allows ability alone to operate, quickly establishes and perpetuates inequality. *Need,* too, must be considered; it adds to the principle of efficiency that of happiness.

CONDITIONS OF POLITICAL DEMOCRACY

Of all the aspects of democracy, the political has top priority. Although political democracy is not identical with democracy as a way of life, the instinct of those who tend to identify the two is not unsound. Experience has shown that political democracy, if practiced over any length of time, leads to the extension of the democratic principle to social, economic, and international problems. So far, there is less evidence that social or economic democracy leads to political democracy. Precisely because political democracy merely defines "the rules of the game," it is more far-reaching than social or economic democracy, which is concerned with one particular substantive area of problems.

The first characteristic of democratic government is the maintenance of a political climate in which *political liberty* can thrive. In every society, those who uphold the orthodox views may freely express them. No one is hindered in Russia today from publicly proclaiming Nikita Khrushchev the greatest statesman of the present. In Yugoslavia, no one is jailed today for referring to President Tito as the greatest president in Yugoslav history. *Political liberty begins at the point where unorthodox opinions may be freely presented, without legal, social, or economic penalties.*

The political liberty of a society can best be measured by the *margin of unorthodoxy* that is *tolerated* in that society. This yardstick enables us to go beyond the crude classification of dictatorship and democracy, which is valid only on a general level. Examining first the totalitarian states by this criterion, we find the least margin of unorthodox opinion in nazi Germany (1933-1945) and in communist states today, a much wider margin of unorthodoxy in fascist Italy (1922-1945) than in either nazi Germany or Soviet Russia, and the relatively largest unorthodoxy in the present Portuguese and Latin American dictatorships.

Measuring the margin of unorthodoxy in democratic societies, we find Britain, France, Scandinavia, Holland, Australia, and New Zealand on the top of the list, while the United States trails somewhat behind. Needless to say, the positions are never fixed, and the range of unorthodoxy constantly changes; by general agreement there is more uniformity and conformity of thought in the United States today than ten years ago, and there may be less again ten years hence.

The *common agreement on fundamentals* is a second condition indispensable to the successful working of political democracy. The most important agreement, and the one no written constitution can by itself guarantee, is the common desire to operate a democratic system. Where there is no written constitution, as in Great Britain, there is no protection of political minorities or individual nonconformists other than the decency and restraint of the majority. Legally, the British government could outlaw the opposition and introduce a totalitarian state overnight. But the government is not doing that, because it is a party to an unwritten agreement to abide by democratic principles.

By the same token, written constitutions are not necessarily a protection: fascism developed in Italy, Germany, Japan, and Argentina despite written constitutions, and the presence of a democratic constitution in Czechoslovakia after World War II did not restrain the communists from distorting and destroying it.

The lesson of all this historical experience is simple: *the strength of a democracy is never greater than the will of the people to uphold it.*

Where agreement on fundamentals is lacking, political democracy suffers from stresses and strains that may well become fatal. An irreconcilable division on fundamentals between major parties may lead to civil war or dictatorship. Such a situation existed in the United States in 1860, when there was no agreement on the basic issue of slavery. In 1930, the German political system was a democracy as far as the paper constitution was concerned; but two-thirds of the electorate wanted to set up totalitarian dictatorships of either the communist or fascist type, the fascists finally winning out in 1933. Obviously, no constitution, however perfect on paper, can save a democracy if the antidemocrats outvote the democrats two to one. A democratic constitution *assumes,* but *cannot* in itself *create,* the will to maintain democratic institutions.

In the French elections of 1956, the parties supporting the republican system (socialists, Catholic democrats, peasants, independents, radical socialists) controlled only 53.5 per cent of the popular vote; on the extreme Left, the communists, with 25.5 of the popular vote, sought to set up a totalitarian dictatorship; and on the extreme Right, the Gaullists and Poujadists, with 16.2 per cent of the popular vote, wanted to do away with the constitution and set up an authoritarian regime based on a strong executive. The contemporary political crisis of France is thus the inevitable result of the fact that the French people are unable to find some common fundamentals upon which they are able to agree.

Is agreement on economic policy a necessary condition of political democracy? A generation ago, this question was answered more often in the affirmative than today. Conservatives frequently expressed apprehension lest the new socialist principle of public ownership undermine the whole fabric of institutions. By contrast, socialists frequently expressed the fear that conservatives would be unwilling to adhere loyally to democratic principles if socialist parties were given a chance to change the economic organization of society by constitutional means, and that the propertied classes would put property above constitutional democracy.

Experience has shown that both sides have been wrong. In theory, the disagreement on basic economic policy between conservatives and socialists looked bigger than it has worked out in practice. The conservatives have abandoned much of their old economic *laissez-faire* position, and the socialists, having considerably modified their economic philosophy, are now satisfied with a program consisting of welfare state legislation and the socialization of the basic industries.

In 1945, the British electorate was faced with a choice, not between socialism and capitalism, but between two programs not too different in nature. The socialists aimed at 20 per cent nationalization of the economy. The conservatives would have preferred 10 to 15 per cent. There was no question of zero versus 100 per cent that was presented in the past as a matter of theory.

The very nature of the democratic process makes the choice of zero versus 100 per cent virtually impossible: since elections are generally decided by the floating independent vote, which by definition is middle-of-the-road, no extreme program has a chance of being accepted.

Government by more than one party expresses the democratic principle, borrowed from the law, that "the other side must also be heard" (*audiatur et altera pars*). The dogmatic, totalitarian viewpoint holds that there is only one Truth, and from that position to the one-party state there is a direct line. The democratic viewpoint holds that different men perceive different aspects of truth, mainly in the light of their lives and experiences, and that there will be at least two sides to any major question.

The Communists say that the two-party system is a product of capitalism; that the opposing interests of capitalists and workers must be represented in opposing parties; and that, since capitalism has been abolished in the Soviet Union, there is no need for an opposition party to the Communist Party.

This line of argument has serious flaws. In the first place, it wrongly assumes that property is the only line of political party. In Europe, party loyalties are frequently based on religious or ideological loyalties; in the United States the regional factor is often important. Also, the communist argument exaggerates the impact of property on party. Only about 60 per cent of the British working class vote Labor, and in the United States the correlation between income and vote is equally indecisive. If income were the only decisive factor, political prediction would be much easier than professional pollsters have found it to be.

Moreover, if inequalities of income are important politically, the need for a multi-party system is more urgent in the Soviet Union than in the capitalist countries, because the inequality between managers and workers, and between skilled and unskilled workers, is much greater in the Soviet Union than in capitalist countries. There is little doubt that if freedom of association were suddenly introduced in the Soviet Union, parties would be formed for the purpose of asserting the claims of peasants, the unskilled workers, and the various nationalities, such as the Ukrainians and White Russians.

Even if capitalism could be abolished in the most democratic manner, there would still be need for more than one party. Assuming a classless society, in which all productive property is owned publicly, and in which incomes, too, are relatively equal, there would still be questions of vital concern to the community, questions admitting of more than one answer. For example, every state, whether democratic, fascist, communist, socialist, or capitalist, has to decide each year what portion of its national product is to be consumed and what portion is to be saved and invested. Another typical question that every community has to face is how much to spend on social welfare, and which groups should be favored: the claims of the old compete with those of the young, education may compete with health—the answer to such questions cannot be found in the form of economic organization.

After all, even when there was no capitalism in the modern sense, there was a multitude of parties. When the suffrage was limited to the propertied classes, as it was in most countries until about one hundred years ago, the existing parties were divided not on the basis of rich and poor, but along other lines—town versus country, secularism versus clericalism, states' rights versus centralism, free trade versus protection, republicanism versus monarchism, slavery versus freedom, to name but a few.

PSYCHOLOGICAL ROOTS OF DEMOCRACY

Man has lived for about a quarter million years on this planet, yet he has had some knowledge of democratic ideas and practice for only about twenty-five hundred years. Even today, democracy as a way of life exists only in a relatively small portion of the world. Democracy, then, can scarcely be called "natural." On the contrary, the democratic way of life is the most difficult of all; it does not emerge spontaneously and by accident, but is the result of deliberate thought, seeking to correct what is natural, all too natural, in human behavior.

Just as the behavior of the child is more natural than that of the adult, the behavior of the authoritarian is more natural than that of the democratic personality. The process of growth and development from childhood to maturity is natural only in the biological and physiological sense, not in the social and cultural sense. Socially and culturally, the transformation of the child into the mature adult demands much forethought, planning, and hard work.

Politically the authoritarian personality is fundamentally the grown-up who has never become mature, the ostensible adult who still accepts the dependency and security characteristic of childhood. By contrast, the democratic personality is the emotionally and intellectually mature adult, the person able to stand on his own feet and shape his life for himself. The mature adult does not need security provided by an external authority; he possesses security within himself. The price of this emotional and intellectual independence is high, since to attain it a person must face responsibilities and make decisions by himself, without being able to blame anyone afterwards if his decisions are wrong.

There is no growing up without making mistakes, and the overprotected child *can* make no mistakes—his father will see to that! Similarly, in a dictatorship, the system prevents the individual from experimenting and acting on his own, so that (in theory, at least) he always does the right thing. By contrast, the process of growing up, of moving away from supervision to personal responsibility, implies the possibility of choosing the wrong thing, of making mistakes; in this sense, *democracy* may be defined as *the right to make mistakes*.

Implied in this concept is not the desirability of erring for the sake of erring, but the recognition that freedom implies choice between alternatives, and that no one can grow to maturity, no one can be truly democratic, without learning to make choices, and without occasionally making the wrong choice.

The 200 per cent American defenders of democracy who want to make it a crime for anyone ever to think or act wrongly, are trying to have a democracy with authoritarian personalities, people who only think and do what authority has allowed them to think or do.

The attitude of the democratic personality toward the leader is markedly different from that of the authoritarian personality. The latter regards the leader of the nation with a mixture of loyalty and reverence resembling the emotions he first felt toward his parents, particularly his father. The traditional reference to a chief of the state as the "father of the country" is the linguistic expression of a profound psychological tie; the adult in such a society has really never outgrown the father-child relationship.

By contrast, *the democratic personality puts more emphasis on the group than on the leader.* This feeling goes back to that of the rebellious child, who joins with his brothers in a league of equals to destroy the authority of their father. "Liberty, equality, fraternity," the three ideals of the French revolution, express the attitude of the democratic personality against authority.

For this reason, democracies frequently act with deep suspicion whenever a great leader appears. Churchill was opposed in England before World War II because he was "too clever," not average enough, and therefore potentially dangerous. Clemenceau was removed from French public life after World War I because he was too much of a leader. Many American voters who cast their ballot against Franklin D. Roosevelt were motivated by the unconscious fear that he was not Mr. Average American. Lincoln attracted the same kind of hatred, although much of it was rationalized in political and ideological arguments.

It is for this reason, too, that impersonal factors like constitutions, charters, and congresses play such an important part in democratic states: leaders come and go, but the institutions continue unimpaired. By contrast, the authoritarian personality thinks in terms of allegiance to a particular person. In Spain and Latin America, for example, political loyalty revolves around the phenomenon of *personalismo*: the political attachment and allegiance are to one particular person, rather than to a party, program, or constitution. Even democratic parties in such countries usually are split into various factions, each led by one man, to whom his group owes allegiance. But this is even more true, of course, of antidemocratic movements: thus we speak of Hitlerism, Peronism, Stalinism, but not of Churchillism or Eisenhowerism.

The formation of the democratic personality is first determined in the *family*. It was Sigmund Freud who emphasized that the first

five years are probably the most decisive years of life, as far as basic
attitudes are concerned. In the early years of life, the home is school,
church, and government all rolled into one. In some societies, parents are accorded absolute power over their children; in such societies the family resembles a miniature absolutist state, in which the
fiat of the absolute ruler (the father) is the law.

By contrast, democratic family relations give the child the first experience of democracy. In the United States, the family unit resembles,
in most cases, a small parliament in which every member feels free
to have his say when family decisions are in the making. Children do
not expect to be told what to do, what line of work to pick, or whom
to marry. Far from being the absolute ruler of an authoritarian family,
the American father has often learned to be satisfied if he has a chance
to be heard. His hope is not of being obeyed *because* he is the father,
but rather (if we can take the cartoonist's word for it, at least) of
getting a fair hearing *although* he is the father.

One of Germany's leading child psychologists, Kurt Lewin, came
to the United States in 1934 and stayed here until his death in 1945.
In 1936 he wrote a paper on "Some Social-Psychological Differences
between the United States and Germany" (reprinted in his *Resolving Social Conflicts,* 1948), in which he makes the following obser-
vations:

"To one who comes from Germany, the degree of freedom and
independence of children and adolescents in the United States is
very impressive. Especially the lack of servility of the young child
toward adults or of the student toward his professor is striking.
The adults, too, treat the child on a much more equal footing,
whereas in Germany it seems to be the natural right of the adult
to rule and the duty of the child to obey. The natural relation of
adult and child in the United States is not considered that of a
superior (*Herr*) to a subordinate (*Untergebener*) but that of two
individuals with the same right in principle. The parents seem to
treat the children with more respect. Generally they will be careful, when requesting the child to bring some object, to ask them
in a polite way. They will let the child feel that he is doing them
a favor in a situation in which the German parent is much more likely
to give short orders. It is more common in the United States to
hear a parent thank the child after such action. The parent may
even do so after he has had to apply considerable pressure in order

to make the child comply, whereas the same situation in Germany would probably lead to 'the next time you should do it right away.' In Germany the adult will tend to keep the child in a state of submission, while the American may want to put the child back on an equal footing as soon as possible."

The *school* is, next to the home, perhaps the most important single source of a child's basic psychological patterns. What children formally learn in school is much less important than what they pick up unconsciously from the way in which the school operates. Authoritarian societies consider the school as little more than a phase of premilitary training, in which the function of the teacher is to inculcate habits of order and discipline.

In a democratic school system, the main function of the teacher is to help the child develop his own personality, and to help him learn *how* to think rather than what to think. The *permissive* attitude of the democratic school is premised on the assumption that people will generally choose the right way if given the proper help and guidance, and that trust will beget trust.

Also, most democratic societies do not hesitate to run the schools on a coeducational basis and to employ women on a large scale. By contrast, authoritarian schools separate boys from girls to make sure that the boys grow into tough men rather than soft sissies; also, men are generally preferred as teachers, mainly because only men can play the necessary role of father-substitute.

The democratic nature of the school is also determined by the relation of teacher and parent, and that of teacher and political authority. In student government, the students are given the opportunity to learn formal self-government, and to make their rules of self-government without interference from the outside. In many colleges, much of the discipline, from exams ("honor system") to staying-out hours, is regulated and enforced by the students themselves. This type of experience teaches a student more about democracy than a reading assignment about the theory and ideals of democracy.

Moreover, the existence of private schools in democracies is a further expression of freedom in education. In authoritarian societies, the state generally abolishes all private schools, since there is only one pattern that is right and the state knows what it is and has the means to enforce it. In democratic societies, many important

"I HATE EVERYBODY, REGARDLESS OF RACE, CREED, OR PLACE OF
NATIONAL ORIGIN!"

educational innovations have been given their first trial in small experimental schools; if successful, such advances then spread to the public school system.

The attitude toward women in society sharply differentiates the democratic from the authoritarian personality. The authoritarian generally desires to keep women in their place; his scale of values is oriented strongly toward masculine traits and preferences. Many legal codes officially recognize the superior position of the man by declaring him to be the head of the family, and by subordinating his wife to him in matters of property and other basic issues.

Feminism is not only the creed of rebellious women who wish to assert their equality, but also the feeling of democratically inclined men, who resent the treatment of women as inferiors just as they resent the treatment of any other human being as an inferior, on the basis of race, for example, or religion, or nationality. As in other cases of intolerance and inequality, the democratic personality is keenly aware of the fact that *unfair and arrogant treatment is harmful not only to the person so treated, but also to the person who metes it out.* This aspect of racial segregation was recognized by the Supreme Court, when it declared racial segregation in public schools unconstitutional in its historic decision of May 17, 1954.

The *range of affection* determines the degree to which a person matures, to which he can be called democratic. The child first knows only himself. Gradually he discovers a world outside of his own body and desires—his mother, father, brothers and sisters, neighbors, and classmates. The degree of his maturation and adulthood is in direct proportion to his capacity to enlarge his horizon and make friends with all kinds of persons.

The immature personality stops early in this process; he can only identify with his own group (the "in-group"), and considers others (the "out-group") as dangerous and hostile. This group-egotism may include the family only, or it may extend to social class, political party, or nation. In all these cases, the attachment to the in-group is frequently more an *expression of hatred for the outsider than of affection for the insider.*

By contrast, the democratic personality is always aware of his own imperfections and those of his social class, party, or nation, and this realization makes him tolerant of different people, different races, different religions, different ideas. His capacity to cooperate and love is not a rigid fixation on one particular object, but the expression of a *general capacity to cooperate, to share, to love.*

Love that is exclusively directed at one person or group is usually not love, but either masochistic self-abasement or sadistic domination. Love and cooperation in the democratic sense imply freedom, equality, and integrity, not exclusiveness and domination. When St. Paul said that there was "neither Jew nor Greek, neither bond nor free," he gave expression to a conception of human relations in which there was no in-group and no out-group, but only one humanity.

The strength of the democratic personality is proportionate to the strength of democratic institutions and practices in the society in which he lives. To the extent that persons are given leeway to develop and to act freely and spontaneously, they will experience less frustration and hatred.

Aggression is generally the *result of frustration,* although the causal relationship does not always appear immediately. Many persons are able to repress temporarily their aggressive impulses following frustration; such delays and repressions do not destroy the aggressive reaction, but merely postpone, exaggerate, and distort it. By contrast, the democratic society minimizes frustration by removing its sources as much as possible. Thus, in a democracy, everybody has the right to criticize any political leader, the government, or any idea.

This *freedom of expression serves as a safety-valve,* preventing resentment and hostility from being repressed and transformed into aggression and hatred. As everybody knows from his own experience, once he has told somebody off he feels better. Freedom of expression is a psychological catharsis, in which the soul keeps itself from accumulating resentment and hostility.

By contrast, a totalitarian society seems to be happy and united, and apparently there is no dissent. Yet this artificial calm builds up tremendous resources of hatred, which can often be expressed only in gossip, jokes, and other informal channels of expression. But when the lid is off, the accumulated frustrations break out into open violence. Hitler at the end of his regime, obsessed with the idea that everybody was conspiring to kill him, finally issued arrests for such close intimates as Goering, his second in command.

The artificiality of the calm and uniformity in totalitarian regimes is best demonstrated by the periodic purges and blood baths that are characteristic of communist and fascist states. Thus, Lavrenti Beria, one of the top three rulers in Russia, was executed in December 1953 for a long assortment of crimes he allegedly committed or planned to commit. A regime in which treason can reach so high up that the man in charge of the nation's secret police and internal security is killed as a spy in the pay of Wall Street, is scarcely a model of internal strength.

Finally, totalitarians invariably misjudge the apparent dissensions and disagreements in a democratic society. It is precisely because such disagreements are openly expressed that there is so little smouldering hatred and hostility within a free society, and it can act unitedly and strongly in the hour of need.

It is generally agreed that the democratic personality is more tolerant, more cooperative, friendlier, and fairer than the authoritarian personality. But the question is often raised whether these human gains are not paid for by the loss of efficiency. Controlled experiments with children and adults have shown that the efficiency of a group can be raised by substituting a democratic group decision for a lecture, request, or command from the top. In industry, management is increasingly using democratic group discussions to raise efficiency. This is still a new field of experimentation, but there is certainly no evidence that the autocratically run group produces more efficient individuals.

In the field of education, too, schools and colleges are trying to get away from the lecture method, where the teacher tells the student that such and such is so and so—period. The advantage of the discussion method over lecturing is that the teacher no longer functions as a little god issuing the law from Mount Sinai, but is more in the nature of an umpire, who sees to it that the rules of debate are properly observed; the discussion itself has to be carried forward by the students, and whatever conclusions they arrive at are the product of their own group thinking, and not of superior authority. Discussion, of course, assumes equality; superiors do not discuss with inferiors, but tell them what to do.

The *feeling of being wanted is one of the strongest driving forces of action and allegiance;* nothing can produce that feeling better than the democratic process of consultation, discussion, and free exchange of ideas. With love, greater things can be accomplished than with hatred. This old religious truth is also borne out by psychology, politics, and history.

In the last two hundred years, not a single major war has been won by the apostles of hatred and strife over the more democratic side, which would indicate that totalitarian efficiency fails even in the one field where it is supposed to be highest: war. The reason for such failure may be the tendency of the totalitarian personality to close his mind to new and changing circumstances, to adhere rigidly to fixed dogma, to aim at unrealistic objectives, or to pursue possible objectives with impossible means. Self-criticism is one of the most crucial correctives in doing any job; and although everybody is somewhat sensitive to criticism, the democratic personality can tolerate more of it than the totalitarian.

INDIVIDUAL FREEDOM AND NATIONAL SECURITY

The best introduction into the problem of individual liberty is still John Stuart Mill's essay *On Liberty* (1859). Mill wrote his essay at a comparatively civilized time, when there seemed to be little need for it. Yet he foresaw that illiberal forces would gain in influence, and he hoped that men would then turn to *On Liberty*. Though Mill modestly disclaimed originality other than that which "every thoughtful mind gives to its own mode of conceiving and expressing truths which are common property," the essay has grown in stature as time goes on, because many of Mill's predictions have come true, and much that he has to say is still valid today, a century later.

As Alexis de Tocqueville had done in his *Democracy in America* (1835-1840), Mill attacks the illusion that evolution of government from tyranny to democracy necessarily solves the problem of individual liberty. *Tyranny can be exercised by one, by a few, or by the majority,* and the latter is potentially the worst of all, since it commands the widest moral support, whereas oppression by one or a few is mainly physical. The power of public opinion in a democracy often exercises more restraint and repression against dissidents than a dictator exercises by physical means in a dictatorship. Protection against political tyranny is therefore not enough. It must be supplemented by protection against social tyranny, which leaves fewer means of escape, "penetrating much more deeply into the details of life, and enslaving the soul itself."

Mill sees that the natural tendency of man is not to be tolerant and open-minded, but to impose his views on others, and that lack of power is frequently the major cause of tolerating dissent. It makes little difference how numerous the dissenting minority is: "If all mankind minus one, were of one opinion, and only one person were of the contrary opinion, mankind would be no more justified in silencing that one person, than he, if he had the power, would be justified in silencing mankind."

Silencing an unorthodox opinion is not only wrong but harmful, because it robs others of an opportunity to get acquainted with ideas that may be true, or partly true. "All silencing of discussion," Mill argues, "is an assumption of infallibility." Therefore Mill states that, unless *absolute freedom of opinion*—scientific, moral, political, and theological—is guaranteed, a society is not completely free.

No individual can grasp more than a fragment or portion of truth; no society can speak for all mankind; finally, whole eras are no more infallible than individuals. History is full of opinions held by one age as the last truth only to be considered false and absurd by subsequent ages.

Just as liberty is not complete unless it is absolute, so discussion must be completely unhampered, and free discussion must not be ruled out when "pushed to an extreme," because the arguments for a case are not good unless they are good for an extreme case. Mill is aware of the argument that some opinions are so useful and important to society that they must be excluded from public discussion and criticism, but he answers that the "usefulness of an opinion is itself a matter of opinion."

Mill does not accept the "pleasant falsehood" that truth inevitably triumphs over persecution; history "teems with instances of truth put down by persecution." In the history of religion in the West, for example, there are numerous sects and churches that have been successfully suppressed, and Mill therefore concludes that "persecution has always succeeded, save where the heretics were too strong a party to be effectually persecuted."

Moreover, *the greatest harm of persecution is inflicted not on those who dissent from established beliefs, but on those who do not*, because the mental development of the latter is stifled by the fear of expressing unorthodox or dissenting views. In an atmosphere of cowed uniformity there may be a few exceptional great thinkers, but not an intellectually active people: "No one can be a great thinker who does not recognize, that as a thinker it is his first duty to follow his intellect to whatever conclusions it may lead."

Moreover, dogmatism robs truth of its vigor and vitality, and is more likely to destroy truth than keep it alive. For its own health, truth needs to be "fully, frequently, and fearlessly" discussed. If possible at all, the opposing opinion should be expressed by someone who really believes in it. Only in the constant process of being challenged can truth grow and remain healthy: "Both teachers and learners go to sleep at their posts, as soon as there is no enemy in the field."

The necessity of the fullest expression of opinion may be based on three grounds. First, the silenced opinion may be *wholly true,* in which case its suppression is wholly unjustified. Second, the silenced opinion may be *partly true and partly false,* as most opinions tend to be, in which case "it is only by the collision of adverse opinions that the remainder of the truth has any chance of being supplied." Third, even if the silenced opinion be *wholly erroneous,* it should not be suppressed, because its very challenge of truth prevents the latter from degenerating into dogma and prejudice.

The purpose of individual liberty is personal self-development. It is the privilege of every person to interpret experience in his own way, and his moral faculties can only be brought into play when he is obliged to choose between alternatives. A person who merely follows custom and tradition makes no choice, nor does he who lets others make his decisions for him. *Different persons should be permitted to lead different lives;* the principle of liberty thus inevitably implies that of variety and diversity.

It should be noted that the progress of industrial civilization does not make it easier for men and women to remain individual personalities, because increasingly "they now read the same things, listen to the same things, go to the same places, have their hopes and fears directed to the same objects, have the same rights and liberties, and the same means of asserting them." People who do the same things tend to think the same thoughts.

This standardization has progressed enormously in the last hundred years; the radio, television, and movie industries have added new dimensions of prefabricated opinion. As to newspapers: the number of daily papers is steadily declining in Britain and the United States (there are hundreds of cities and towns with only one daily paper) and the number of newspaper readers is constantly increasing, so that more and more people are reading fewer and fewer papers. Moreover, standardization has now reached the point where not only is identical news coverage published in thousands of papers, with the same headlines and all, but even editorials, purporting to present the viewpoint of the local paper's editor, are actually "canned," prepared in a New York or Washington agency and then "farmed out" all over the country.

Mill reminds those who are willing to repress individual liberty for the sake of a strong state that the worth of a state is no more than the worth of its individual citizens. When the state "dwarfs" its men, and reduces them to docile instruments, it will find that "with small men no great things can really be accomplished."

Mill is still the best guide to liberty based on reason. Yet *On Liberty* is a century old, and it cannot be expected to give clear-cut answers to the problems that baffle us today. In particular, Mill did not deal with two problems that did not exist in his day but are of paramount importance today.

First, Mill always assumed that in every debate both sides were after the truth, and were honestly searching for it. Today we face a situation where totalitarian movements, like fascism or communism, disseminate statements which not only are false, but which the communist or fascist propagandists *know to be false*—for example, the communist stories of American germ warfare in Korea.

The second problem that did not exist in Mill's day, and that has tremendous practical importance today, is the phenomenon of a *revolutionary, subversive party directed from abroad*. In Mill's day, apart from a few mild anarchists or theoretical revolutionaries whom no one took seriously, there was no organized movement of a revolutionary, subversive nature. Today, revolutionary subversion is organized in powerful movements, movements that are particularly difficult to cope with because they are not homegrown but instruments of a foreign power, whose purposes alone they serve.

In the United States, the curbing of revolutionary movements by legal means is based on the Smith Act of 1940, Section 2 of which makes it unlawful for any person knowingly or wilfully to "advocate, abet, advise, or teach the duty, necessity, desirability, or propriety of overthrowing or destroying any government in the United States by force or violence, or by the assassination of any officer of such government." In 1948, eleven top communist leaders were indicted for violation of the Smith Act. The trial, one of the most important political trials in American history, lasted over nine months, the record running up to 16,000 pages. Finally, the Supreme Court took up the case, and decided against the communist leaders on June 4, 1951.

The main constitutional issue involved was *whether the Smith Act violated the First and Fifth Amendments.* The First Amendment provides that Congress shall make no law "abridging the freedom of speech, or of the press; or the right of the people peaceably to assemble, and to petition the government for a redress of grievances." Under the Fifth Amendment, no person "shall be deprived of life, liberty, or property, without due process of law." By a majority of six to two, the Supreme Court held the Smith Act constitutional.

A central concept in the conflicting opinions of the Court was the *clear and present danger* doctrine, as expressed by Mr. Justice Holmes in 1919: "The question in every case," Holmes wrote, "is whether the words used are used in such circumstances and are of such a nature as to create a clear and present danger that they will bring about the substantive evils that Congress has a right to prevent. It is a question of proximity and degree."

Writing for the majority in the case of the communists, Chief Justice Vinson declared that the communists *did* create a clear and present danger in recommending the overthrow of the government by force and violence. Chief Justice Vinson even went beyond the "clear and present danger" doctrine by accepting a narrower concept of *probable danger:* "In each case [courts] must ask whether the gravity of the 'evil,' discounted by its improbability, justifies such invasion of free speech as is necessary to avoid the danger." In a concurring opinion, Mr. Justice Jackson denied that the "clear and present danger" doctrine could properly be applied to the case; otherwise communists plotting a revolutionary conspiracy would be protected during its period of incubation, and the Government could move "only after imminent action is manifest, when it would, of course, be too late."

In his dissenting opinion, Mr. Justice Black emphasized that the communist leaders were not charged with any nonverbal acts designed to overthrow the government, and that the outlawry of verbal expressions of revolution constitutes a drastic qualification or complete repudiation of the "clear and present danger" doctrine. Mr.

Justice Douglas, in his dissenting opinion, concedes that "the freedom to speak is not absolute," and accepts, in general, the Holmesian principle. However, whereas Holmes left the meaning of his principle rather vague, Douglas quotes approvingly Mr. Justice Brandeis in *Whitney* v. *California* (1927) that "no danger flowing from speech can be deemed clear and present, unless the incidence of the evil apprehended is so imminent that it may befall before there is opportunity for full discussion." Following Brandeis, Douglas argues that free speech *has* destroyed communism in the United States, and that it is "inconceivable" that advocates of communist revolution in the United States would have any success.

Under the Brandeis doctrine, it might be one thing to preach publicly against conscription when there is ample opportunity to rebut pacifism in public debate, and quite another thing to preach pacifist doctrine outside a draft board, when such opportunity to rebut does not exist. Similarly, a person may publicly attack income taxes as harmful to liberty and full personal development, but such propaganda would hardly be tolerable outside an office of the Bureau of Internal Revenue, because there would be no opportunity to debate the issue, and the harm of such anti-tax propaganda might be done before the other side of the debate could be presented.

The Brandeis doctrine was expressed much earlier by Thomas Jefferson, who was willing to "tolerate error so long as reason is left free to combat it." In his first inaugural address Jefferson said that "having banished from our land that religious intolerance under which mankind so long bled and suffered, we have yet gained little if we countenance a political intolerance as despotic, as wicked, and capable of as bitter and bloody persecutions." Going into the fundamental question of how to deal with those who advocate basic change, Jefferson had this to say: "If there be any among us who would wish to dissolve this Union or to change its republican form, let them stand undisturbed as monuments of the safety with which error of opinion may be tolerated where reason is left free to combat it."

Jefferson was willing to allow even antirepublican (or antidemocratic, as we would say today) doctrines, not only on the basis of rational argument, but also because he had tremendous faith in a free America, "the strongest government on earth." It is possible that our present wavering with regard to the Jeffersonian doctrine coincides with something deeper: a loss of self-confidence in the strength of liberty, and the growing fear that antidemocratic propaganda, if un-checked, might gain too many converts.

There are indications that a return to more traditional American concepts is under way. Virtually reversing its position of 1951, the Supreme Court ruled on June 17, 1957, that in the case against fourteen West Coast communist leaders a distinction must be made "between advocacy of forcible overthrow as an abstract doctrine and advocacy of action to that end," and that "mere membership or the holding of office in the Communist Party" did not constitute sufficient evidence of the intent to overthrow the government by force. While this decision did not explicitly invalidate the constitutionality of the Smith Act, it marked, at least, a return to the "clear and present danger" doctrine that had been strongly modified, if not abandoned, in 1951. In any case, the 1957 decision of the Supreme Court reestablished the traditional democratic (and American) concept under which all doctrines, including revolutionary ones, may be law-fully advocated and propagated. In other words, the validity of democracy is no longer a taboo issue that must not be challenged.

It is noteworthy that this new approach of the Supreme Court to the issue of individual political liberty and freedom of expression occurred four years after the end of the Korean war, nearly three years after the Senate's censure of the late Senator McCarthy, and a month after the latter's death. Equally noteworthy is the fact that of the nine justices of the Supreme Court, six concurred in the decision, whereas only one (Mr. Justice Clark) dissented (two did not take part in the decision). Justices Black and Douglas, who in 1951 were the only dissenters from the majority opinion upholding the constitu-tionality of the Smith Act, were not satisfied that the Court majority in 1957 had fully adopted their viewpoint, and Mr. Justice Black wrote a separate opinion (joined by Mr. Justice Douglas) containing the following passage: "Unless there is complete freedom of expres-sion for all ideas, whether we like them or not, concerning the way government should be run and who shall run it, I doubt if any views in the long run can be secured against the censor. The First Amend-ment provides the only kind of security system that can preserve a free government—one that leaves the way wide open for people to favor, discuss, advocate, or incite causes and doctrines however obnoxious and antagonistic such views may be to the rest of us."

The history of the Supreme Court is full of instances in which the minority of yesterday becomes the majority of today, and while the minority viewpoint of Justices Black and Douglas in 1951 did not fully convert the majority in 1957, the conversion went far enough to satisfy most defenders of the traditional liberal concept of individual freedom as the chief aim of the Constitution.

From a broader viewpoint, the important issue is not only what the security program, first set up by President Truman in 1947 and later revamped by President Eisenhower in 1953, has done to communists and fellow-travelers. What is perhaps more important is the growing trend toward conformity among ordinary people. After all, of 4,500,000 federal employees and applicants only about 30,000 were ever reviewed by the Loyalty Review Board, which is less than one per cent. Of the cases reviewed, only about three per cent were dismissed.

Too much has been said of the impact of the program on the one per cent directly affected by it, and too little about the 99 per cent who have no personal or painful experience with it. Two social psychologists, Marie Jahoda and Stuart W. Cook, made a study called "Security Measures and Freedom of Thought: An Exploratory Study of the Impact of Loyalty and Security Programs" (*Yale Law Journal*, March, 1952) They found that federal employees are learning to keep out of discussions of controversial subjects, such as atomic energy, religion, and racial equality: "One person carried his avoidance of conversations involving controversial subjects so far that he decided to take an earlier bus to work every morning because he had overheard some regular bus riders on his original route discussing politics." Reading habits are changing, but one employee said he felt there were no restrictions worth mentioning: "There is no reason to refrain from reading the *Saturday Evening Post* and *Collier's*."

In the minds of the employees, some persons nowadays are liable to become *targets of unfounded suspicion,* not because they have ever done or said anything disloyal or subversive, but because they have certain personal characteristics that are not desirable at present. The following were specifically listed as targets of unfounded suspicion:

"Those who are useful in organizations. If you don't do anything,
   you are never questioned."

"Those who actively work in election campaigns."

"A person willing to hire a Negro secretary."

"People whose job is international affairs."

"People with many friends and associates."

"People who have been in college during the depression."

© 1950 The New Yorker Magazine

"IT'S TRUE, SIR, THAT THE STATE DEPARTMENT LET ME GO, BUT
THAT WAS SOLELY BECAUSE OF INCOMPETENCE."

In such an atmosphere the public service will have difficulty at-
tracting men and women of imagination, independence, and daring.

In the protection of traditional liberties, the judiciary has held up
best in the current crisis; and the executive branch also has at least
made an honest effort to administer a complex program fairly and
equitably.

Several judicial decisions deserve particular attention. On June
23, 1955, the United States Court of Appeal upheld the "natural
right" of American citizens to travel abroad, thus denying the Depart-

ment of State the authority to arbitrarily decide who may travel abroad. Since that decision, the government can deny the issuance of a passport only after due process of law, whereas until that time it could, and did, make such vital decisions on its own discretion.

An even more important decision was that of the Supreme Court on July 11, 1956, when it ruled that the security program for federal employees could be applied only to "sensitive" jobs, that is, jobs concerned with "the nation's safety" (such as in national defense, intelligence, secret scientific research, and similar activities). Since half the number of persons dismissed under the security program had held non-sensitive jobs, this decision of the Supreme Court had immediate practical results; more importantly from an overall viewpoint, it helped to create a new, and more rational, climate of opinion in matters relating to loyalty and security in the government. In this new atmosphere, the Supreme Court ruled on June 17, 1957, that John Stewart Service, a foreign service officer and one-time main target of the late Senator McCarthy, had been illegally dismissed by the State Department in 1951, after he had been cleared by its own Loyalty Board six times in the preceding six years. Mr. Service fought his case in the federal courts for nearly six years after his dismissal. The lower courts sided with the government, but the Supreme Court upheld his claim that his discharge had been unlawful.

Finally, on June 3, 1957, the Supreme Court decided in the Jencks case that the defense has the right to see secret F. B. I. data on which the charges against the accused are based. Mr. Clinton E. Jencks, a New Mexico leader, had been convicted of falsely swearing that he had never been a communist, but had been denied access to the F. B. I. files for his defense. The Sixth Amendment provides the accused in all criminal prosecutions with the right "to be confronted with the witnesses against him," but the government maintained that F. B. I files must remain secret in order to protect sources of information from exposure. In the Jencks decision, the Supreme Court ordered a new trial for Mr. Jencks, because his constitutional rights had been violated by the use of secret charges against him. The effect of the decision in the Jencks case is not, of course, to make F. B. I. files available for general inspection by the public; the data will remain secret. Only when the government wishes to use them in a criminal prosecution will the defense have access to them. By its ruling in the Jencks case the Supreme Court helped to redress the balance of rights and liberties still further in favor of the individual. The interest of the United States, the Court said, "is not that it shall win a case but that justice shall be done."

It is the lawmaking branch of the government that in the eyes of many has violated elementary principles of justice and fair play. Zechariah Chafee, the leading American authority on the problem of free speech, writes in *Thirty-Five Years with Freedom of Speech* (1952) that it is not just a question of violating freedom of speech, press and assembly:

"Equally disquieting is what those inroads are doing to our traditions of a fair trial. A person who is subpoenaed into a legislative investigation, where his reputation and perhaps his livelihood are at stake, is denied much of the protection long enjoyed by those who risk imprisonment or a fine. He is not told what he is charged with before he prepares his defense and starts answering questions; the investigators have a roving commission to find out anything whatever that will damage him. He cannot demand to be confronted with the witnesses against him, for they may be spies whose identity the secret police do not want disclosed. So he may not know who his accusers are, and in any event he cannot cross-examine them. The normal right to counsel is denied. Sometimes he cannot even bring a lawyer into the room with him. When a lawyer is graciously admitted, he must usually be just a bystander with no chance to conduct the defense."

On June 17, 1957, a day on which it made history in several issues affecting individual liberty, the Supreme Court also dealt with the scope and authority of legislative investigatory committees. The first case was that of John Thomas Watkins, a labor organizer in the automobile industry. Watkins appeared before a subcommittee of the Committee on Un-American Activities of the House of Representatives in 1954, where he candidly told about his own past political activities, but refused to talk about persons who years ago may have been Communists but were so no longer. As a result, he was sentenced, for contempt of Congress, to one year in prison and fined. The Supreme Court reversed the decision of the lower court, arguing that the purpose of a legislative inquiry must be explicitly stated and that the questions asked of witnesses must be pertinent to a legitimate legislative purpose. While conceding that Congress must have the authority to conduct investigations, and that such investigative powers are broad, the Supreme Court also emphasized that such powers are "not unlimited," that Congress is not a "law enforcement or trial agency," and that it has no power "to expose for the sake of exposure." Indirectly referring to the use by some legislators of investigative publicity as a principal means of political fame and advancement, the Supreme Court finally issued this weighty reminder: "Investigations conducted solely for the personal ag-

TORCH OF LIBERTY

Herblock in the *Washington Post*

1949   1957

grandizement of the investigators or to 'punish' those investigated are indefensible."

The second case, also passed on by the Supreme Court on June 17, 1957, dealt with the issue of academic freedom. Professor Paul Sweezey, after lecturing at the University of New Hampshire on economics, was questioned by the state's Attorney General about his political activities and beliefs. He denied the charge that he had ever been a member of the Communist Party, but refused to give any information about his teaching or his political opinions and associations. As a result, he was held to be in contempt by the New

Hampshire Supreme Court. The United States Supreme Court decided that Professor Sweezey's conviction was invalid, and added the warning that government should be "extremely reticent" to tread in the areas of academic freedom and political expression: "No one should underestimate the vital role in a democracy that is played by those who guide and train our youth. To impose any strait-jacket upon the intellectual leaders in our colleges and universities would imperil the future of our nation."

CLASSICAL CAPITALISM

Capitalism developed historically as part of the great movement of *rationalist individualism*. In religion, that movement produced the Reformation; in learning, the growth of the physical sciences; in human relations, the social sciences; in politics, democratic government; and in economics, the capitalist system. The concept of *capitalist civilization* is therefore a legitimate one; it suggests that capitalism is more than an economic system, that it reflects a way of life. It first developed in eighteenth-century Britain; later it was transplanted to northwestern Europe and North America. A few basic traits have characterized capitalism from the beginning.

Ownership of the means of production (land, factories, machinery, natural resources) is, in the capitalist system, *held by individuals, not by the state*. This does not exclude public ownership of natural monopolies or basic public services (post office, atomic arms), but such cases are considered the exception rather than the rule.

The bias of the capitalist civilization in favor of private ownership of the means of the production is based on two considerations. First, ownership of productive property means power over the lives of other people; it is preferable that such *power* be *diffused among many property owners* rather than held by one owner, the state. Moreover, the economic power of private property owners can be curbed by the popularly elected government; were the state to own all productive property, economic and political power would coincide, and the outlook for personal economic liberty would be dim. Second, the assumption of capitalist thinking is that *technological progress* is more easily attained when each person minds his own business, and has a personal incentive to do so.

The second principle of the capitalist system is that of the *market economy*. In the precapitalist era, the economy was generally local and self-sufficient; each family produced just about what it needed, supplementing its simple needs with some barter or exchange operations in a primitive local market. *Division of labor* was barely known, and each family had to do many jobs that nowadays are spread among hundreds of various crafts and specialties. Also, the type of occupation a person was in and the price he could charge for his goods and services were largely predetermined for him by custom and usage. By contrast, the market economy of the capitalist system is based on specialization of labor. Each person supplies only a very small part of his needs through his own skills and labors. The products or services are designed not for the producer's own household, but for the market.

Neither custom and usage nor the commands of a political authority determine the *price* in the market; this function is fulfilled by supply and demand. If prices are high, the market provides a signal that the supply of certain goods or services would be profitable; if prices are low, the market seems to say, "Try your luck in something else."

In the totalitarian economy (fascist or communist) the state, in trying to plan the whole economy, runs up against the difficulty of the limitations of the "span of control." No human being can anticipate all the possible developments in an intricate economic system, encompassing many millions of persons and operated by economic decisions running daily into tens of millions.

In the capitalist market economy, each decision-maker has to watch over a much smaller area, and his span of attention and control is more limited and manageable.

The market economy is the touchstone of all economic systems. Neither communism nor fascism believes in it; in fascism, ownership of the means of production is formally still in the hands of private individuals, but this is not too important, because fascism does away with the market economy, and substitutes for it the *command economy*. The state tells the individuals where to work, what jobs to choose, what to eat, what to produce, what prices to charge, and how to invest savings and profits. Communism abolishes private ownership of the means of production and the market economy. The communist economy, too, is a totalitarian command economy, in which economic decisions are made by a totalitarian state. By contrast, the market economy is an economy in which free individuals make their own economic decisions in the light of their interest, experience, and intelligence.

The tremendous political implications of the market economy have finally been recognized by socialist economists. W. Arthur Lewis, a British economist, examines this question in a book written for the Fabian Society, *The Principles of Economic Planning* (1949). As a socialist, Lewis is opposed to the orthodox concepts of *laissez-faire* (as are most nonsocialist economists today).

The real issue, Lewis argues, is not between planning and no planning, but between *planning by direction* and *planning by inducement*. In the former, the government (as under fascism or communism) tries to get the right things done by direct control and regulation of output, prices, and wages. A government agent watches every step in the plan, and those workers or managers who fail to fulfil their quota are punished as traitors and saboteurs, although neglect or incapacity rather than wilful disregard may have been the cause of their failure. The key mechanism in such a command economy is terror, specifically the fear of the prison or the slave labor camp.

In a democratic state, the government indirectly stimulates certain economic activities through the budget, taxation, interest rates, and other policies of planning by inducement, thus avoiding the two main defects of planning by direction: bureaucratic centralization and economic inefficiency. Far from rejecting the free market as the normal mechanism of economic adjustment, Lewis holds that "our aim should be to preserve free markets wherever possible." It is also of no little interest that Lewis, in accepting the principle of the market economy, is driven to the conclusion that the nationalization of all industry is undesirable, because of the usual reasons against monopoly: inefficiency, lack of initiative, and concentration of power.

Thus, the *function of the free market as a mechanism of political liberty* is now increasingly being recognized by socialists, and it gradually dawns on them that the question of ownership is less important than the question of whether economic decisions are made by free, independent individuals or corporations on the one hand, or by the state on the other.

The distinction between the command economy and the market economy thus reflects in the economic field the more basic political distinction between totalitarianism (fascism and communism) and liberalism (socialism and capitalism).

The most important specific liberties of the free market economy are the following: for the *worker,* to choose his line of work and his particular job; for the *businessman,* to choose his type of business, and set it up at the place of his choice; for the investor, to invest his capital in whatever enterprise he chooses; finally, for the *consumer,* to buy the product he prefers.

This last freedom ("consumer sovereignty") is, in many respects, the most important of all, because it is the preference of the consumer that ultimately decides in a free market what is to be produced, at what quality, and in what quantities. In totalitarian economies, fascist or communist, consumer sovereignty is seriously curtailed. In the totalitarian economy, the state decides what is to be produced for consumption purposes, and how it is to be distributed.

Thus, a person with a high income in Russia may be unable to buy an automobile, because the government has decided that only a small number shall be produced, and that that small number shall be rationed among a small group of meritorious persons—who also, generally, happen to be high government officials. Russia diverts only enough material from armaments production to permit an annual production of about 100,000 automobiles, as compared with an annual production of over 6 million in the United States. Although there are more cars than families in the United States, only about one in every 1,000 Russian families owns a car. Consumer sovereignty is thus replaced by that of the commissar.

Another essential characteristic of the capitalist economy is *competition.* In the precapitalist economy, custom and usage dictated what goods and services were worth, and there were many persons who could not compete at all, because they were excluded from certain occupations. In the capitalist economy, everybody is free to choose whatever line of work he prefers ("freedom of occupation"), and there is to be no artificial restriction or exclusion (such as on the basis of racial or religious prejudice) from any occupation or profession. Similarly, the capitalist market provides the place where goods and services are offered for sale, the quantity and quality of which are regulated by free competition. The basic assumption of the classical capitalist economy is that there is relative equality of bargaining power within, and between, buyers and sellers.

The freedom to compete in the market results from four basic capitalist freedoms: freedom of trade and occupation, freedom of contract, freedom of property, and freedom of profit-making. To the extent that any of these four freedoms is curbed, free competition is reduced.

The alternative to competition is either (a) private monopoly or (b) the omnipotent state. In both cases, the arbitrary determination of the prices of goods and services by a *de facto* authority (as in the case of private monopoly) or a legal authority (as in that of the state) takes the place of the free interplay of buyers and sellers, following their own choice.

The economic justification of competition is that it keeps everybody—worker, businessman, investor—on his toes, constantly alert to changes in the market, and constantly on the lookout for ways to increase his efficiency and thereby improve his chances in the market. By increasing his own efficiency, the individual worker or entrepreneur proportionately increases the efficiency and productivity of the whole market. Better products, lower prices, better services—ultimately higher living standards for all—result from the constant incentive to keep up with, and if possible to outdo, one's competitors.

In industry, *research* has become one of the keenest areas of competition. Research today means cheaper and better products tomorrow, and the vitality of competition is seen in the fact that companies are spending an increasingly larger share of their budget on research. Twenty-five years ago, private annual expenditure on industrial research was about 100 million dollars; today, it is approaching 6 billion dollars. Research, by accelerating the rate of change in the economy, promotes competition at an early stage, long before the product or service reaches the market.

The *profit* principle is another basic principle that characterizes the capitalist system. So far, no historian has been able to show that before capitalism the profit principle was absent—the merchant in ancient Greece, for example, did not stay in business for his health.

Yet there is one tremendous difference between capitalism and pre-capitalist systems: the capitalist economy provides more opportunity for profit than any previous economy, because it guarantees three freedoms that were not commonly found in precapitalist systems: freedom of trade and occupation, freedom of property, and freedom of contract. Obviously, where the institution of slavery exists, the slaves cannot enter the profit system: their economic fate is deter mined by their social position; not possessing any of the other three basic economic freedoms, they have no access to the profit system.

In the middle ages, products were made by guilds and sold at prescribed prices. The profit system was thus doubly limited: only a member of the guild could enter the process of production; furthermore, prices were defined not by freedom of contract between buyer and seller, but by the authority of custom, the church, or the state.

Even in modern states like Germany and Japan, the American occupation authorities after World War II were amazed to find how many professions and trades were virtually closed to outsiders, and they found it no easy task to induce the German and Japanese lawmakers to allow more freedom of trade and occupation.

The expansion of the profit system under capitalism thus does not necessarily show that the greater chance of profit makes capitalism more unethical; rather, it shows that capitalism is more democratic in opening profit opportunities for persons and classes which traditionally have been excluded from them. The profit concept goes beyond the entrepreneur, of course; the worker who takes a job at the place of his choice, for example, has an access to profit that he would not have had in a precapitalist society.

Moreover, whenever the capitalist system is described as a profit system, it is frequently forgotten that the other side of the medal is equally important—that capitalism is also a *loss* system. Although it is true to say that never have so many made so much profit as under capitalism, it is equally true that in no other system have so many lost so much as under capitalism. In American economic development, for example, losses, bankruptcies, and failures were very heavy in the early mining, railroading, and automotive industries. In the more recent field of television, for example, a pioneering company like the Radio Corporation of America lost many millions of dollars (seven millions in 1956 alone) when it first introduced color television. The first stages of black and white television were also loss operations.

The unparalleled opportunities of profit and loss in capitalism have one thing in common: *personal risk-taking.* Capitalism does not order anybody to take risks; it merely holds out the promise of profit to the person who is willing to take risks. Where the spirit of risk-taking is weak, investors prefer secure investments in bonds, which offer a guaranteed (and lower) return. Where the spirit of risk-taking is strong, investors prefer the common stock of corporations, which usually yield 50 to 75 per cent higher returns than bonds.

However, if the quest for security is so strong that most investors shy away from risk investments, as in France, for example, economic stagnation is inevitable. The sudden and phenomenal growth of the air-conditioning industry in the United States today is due to the fact that enough investors were willing to take a chance on an unknown industry rather than invest their capital in a sure thing.

STRESSES AND STRAINS IN MODERN CAPITALISM

The theory of capitalism approximated reality most closely in its classical period, roughly from the middle of the eighteenth to the end of the nineteenth century. In the twentieth century, capitalism has had to face stresses and strains, some internal, such as techno-logical developments of industry itself, others external, such as wars.

The separation of ownership from management and financial con-trol was made legally possible by the invention of the *corporate form of business:* each shareholder in a corporation is liable only to the extent of the shares he owns, no more and no less. In the pre-capitalist economy, a partnership involved full personal responsi-bility of each partner for the operations of the business. Partnerships tended to be relatively small, and each partner had a sense of per-sonal involvement, financial and moral, in the business. In a big modern corporation, where fifty million or one hundred million shares are owned by more than half a million shareholders, the link between the individual shareholder and the corporation, of which he is part owner, is very tenuous. The corporation may be located thousands of miles away from most of the shareholders, and in most corpora-tions only a small fraction of shareholders, generally less than one per cent, attend the annual meetings in which officers are elected and other important business is transacted.

Management draws up the list of officers to be elected, manage-ment presides over the elections, management explains why its pro-

"THE MOTION HAS BEEN MADE AND SECONDED THAT WE GIVE OUR-SELVES A RAISE IN SALARY. ALL THOSE IN FAVOR SAY 'AYE.'"

posed policy decisions should be adopted, management decides the salaries of management, management finally submits all its proposals to a vote: the vote is normally between 95 and 99 per cent in favor of management. This is a comfortable majority, as compared with average majorities of 52 to 55 per cent in political elections. "Like a stockholders' meeting" is a common phrase used to describe any perfunctorily run meeting.

In fact, whenever there is a real fight between management and a strong opposition, as there was over the New York Central Railroad in 1954, the controversy makes the front page. Of course, when the unusual happens and the opposition manages to acquire control, a new cycle of one-party rule starts again, until after several more decades there is some new revolt.

The essence of the problem is simple: in government, democracy has established the principle that *those who wield power must be accountable to the public.* The people are the boss, the government their agent. Political power—in a democracy—must not be held for the benefit of the rulers; it is a trust, the purpose of which is to protect the interests of the people.

In the economic realm, on the other hand, a constitutional situation prevails that runs counter to the basic concept of democracy: the owners of capital (or their hired managers) wield far-reaching power over their employees, and they constantly make decisions affecting the public interest, without any clearly defined responsibility to the public. Whereas in a capitalist democracy political policies are arrived at through processes of consent that begin at the bottom and end at the top, in corporate business economic policies are made from the top and passed on to the bottom. The character of modern industrial organization is hierarchical, founded on discipline and obedience.

More recently, however, the traditional pattern in industry has been considerably modified and made more democratic, mainly by organized labor, legislation, public opinion, and the growth in the business class of a sense of responsibility toward the community.

The more capitalism succeeds, the more it destroys—paradoxically enough—its original institutional and ideological character by collectivizing and socializing the framework of business. The first collectivists in the capitalistic era were not its critics, but the most successful capitalistic entrepreneurs, men like Andrew Carnegie,

John D. Rockefeller, and Henry Ford who created vast industrial empires.

Like other empires, industrial empires tend to become bureaucratic and conformity-minded, to follow routine and precedent, and, above all, to transform personal initiative and enterprise into impersonal rules of administrative routine. Whereas the original individual capitalists were men of bold, daring adventurousness, the bureaucratic administrators of the new vast industrial empires tend to put security above everything else. If risk-taking was one of the most characteristic traits of original capitalists, large corporate business has tended to shy away from risk-taking investments, and stick to "safe bets."

The danger is that, as business becomes bigger, the free-enterprise system may gradually become a "safe enterprise" system.

Psychologically, there is *less difference between large-scale capitalist enterprise and large-scale socialized enterprise on the one hand than between small-scale capitalist enterprise and large-scale capitalist enterprise on the other.* It is for this reason that such defenders of capitalism as Justice Brandeis and President Wilson were afraid that the "curse of bigness" might eventually destroy not only big private enterprise, but private enterprise itself. Again, this problem of bigness is not peculiar to the economic institutions of liberal capitalism; in politics, too, there is the threat of "big government" destroying the very elements that give life and color to democracy.

Who owns American business? Until recently, there were only guesses on this question, but now the facts begin to come to light. About 70 per cent of all corporate stock is owned by individuals, the rest by investment companies, insurance companies, foundations, and institutions. In 1952, the Federal Reserve Board found that of 53.1 million American families only 3.7 million held any stock. Among stock-owning families, half a million, or one per cent of all American families, own two-thirds of all the stock by value, the remaining one-third being largely owned by another half a million families. The remaining 2.7 million own only "a very limited part" of all corporate stock. What this amounts to is this: *a little over one million families own virtually all of the corporate stock held by individual owners.*

To get some idea of the role of big business in the American economy: in 1948, the 200 largest corporations accounted for 19.8 per cent of the nonagricultural private labor force, and for 12.4 per cent of the total civilian labor force. These same 200 corporations hold 40 per cent of all corporate wealth, or between one-fourth and one-fifth of all income-producing national wealth. Taking industrial research as the key to industrial progress and effective competition: the largest 75 corporation laboratories employ about one-half of all professional research personnel in industry.

The phenomenon of concentration can best be illustrated by a giant corporation like General Motors. In 1955, its assets were $6.3 billion, or about 1 per cent of all corporate assets; it employed 624,000 employees, or about 1.5 per cent of all employees in private, non-agricultural establishments, or nearly 4 per cent of all employees in manufacturing; its payroll was $3.1 billion, or nearly 2 per cent of all wages and salaries in private business; its tax bill was $1.4 billion, or 2 per cent of all receipts of the United States Government, or 7 per cent of all corporate taxes; its net profit (after taxes) was $1.2 billion, or equal to the combined profits of 82 per cent of all corporations in the country. In its own (automotive) industry, General Motors produces about 50 per cent (in some years even more) of all cars. The Big Three—General Motors, Ford, and Chrysler—account for over 95 per cent of all passenger cars. In 1921, there were 87 manufacturers of cars; in 1957, only five.

Yet there is another side to the picture. In the first place, it is not known whether concentration is increasing, decreasing, or standing still. In "The Measurement of Industrial Concentration" (in *The Review of Economics and Statistics,* November 1951), M. A. Adelman argues that in 1901 nearly one-third of manufacturing was produced in industries of high concentration, whereas by 1947 only about one-fourth of value added by manufacturing was produced in highly concentrated industry. Adelman realizes the difficulty of considering such figures as final, but he concludes as follows: "The odds are better than even that there has actually been *some* decline in concentration. It is a good bet that there has at least been no actual increase; and the odds do seem high against any substantial increase."

Moreover, it is argued, though a high proportion of American industry is dominated by big business, its composition constantly changes. There is *no hereditary aristocracy in big business.* Taking the 100 largest corporations of 1909 as a starting point, 64 had lost their top ranking by 1948, giving place to newcomers. The competition is not only between individual firms in this top group; changing conditions of the economy entail keen *competition between whole industry groups*. Thus, steel, coal mining and textiles were relatively much more important in 1909 than in 1948, whereas the petroleum, chemical, and electrical equipment industries rose sharply in their relative importance in the top 100 corporations. This rapid change in the composition of the top group during four decades further illustrates the point that bigness is not to be identified with monopoly.

Defenders of big business maintain that a big country and a big market need big business. The very survival of the United States may depend on the productivity of big business, not only in turning out the necessary armaments and civilian goods and services, but also in giving economic and military assistance to the free nations whose freedom and security are linked with those of the United States.

Individual security, too, has a better chance in big business than in small enterprises, because the former can do a better job in long-term planning of production, stability of employment, and the provision of services like pension and sickness benefits. In the field of labor-management relations, the greatest progress has been made in the mass production industries, like steel and automobiles, in which big business predominates; by contrast, labor unions have made little progress in agriculture and retailing, where the small unit prevails.

In research, too, as has been pointed out above, big business carries most of the work and responsibility. Occasionally important inventions are still made in small laboratories; then it takes the resources and organization of larger corporations to translate the inventions into economic realities. More and more, however, industrial research is carried out by big corporations, because it requires large financial resources and many years of waiting. Thus, du Pont spent $27,000,000 and 13 years of research before nylon could be marketed commercially.

Concerning the impact of big business on competition, it is argued that the two are not incompatible. Big business produces a new kind of competition—internal competition. Thus, not only is there competition between General Motors and Ford, but within General Motors itself the Chevrolet competes with the Pontiac, the

Buick with the Oldsmobile. Moreover, there is competition between the automobile and the railroad, as far as passenger transportation is concerned.

The problem of competition in the changing American economy is the key issue in *American Capitalism: The Concept of Countervailing Power* (1952), by John Kenneth Galbraith. In classical economics, competition was conceived in terms of many sellers, each with a small share of the market, and restraint of excessive private economic power was provided by competing firms on the same side of the market. Galbraith concedes that this classical model of competition has largely disappeared, since many markets have become dominated by a few firms, and since there is frequently tacit collusion among these firms on major policy decisions.

Yet Galbraith does not conclude from the widespread disappearance of traditional competition that there is no longer any restraint of private economic power left. In fact, new restraints have taken the place of the old competitive mechanism, and these restraints —termed by Galbraith "countervailing power"—are the very product of concentration and bigness.

These new factors of restraint appear not on the same side of the market but on the opposite side, not with competitors but with customers and suppliers. The concentration of industrial enterprises not only has led to a relatively small number of sellers, but also has brought about the predominant position of a few buyers. Galbraith explains the growth and expansion of retailers like Sears, Roebuck or the A & P in terms of countervailing power; by contrast, the absence of a few large firms in the housing industry has meant more traditional competition and less efficiency, since the many small enterprises in the housing industry are unable to use countervailing pressure against labor unions and suppliers of materials.

In the field of labor, too, Galbraith is impressed by the fact that strong unions have developed mainly when faced by strong corporations, as in the steel, automobile, and electrical industries. By contrast, there is no major union of any consequence in the retail business or in agriculture, the closest approach, in the United States, to pure competition. Galbraith concedes that countervailing power is not universally effective as a restraint on private economic power, and that it fails to operate in inflation, when relative scarcity of demand disappears, and too many buyers compete for available goods and services. If supply is small in relation to demand, the seller need not surrender to the bargaining power of the buyer, who thus loses his capacity to function as a countervailing power.

The weakness of the concept of countervailing power lies in the fact that, though the power of the large seller may be checked by that of the large buyer, the resulting benefit need not be passed on to the consumer. Monopoly benefits may be amicably split between the large buyer and the large seller at the expense of the consumer.

In substituting the *few giant* competitive units of the twentieth century for the *many small* ones of the eighteenth, the theory of countervailing power still assumes that a socially fair market equilibrium may be obtained without the intervention of the community in defense of the public interest. In a sense, therefore, the concept of countervailing power, illuminating and provocative as it is, is essentially a sophisticated restatement of the doctrine of the self-regulating market of classical economics, imaginatively adapted to the economic facts of today.

This reasoning was adopted by the Supreme Court in the du Pont case (June 3, 1957), the most important antitrust decision in over forty years. In 1917, du Pont acquired 23 per cent of the stock of General Motors, and consistently supplied the bulk of that company's needs in automotive fabrics and paints. Since General Motors produces about one half of all automobiles, the question arose whether du Pont's part ownership of General Motors was a violation of the Clayton (antitrust) Act.

Until 1957, the courts took the view that only "horizontal" acquisitions (that is, acquisitions of corporations in the same industry) constituted a possible violation of competition; since du Pont and General Motors are in different industries, the large share of General Motors owned by du Pont was not considered a violation of the Clayton Act. But in the du Pont case of June 3, 1957, the Supreme Court abandoned the theory of countervailing power between buyer and seller, and ruled that acquisition of the stock of a customer corporation, or "vertical" acquisition, also constituted a violation of the antitrust laws, if competition is thereby likely to be diminished. In the specific instance of du Pont's owning 23 per cent of General Motors and supplying it with the bulk of its paints and fabrics, the Supreme Court found that "the inference is overwhelming that du Pont's commanding position was promoted by its stock interest and was not gained solely on competitive merit."

SOURCES OF STRENGTH OF CAPITALIST DEMOCRACY

Capitalism, it has been said by a close student of the subject,

. . . during its rule of scarce one hundred years, has created more massive and more colossal productive forces than have all preceding generations together. Subjection of nature's forces to man, machinery, application of chemistry to industry and agriculture, steam-navigation, railways, electric telegraphs, clearing of whole continents for cultivation, canalization of rivers, whole populations conjured out of the ground—what earlier century had even a presentiment that such productive forces slumbered in the lap of social labor?

The author goes on to say that capitalism "has accomplished wonders far surpassing Egyptian pyramids, Roman aqueducts, and Gothic cathedrals; it has conducted expeditions that put in the shade all former migrations of nations and crusades." This eulogy of capitalism was written, not by the research director of the National Association of Manufacturers or of the United States Chamber of Commerce, but by Karl Marx, in the *Communist Manifesto*. Few students of capitalism have been as aware as Marx of the fact that capitalism is a *revolutionary way of life,* creating a new material world as well as new intellectual and ethical values. To put the strength of capitalist democracy in one brief sentence: never before have so many had it so good. A brief glance at the United States: its population increased six times between 1850 and 1950, yet its national income increased thirty times (in constant dollars, to allow for changes in purchasing power). At the same time, the suffrage has been steadily broadened; education has been made available to more persons than ever before, work hours are shorter than ever before, and there is more leisure than man has known hitherto. Above all, *never before has there been so much concern with the welfare of the underprivileged classes in society.*

The abolition of slavery, education for all, health facilities on an unprecedented level, social security for everybody, the doubling of longevity within a century, the highest increase of population on record—all coincide with the development of capitalism. None of these could have been accomplished in a civilization motivated primarily by greed. Looking at precapitalist civilizations today, one is impressed by the survival of social inequalities (the caste system in India, the peon class in Latin America) that reflect a profound disregard of human dignity, an attitude that is no longer feasible in most capitalist societies.

In the fields of education, health, and welfare, more has been ac-

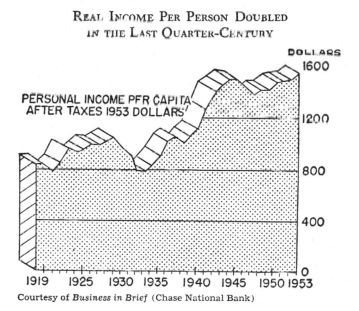

REAL INCOME PER PERSON DOUBLED
IN THE LAST QUARTER-CENTURY

Courtesy of *Business in Brief* (Chase National Bank)

complished in capitalist societies in a spirit of service and disinterestedness than ever before in history. In the world today, the great charitable foundations are to be found primarily in the capitalist nations, particularly in the English-speaking world, not because there are no wealthy people in Asia or Latin America, but because wealthy persons in precapitalist societies rarely believe in the capitalist concept that *wealth can ultimately be justified only through service to the community.*

In the United States, there are over 7,300 private charitable foundations, with total assets of over $8 billion. The Ford Foundation alone,

the largest of them all, has assets in excess of $3 billion. In the fiscal
year of 1956 (October 1, 1955, to September 30, 1956), it spent, in
the United States and abroad, $602 million on education, human wel-
fare, and international aid.

While Indian statesmen, for example, lecture the United States
on capitalist greed and imperialism, as contrasted with Indian spiritu-
ality and love of mankind, the United States Government and private
American foundations gave India, in the years 1952-1956 alone, 1
billion dollars. About half of this sum was donated as an outright gift,
and the other half loaned. To get an idea of the size of the American

"SURE, RUSSIA IS ALWAYS RIGHT THERE WITH MILITARY COMMIS-
SIONS, TECHNICAL ADVISERS, AND ALL THAT, BUT UNCLE SAM GETS
UP THE MOOLA."

contribution to India's economic development: 8 per cent of the cost of India's first five-year plan, ending in the spring of 1956, was paid by direct American aid, and in the field of agriculture and community development—the key to India's economic progress—the United States bore 15 per cent of all expenditures.

Yet this attitude is not new, and not a product of the cold war, because it was practiced on a large scale long before communism existed, and long before it became a world menace. The Rockefeller Foundation, set up in 1913, spent over $500 million in the first forty years of its existence; most of this money was spent on education, much of it abroad. The Carnegie group (Carnegie Corporation, Carnegie Endowment, and Carnegie Foundation) has been mostly active in the field of education and international cooperation. None of these major charitable foundations confines its benefits to American institutions or individuals; they all had their own "Point IV" programs long before the government stepped into the picture after World War II.

Moreover, *never before has a ruling class been willing, as under capitalism, to finance the very people who seek to change the existing social system.* Reform economics need not hide, in the United States, in secret, illegal sheets, but may be taught at private and public colleges and universities endowed by large capitalist fortunes or maintained by state legislatures. A good deal of the progress in social science and social reform in the United States in the last 30 years is directly traceable to research and scholarship subsidized by foundations that owe their existence to the great fortunes built up in previous generations.

Because charitable foundations are tax-exempt, Congress has taken an interest in them from time to time. In May, 1954, the Special House Committee to Investigate Tax-Exempt Foundations came out with sharp criticisms that many of the foundations supported research and education "toward an international viewpoint." Also, the charge was made that much of the research subsidized did not lead to conclusions favorable to conservative economic theory. Such charges have been made in the past, and will be made in the future again. Although they may be considered an improper interference with the freedom of research and education, they can scarcely be said to prove Moscow's occasional contention that capitalism in the United States has imposed an Iron Curtain, behind which only adulation of existing institutions is permitted.

The progress of social science in the United States—one of the most important vehicles of social reform—has been largely financed by private foundations. Conservatives' suspicion of social science is well founded: their frequent confusion of social science with socialism is not quite as obtuse as it may appear to the reformer—since social science, by digging up the facts, may well lead to the very social changes the conservatives fear most.

The political implications of capitalism can now be clearly seen: first, *individual risk-taking,* the desire and capacity to make decisions, to assume responsibility, to determine one's own life. Without this kind of motivation, there can be no democracy, and historically there has been no democracy without it.

Logically, it is conceivable that democracy may develop in the future without this economic background, but so far it has not happened that way. Capitalist economy developed before democratic government, but the one was bound to lead to the other. Persons who constantly faced danger, risk, and responsibility in their economic affairs were ultimately unwilling to accept authoritarian government from kings and aristocracies, and when the capitalist middle classes could not obtain their objectives peacefully, they resorted to revolution: the English civil war in the seventeenth century, and the American and French revolutions in the eighteenth century.

In fighting for itself, the capitalist middle class appealed to the principles of universal human liberty, the rights of man, and natural law. It is for this reason that democracy became an intrinsic part of capitalist civilization, and for this reason also that the greatest advances in democratic government and human liberty have so far been made in capitalist societies.

The second principle of capitalism that directly affects government is the *diffusion of decision and power.* Instead of one central authority's laying down the law of the market, thousands of little decisions hold each other in balance. Many of these decisions are based on erroneous facts and bad judgment, but such defects are preferable to the big errors made by a central authority, particularly if the central authority is subject to no political checks. Every type of democracy seeks to diffuse power by various devices in order to avoid the abuse and corruption that follow the concentration of power. By strengthening the diffusion of power in the economic area, capitalism thus supports one of the key principles of democracy.

Taking a larger, worldwide view, it should be remembered that capitalist civilization, as represented primarily by Britain in the nineteenth and the United States in the twentieth century, revolutionized the underdeveloped continents. The masses of Asia, Africa, and Latin America learned from their contact with capitalism the appreciation of more and better material things. What is less often understood is that the West also taught the underdeveloped continents the principles of the dignity of man, the right of national self-determination, and the evil of racial superiority. Gandhi, Nehru, and the other leaders of the Indian independence movement were educated in England, and it was the ideas of John Locke that taught them individual and national liberty.

Asian communism, distorted and perverted as it may appear in the light of Western democracy, owes its existence partly to western ideas—promises that western capitalism made but failed to live up to. Marx gathered his ideas, not in the steppes of Central Asia or Siberia, but from German philosophy, English political economy, and French revolutionary politics. The communist promise of a happier, better life for all people regardless of class or race is the original promise of capitalism; to the extent that capitalism lives up to it, communism loses its appeal. If offered a fair choice, mankind will prefer economic welfare and political freedom to economic warfare and political slavery.

WHY SOCIALISM HAS NOT SPREAD IN THE UNITED STATES

The question is often asked why socialism has never been able to gain a strong foothold in the United States. According to socialist writers, the United States as the leading capitalist country in the world was bound to develop the "inner contradictions" out of which socialist mass movements would develop. Yet nothing of the sort has happened. Is it because socialism is European? There are strong socialist parties in Canada, Australia, New Zealand, Chile, Brazil, Japan, and other countries outside of Europe. Why the failure in the United States?

The basic reason probably lies in the fact that American capitalism —more than any other economic system in the world—has given to the people *now* much of what socialism promises them for the future. Specifically, socialism bases its appeal on two basic promises: (1) *social equality;* and (2) the *abolition of poverty.* Although no one will argue that American capitalism has lived up 100 per cent to these two principles, it must have done so to a very large extent, since socialist propaganda so far has had little effect.

A GREATER SHARE FROM WAGES: CASH INCOME AFTER TAXES

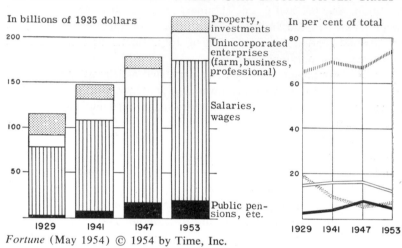

Fortune (May 1954) © 1954 by Time, Inc.

The tremendous swelling in real cash income since 1929 has been accompanied by a steady shift in the kinds *of incomes Americans receive. Income from pensions and other governmental aid programs, though still only a sliver of the total, has increased sevenfold. Property income—rents, royalties, etc.— dropped sharply, from 18 to 7 per cent of total, principally because of the impact of taxes on the upper-income brackets. But the wage-and-salary component grew from less than two-thirds in 1929 to almost three-quarters today.*

This last change is intimately related to the blooming of the vast new $4,000-to-$7,500 group, which now receives 42 per cent of all personal income.

As to the principle of equality, the Constitution of the United States and the reality of economic life keep opportunity open to anyone who looks for it. Since in public opinion polls over 80 per cent of the American people describe themselves as "middle class," it is clear that psychologically, at least, there is little class-consciousness in the United States. Social mobility is very great, mainly because higher education is available to more persons than anywhere else in the world (there are, for example, more college teachers in the

United States than college students in Britain, although the American population is only about three times the British).

As to the second basic promise of socialism—the abolition of poverty—American capitalism has had its serious flaws, crises, and depressions. Yet when all is said and done, and although things could

THE "WORKERS" ARE BECOMING MIDDLE-INCOME

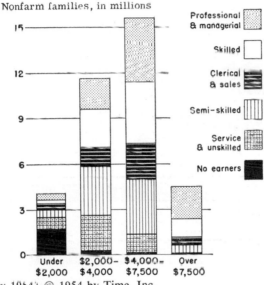

Fortune (May 1954) © 1954 by Time, Inc.

What kind of families inhabit the vast $4,000-$7,500 group? Many are professionals and managers, of course, but more than one-fourth are headed by skilled workers, another 23 per cent by semi-skilled workers, still another 10 per cent by service workers and laborers. All together, nine million of these 15,500,000 middle-income families are "working class."

be better still, living standards in the United States are by far the highest in the world, and they are constantly rising. Vast resources, a single national market, and huge government spending have all contributed to the success of the American economy, quite apart from its spirit of dynamic enterprise and technological progressiveness. By contrast, where capitalism has shown itself restrictionist, timid, inefficient, and tied to a rigid class system, as in many other countries, socialism has grown up in the shadow of capitalist inefficiency and inequality.

Intelligent foreign socialists are beginning to realize that the socialist-capitalist controversy does not make much sense in the United States. Thus a leading British socialist economist, C. A. R. Crosland, writes in *The Future of Socialism* (1957), the most searching analysis of socialism in the last twenty years, that in Britain a Leftist would be a socialist, whereas in the United States he would be

HOURLY OUTPUT PER U. S. WORKER

Each symbol represents 25 cents worth of output at 1954 prices
Twentieth Century Fund, *USA in New Dimensions,* Macmillan, 1957

much less concerned "to promote social equality or material welfare, of which plenty exists already, than with reforms lying outside the field of socialist-capitalist controversy" (p. 521), such as civil liberties, racial equality, juvenile delinquency, and foreign policy.

Hugh Gaitskell, the Leader of the British Labor Party and next Labor Prime Minister, writes in a similar vein. In analyzing the causes of Labor's defeat in the general elections of 1955, he argues that improved living conditions had changed many people's ideas: "Call it if you like a growing Americanization of outlook." (*Socialist Commentary,* July, 1955, p. 205)

For generations European socialists assumed that the absence of a strong socialist movement in the United States proved that the latter was reactionary, or at least conservative, in politics. Now, there is a growing realization in Europe that the two primary problems that socialism seeks to solve—material welfare and social equality— have been largely solved in the United States by the capitalist system, and that therefore the major issues of American public life—such as civil liberties, racial equality, or foreign policy—have no relation whatsoever to the issue of socialism versus capitalism. That issue may, in fact, die out in European and other nations, too, once they manage to abolish poverty and social inequality.

THE WELFARE STATE

The main principles of the welfare state are relatively simple: first, the recognition that every member of the community is entitled, solely because he is a human being, to a *minimum standard of living;* second, the welfare state is committed to putting *full employment* at the top of social goals to be supported by public policy.

The Great Depression of 1929-1939 showed not only the economic ravages of unemployment, but also the human degradation imposed upon those who are able and anxious to work but cannot find a job for reasons over which they have no control.

Particularly in the United States, the adherents of the welfare state believe that free enterprise can be preserved and strengthened by full employment measures without having recourse to nationalization. Taxation properly adjusted to periods of prosperity and depression, interest rates determined by governmental decision according to economic needs, fiscal policies designed to redistribute purchasing power in harmony with the best interests of the nation, investment incentives in times of contracting business, public works for direct unemployment relief, government credits to builders or buyers of homes— these are but a few of the measures the government can adopt in stabilizing the economy without changing its foundations.

In the field of *social security,* protection against the worst dangers of want, sickness, and old age not only is indicated by humanitarian considerations, but also has important economic effects, since such measures of social security provide people with a minimum purchasing power indispensable to the functioning of industry in prosperity and depression.

Collective bargaining between labor and capital is another basic contribution toward a more stable and prosperous economy, because higher wages—if based on higher productivity—create a bigger market for the products of industry and agriculture. Similarly, an active support program for agriculture, guaranteeing the farmer a minimum price level for his products, is of benefit not only to the farmer but also to the worker and the industrialist, since a prosperous industry depends upon a prosperous agriculture.

In the United States, the Great Depression undermined faith in the orthodox philosophy of *laissez-faire,* according to which the disequilibrium of the market would eventually be restored to a new equilibrium without any interference from the outside. When the American economy reached the stage in which one out of every four employable persons found himself out of work, in which the farmer could not sell his products at reasonable prices, in which more and more business enterprises went bankrupt or were unable to pay wages to their employees or earn profits for their shareholders, something had to be done. The New Deal, starting with the first term of President Franklin D. Roosevelt in 1933, was not so much a set of premeditated philosophical principles to be superimposed upon the American people as a series of emergency measures in response to urgent practical problems.

The Agricultural Adjustment Act (May 12, 1933) attempted to help the farmer by raising farm prices to a level that would enable farmers to buy industrial products as they had been able to do in the years 1909-1914. In order to make such "parity" possible, farmers were to reduce production, in return for which they would receive higher prices (as a result of decreased supply) from the consumer and subsidies from the government. The Act was declared unconstitutional by the Supreme Court in 1936, but Congress enacted subsequently the Soil Conservation Act, the Domestic Allotment Act, and, in 1938, a new Agricultural Adjustment Act. Traditionally opposed, in theory at least, to government interference, the farmers have been very content with that part of the welfare state which directly protects their interests.

Whereas in most countries relief to the unemployed was paid out in cash as a "dole," the American method of relief showed more understanding of the human problems involved. The federal government set up the Works Progress Administration in 1935 (renamed the Works Projects Administration in 1939) in order to provide *work relief* rather than cash doles. Though some of the projects were properly criticized for being excursions into boondoggling, the total impact of the program was highly beneficial, not only for providing financial help to those who needed it, but—and above all —for preserving a sense of self-respect in those who were employed by it. The peak of employment by WPA was reached in November 1938, when 3.3 million persons were on its payrolls. All in all, 8.5 million persons were employed at some time on WPA projects during the eight years of the agency's existence, and nearly $11 billion was spent.

The National Labor Relations Act (July 5, 1935), commonly known as the Wagner Act, established for the first time full statutory regulation of labor-management relations in the United States. In the preceding half century, the employer in the United States was free to recognize or not to recognize labor unions, and to deal or not to deal with them. Employers frequently discharged employees for union activities, and if unions become too strong, employers would use various means to break them, such as company unions, private police, labor spies, lockouts, and professional strikebreakers. In the absence of statutory regulation, court rulings were frequently sought to protect the interest of management, particularly during strikes. The Norris-LaGuardia Act of 1932 was the first major step in creating a more equitable balance between labor and capital, by limiting the use of court injunctions against labor unions; but since this act failed to establish an administrative agency to enforce its provisions, much of its original intent did not materialize.

The Wagner Act is the Magna Carta of American labor. Its main purpose was to encourage collective bargaining between labor and management, thus substituting peaceful discussion for violence. Just as the Constitution of the United States does not prescribe the contents of statutes to be passed by Congress, but merely sets down the rules and procedures of the legislative process, the Wagner Act, too, merely created a set of rules and an atmosphere in which labor and management could talk to each other. Although the law did not, and could not, compel both sides to agree, strikes and lockouts still remaining legal, the experience of collective bargaining quickly proved that the application of democratic methods of negotiation usually leads to results beneficial to both parties.

Dissatisfaction of management with some provisions of the Wagner Act led to its replacement in 1947 by the Labor-Management Relations Act, commonly known as the Taft-Hartley Act. Though spokesmen for labor voiced deep dissatisfaction with the Taft-Hartley Act, it left the basic principle of the Wagner Act—collective bargaining—substantially unchanged.

The issue of public policy will henceforth be not the principle of collective bargaining itself, but the establishment of the proper balance between labor and management. It is to be expected that each side will have its own ideas on what constitutes the proper balance of forces. However, it is the function of the state, not to give any one side an *a priori* superiority over the other, but to see to it that democratic procedures are observed in the settling of industrial disputes.

The Social Security Act (August 14, 1935) marked another milestone in the movement for social reform in the United States. In modern industry the individual is frequently at the mercy of large impersonal forces over which he has no control. The efforts of the family, private charity, and the local community have all too frequently proved insufficient to protect the individual against the hazards of old age, sickness, unemployment, or death. The passage of the Social Security Act marked the recognition that the community, on the local, state, and federal levels, is partly responsible for assuring its citizens of some protection against want and insecurity.

The program is financed mainly by contributions of workers and employers; since the state can only give what it takes, citizens are reminded that if they want higher social security benefits, the only way to get them is to work harder, produce more, and pay for them before the need arises. In 1957, over 58 million workers and their families were covered by old-age and survivor insurance; special programs for railroad workers and government employees covered an additional 4 million persons. Only about 3 million of a total civilian labor force of over 65 million still remained to be covered and most of them were slated for inclusion by the Eisenhower Administration.

PEOPLE HELPED BY MAJOR PUBLIC WELFARE PROGRAMS (1952)

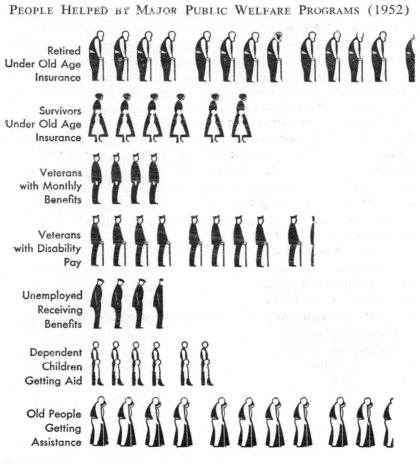

Retired
Under Old Age
Insurance

Survivors
Under Old Age
Insurance

Veterans
with Monthly
Benefits

Veterans
with Disability
Pay

Unemployed
Receiving
Benefits

Dependent
Children
Getting Aid

Old People
Getting
Assistance

Each symbol represents 250,000 people

Twentieth Century Fund, *USA in New Dimensions,* Macmillan, 1957

In the fields of housing, education, and health, too, there have
been notable advances in the United States in the last 25 years. The
general policy of the federal government has been to provide funds
for basic research, as in health and education, or provide loans, as in
housing or industrial expansion generally. If possible, private industry
or the local authority is to do the actual job, so as not to expand
the range of direct federal activity and authority too much.

In the field of health, it has been argued that existing conditions and facilities are inadequate in relation to needs. In 1949, President Truman urged the creation of a comprehensive national health program based on a prepaid compulsory insurance scheme, but administered primarily by state and local authorities. So far, such a program has been rejected on the grounds that it would lower standards of medical service, that it would cost too much, and that it would subject the medical profession to centralized bureaucratic direction.

The main positive effect of the debate on a national health service has been a greater public awareness of the problem and an increase of privately financed insurance schemes to provide medical and hospital facilities. At present, about 25 million persons, or slightly less than one-sixth of the population, receive some form of federal medical care. The principal categories covered by federal medical care are veterans, members of the armed forces and the Coast Guard, Indians, and inmates of federal prisons.

In Great Britain, the impact of the welfare state on the *redistribution of income* has been measured fairly accurately. In the lower-income group of the population, in which earnings are under £500 per annum (£1 = $2.80), each person receives annually about £18 more in social welfare benefits than he has paid in. Since the lower-income group of under £500 per annum includes nearly 40 million persons, or 80 per cent of the British population, it can be seen that the effects of redistribution through welfare state policies are not insubstantial. However, this picture is changed somewhat by the fact that redistribution cuts across class lines; for example, persons who smoke and drink pay a proportionately higher share of taxes than those who do not.

In the United States, it has been estimated that the lowest third of income recipients, with annual incomes of under $2,000 in 1950, comprised about 17 million spending units. The original income of this lowest third of the nation was $24.79 billion, and the redistributed income rose to $27.584 billion. Assuming about 2.5 persons per spending unit, the average gain of the 42 million persons in the lowest income groups amount to about $64 per person (A. T. Peacock, ed., *Income Redistribution and Social Policy*, 1954).

According to this estimate, only one-third of income recipients gain from redistribution in the United States, as contrasted with about four-fifths in Britain. The reason for this difference is simple:

DISTRIBUTION OF CONSUMER UNITS BY SIZE OF
FAMILY PERSONAL INCOME IN 1950

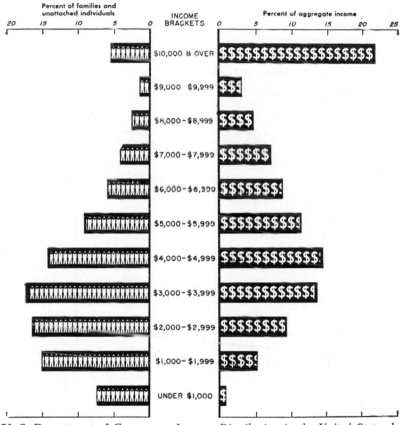

U. S. Department of Commerce, *Income Distribution in the United States by Size, 1944-1950*

there is more poverty in Britain. The national per capita income is less than one-half of that in the United States; as a result there is more need for redistribution. Moreover, *high social mobility in the United States* is, in a sense, a *permanent mechanism of redistribution;* with less social mobility in Britain, there is more need for monetary redistribution. Finally, since the British conception of the welfare state goes further than the American, Britons are willing to push redistribution further than the American public has been willing to do so far.

The main mechanism for bringing about redistribution is *taxation*. Thus in 1950 the top 20 per cent of consumer units in the United States received 46 per cent of the national income, but paid 70 per cent of all income taxes. The top 5 per cent received 20 per cent of

PER CENT DISTRIBUTION OF FAMILY PERSONAL INCOME, FEDERAL INCOME TAX, AND AFTER TAX INCOME IN 1950

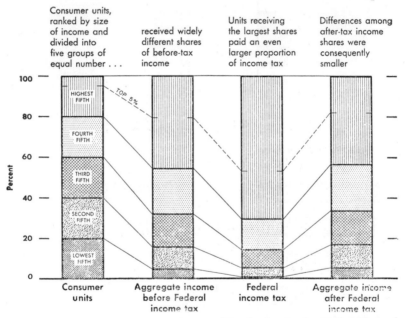

U. S. Department of Commerce, *Income Distribution in the United States by Size, 1944-50*

the national income, but paid 47 per cent of income taxes. By contrast, the lowest 20 per cent received 5 per cent of the national income, but paid only 1 per cent of taxes. The proportionate share of the top 1 per cent of income receivers has suffered the most drastic decline. In 1929, the top 1 per cent received 14.5 per cent of total personal income, and in 1948, 8.4 per cent. In the same period, the share of the top 5 per cent dropped from 26.1 per cent of total personal income to 17.6 per cent.

Equalization of incomes can be brought about by bringing down the high incomes or raising the low incomes. If allowance is made for the changed value of the dollar in the period 1929-1948, it is found that the average incomes of the top 7 per cent have gone down, and that the average incomes of the remaining 93 per cent have gone up. Thus *equalization in the United States has been primarily accomplished by leveling up incomes.*

Inequality within the United States is much smaller than between

THE MOVE INTO HIGHER INCOME BRACKETS

| INCOME UNDER $2000 | $2000-$3999 | $4000 & OVER |

1935-36

1941

1950

Each symbol represents 10 per cent of all consumer units
All incomes are figured in dollars of 1950 purchasing power

Twentieth Century Fund, *USA in New Dimensions*, Macmillan, 1957

the United States and the rest of the world. Thus, the top 6 per cent of income receivers in the United States receive about 19 per cent of the national income. The whole population of the United States is about 6 per cent of the world's population, yet it annually produces about 33 per cent of the world's goods and services.

Just as redistribution is a way of achieving internal peace and stability within the United States, our foreign aid programs apply the same principle to the community of nations, particularly the underdeveloped countries. If the welfare state at home is cheaper than unrest and revolution, international welfare policies are cheaper than war and communist expansion.

As time goes on, the realization grows that *the welfare state is not a way of getting something for nothing, that every piece of welfare has to be paid for.* Since taxation in countries like England and the United States is reaching a level where there is not much left that can be obtained by soaking the rich, every increased social benefit must be paid for by increased taxation of the lower-income groups. The problem of the welfare state is less and less one of which philosophical principle one advocates or opposes, and more and more one of actuarial calculation and specific taxation.

In the welfare state, the people agree that a high portion of their income should be spent by the government in a certain way. Experience shows that people tend to save more easily if they have committed themselves to an insurance policy or a mortgage with monthly payments, than if they rely on irregular voluntary deposits in a savings account.

In the welfare state the situation is similar. The individual hands over to the state the job of saving for him in case of an emergency such as sickness, old age, or death. If people themselves could save for all such emergencies, much of the welfare state would be unnecessary. But the average person finds it easier to pay higher taxes every month or every year, out of which his social security is ultimately to be paid for, than to save for such eventualities in a personal savings account.

There is nothing wrong in admitting this human weakness and entrusting the state with the efficient administration of a comprehensive insurance system, as long as it is understood that the costs of such a system have to be largely borne by taxation, and that therefore the financial principle behind the welfare state is *forced personal and communal saving today for the needs of tomorrow* rather than a simple method of transferring property from the rich to the poor.

Is the welfare state compatible with capitalism? When the first basic measures of the welfare state were introduced twenty-five years ago, the dire prediction was made that the welfare state was the first step to communism, or at least to creeping socialism. Events have disproved that fear: after two decades of the welfare state, the American economy is healthier than ever before, living standards have reached an all-time high, productivity is higher than ever,

people live longer and better, and there is more economic equality
between the various income groups than in the past. Above all, the
welfare state has in no way sapped the spirit of incentive and effort
in the American economy; the whip of want and insecurity is not
the best guide to progress, and in providing a minimum of social
and economic security the welfare state has strengthened the economy as a whole. The performance of the American economy in
World War II and in the years since has astounded the world; far
from being coddled into softness and stagnation by the welfare
state, the American economy has demonstrated enormous dynamism,
drive, and initiative in the last two decades.

After Roosevelt's death in 1945, President Truman's Fair Deal

GROWTH OF WELFARE ACTIVITIES

PRIVATE | PUBLIC

1930

1940

1950

Each symbol represents 1 billion dollars

Twentieth Century Fund, *USA in New Dimensions*, Macmillan, 1957

continued and expanded the policies of the New Deal. When the
Republican Party won the presidential election of 1952 it was feared
by some that there would be a roll-back of welfare state policies. Yet,
during both its terms the Eisenhower Administration vigorously
broadened the scope and range of social welfare, covering more
people than ever before, and increasing benefits to a record level.
When President Eisenhower was reelected in 1956, his victory was
attributed, among other reasons, to the fact that he had convinced the
American public, particularly the lower-income groups, that he was
sincerely committed to the principle of public responsibility for social
and economic welfare for all.

The welfare state—accepted by both the Democratic and Republican Parties—has thus ceased to be a political football, as it used to

be in the 1930's, and has become part of American life, an issue of efficient administration rather than high policy. Whatever the economic and social aspects of the welfare state, its political consequences are even more important: without changing the basic form of government or way of life, the welfare state has strengthened democracy by strengthening the security, self-respect, and freedom of democracy's citizens.

FOR FURTHER READING

Allen, Frederick L., *The Big Change: America Transforms Itself, 1900-1950* (Harper, 1952)

Arnold, Thurman W., and others, *The Future of Democratic Capitalism* (University of Pennsylvania Press, 1950)

Barth, Alan, *The Loyalty of Free Men* (Pocket Books, 1952)

Bell, Daniel (ed.), *The New American Right* (Criterion Books, 1955)

Berle, Adolf A., *The 20th Century Capitalist Revolution* (Harcourt, Brace, 1954)

Beveridge, William, *Full Employment in a Free Society* (Norton, 1945)

Chafee, Zechariah, *The Blessings of Liberty* (Lippincott, 1956)

Cohen, Morris R., *The Faith of a Liberal* (Holt, 1946)

Curti, Merle, *The Roots of American Loyalty* (Columbia University Press, 1946)

Cushman, Robert E., *Civil Liberties in the United States* (Cornell University Press, 1956)

Davenport, Russell W., *The Dignity of Man* (Harper, 1955)

Davis, Michael M., *Medical Care for Tomorrow* (Harper, 1955)

Dollard, John, and others, *Frustration and Aggression* (Yale University Press, 1939)

Ebenstein, William, *Modern Political Thought* (Rinehart, 1954), chaps. 2, 3, 10, 13

Frankfurter, Felix, *The Public and Its Government* (Yale University Press, 1930)

Fromm, Erich, *The Sane Society* (Rinehart, 1955)

Galbraith, John Kenneth, *American Capitalism: The Concept of Countervailing Power* (Houghton Mifflin, 1952)

Gellhorn, Walter, *Individual Freedom and Governmental Restraints* (Louisiana State University Press, 1956)

Glueck, Sheldon (ed.), *The Welfare State and the National Welfare* (Addison-Wesley Press, 1952)

Hacker, Louis M., *American Capitalism* (Anvil Books, 1957)

Handlin, Oscar, *Race and Nationality in American Life* (Little, Brown, 1957)

Hayek, F. A. (ed.), *Capitalism and the Historians* (University of Chicago Press, 1954)

Kahn, E. J., Jr., "Big Potato for a Day," *The New Yorker* (June 17, 1950)

Karr, David, *Fight for Control* (Ballantine Books, 1956)

Kuznets, Simon, *Shares of Upper Income Groups in Income and Savings* (National Bureau of Economic Research, 1953)

Lekachman, Robert (ed.), *National Policy for Economic Welfare at Home and Abroad* (Doubleday, 1955)

Lilienthal, David E., *Big Business: A New Era* (Harper, 1953)

Lindner, Robert, *Must You Conform?* (Rinehart, 1956)

Lindsay, A. D., *The Modern Democratic State* (Oxford University Press, 1943)

McKeon, Richard (ed.), *Democracy in a World of Tensions* (University of Chicago Press, 1951)

Maurer, Herrymon, *Great Enterprise: Growth and Behavior of the Big Corporation* (Macmillan, 1955)

Meiklejohn, Alexander, *Free Speech and Its Relation to Self-Government* (Harper, 1948)

Peacock, Alan T. (ed.), *Income Redistribution and Social Policy* (Macmillan, 1954)

Perkins, Dexter, *The American Way* (Cornell University Press, 1957)

Rappard, William E., *The Secret of American Prosperity* (Greenberg, 1955)

Rauch, Basil (ed.), *Franklin D. Roosevelt: Selected Speeches, Messages, Press Conferences, and Letters* (Rinehart Editions, 1957)

Rozwenc, Edwin C. (ed.), *The New Deal: Revolution or Evolution?* (Heath, 1949)

Russell, Bertrand, "The Best Answer to Fanaticism—Liberalism," *The New York Times Magazine* (December 16, 1951)

Saul, Leon J., *The Hostile Mind: The Sources and Consequences of Rage and Hate* (Random House, 1956)

Selekman, Sylvia and Benjamin, *Power and Morality in a Business Society* (McGraw-Hill, 1956)

Stouffer, Samuel A., *Communism, Conformity, and Civil Liberties* (Doubleday, 1955)

Sutton, Francis X., and others, *The American Business Creed* (Harvard University Press, 1956)

Tawney, R. H., *Religion and the Rise of Capitalism* (Mentor Books, 1947)

Wahlke, John C. (ed.), *Loyalty in a Democratic State* (Heath, 1952)
Warner, W. Lloyd, and James Abegglen, *Big Business Leaders in America* (Harper, 1955)
Whyte, William H., *The Organization Man* (Anchor Books, 1957)
Wright, David McCord, *Capitalism* (McGraw-Hill, 1951)

4

DEMOCRATIC SOCIALISM

HISTORICAL BACKGROUND

It is not easy to state when socialism first appears. Some have asserted that the ideal commonwealth in Plato's *Republic* is socialist, inasmuch as its ruling class has no property of its own, and shares all things in common. Others have claimed that the Bible, particularly the Old Testament, constitutes the first socialist code, covering as it does the protection of workers, women, and the weak. The early Christians rejected the concept of "mine and thine," and practiced socialism in their everyday lives; and in the Middle Ages numerous sects and movements, mostly religious, attacked wealth and commerce as wicked and incompatible with the Christian life. Such sects frequently withdrew into isolation, living an austere existence, and sharing poverty in brotherly love as a protest against the prevalent greed in the world around them.

During the Renaissance and the Reformation, there was a revival of protest against inequality based on wealth. The new arguments increasingly combined the older faith with the newer rationalism, as evidenced, for example, in Thomas Moore's *Utopia* (1516). In the Puritan revolution of the seventeenth century, there arose, side by side with the main movement of middle-class origin, a more radical group—called Diggers or True Levelers—that sought to attain communal ownership of land not currently in use. The movement was short-lived, but its radical protest against private landed property was not to be entirely forgotten.

Yet despite all such illustrations from earlier times, *socialism* as a major political force can properly be said to have originated as the *result of modern industrial capitalism*. To the extent that socialism contains within itself an element of protest against social inequality —and no movement can call itself socialist unless it expresses that kind of protest—it is as old as western civilization itself: both Greek and Jewish-Christian thought categorically reject the conception of wealth as the basis of the good life.

Another feature of socialism, the protest against money as the chief tie between human beings, is also not confined to the socialist tradition; many nonsocialists have voiced their disapproval of the "cash nexus." If we thus look to something more specific and historically more concrete than a vague protest against social injustice, we find that socialism as an effective, organized political movement is the product of the Industrial Revolution.

Just as communism has happened—and is likely to happen—only in countries *before* they have undergone the full impact of the Industrial Revolution, democratic socialism develops only in societies *after* they have experienced considerable industrialization.

Wherever industrialization has taken place in societies without deeply rooted liberal institutions, the political adjustment to the resulting tensions is likely to be either some sort of fascism (as in modern Germany, Italy, Japan, and Argentina) or communism (as in Russia and China). Because industrialization in these societies is promoted and controlled by an authoritarian state, its purpose is the power of the state, not the welfare of the individual.

By contrast, *where industrialization has occurred in relatively liberal societies* (as in northwestern Europe, North America, Australia, and New Zealand), the purpose of the economy is the welfare of the individual, and the adjustment to the inevitable tensions and conflicts of industrial capitalism assumes some form of democratic socialism or social democracy, rather than fascism or communism.

This basic distinction between the authoritarian and the liberal society can cut away a lot of confusion. Thus, the question is frequently debated whether a fascist economy is socialistic (because of the complete regulation of economic activity by the state) or capitalistic (because the means of production are left in private hands).

Such discussions are endless and insoluble, because they are based on a false premise: that the basic distinction in the world's economic systems is between socialism and capitalism. In actuality, the line of division runs differently: between *welfare economies* (which operate democratically and aim at freedom, welfare, and happiness) and *police state* or *command economies* (which operate by command and coercion, and aim at the power of the state through military expansion). Both capitalism and socialism fall into the group that is dominated by the concept of welfare economics, whereas fascism and communism fall into the second group, the command economy.

Differences among the species within each major group are important, but they are not crucial. Thus, capitalism and socialism disagree on the best method of how to bring the maximum welfare to all the people, the former stressing individual property and effort, the latter putting its faith in collective productive property and effort.

Comparably, fascism and communism do not see eye to eye in every detail on how best to operate an economy in the service of the state. Differences between fascism and communism, however, tend to fade into insignificance if it is recalled that the objective— the power of the state to wage aggressive war—is the same, and that the means—ranging from friendly pressure to slave labor and the concentration camp—are amazingly similar and frequently identical.

In some ways, of course, socialism opposes capitalism, but it is the rebellion of the child against the father, not the total war of stranger against stranger. Just as the rebellious child uses arguments he has learned from his own father, socialism employs, in the controversy with its progenitor, a whole arsenal of capitalist values and attitudes, especially critical rationalism and pragmatic utilitarianism.

As to the specific problem of property, socialism inherits from capitalism one basic goal: *to preserve the unity of work and ownership.* In the seventeenth and eighteenth centuries, the early phase of modern capitalism, that unity was a reality. In the England of John Locke, or in the America of Thomas Jefferson, the average farm, store, or workshop was generally small enough to be owned and operated by one person or family. *Work and ownership coincided.* The chief threat to this unity came from the state, which sought to prescribe, to regulate, to snoop, in short to play the role of an om-

niscient busybody in economic matters—all this when the individual
entrepreneur knew that he could best run his own business without
any unsolicited advice from pompous and self-confident state officials.

As the capitalist economy progressed, however, the individual (or
single-family) form of ownership and work was gradually replaced,
owing primarily to technological progress, by an economic system in
which large-scale enterprise swallowed up the original capitalist-
owner-manager. *As the size of industrial enterprise grew larger and
larger, work became more and more socialized, collective, whereas
ownership remained private.*

In seeking to restore the classical harmony between work and
property, the reformer faces two alternatives. He can divide up
large-scale enterprises into small units, so that both work and ownership can coincide again in one person or family. This method is
feasible in agriculture, where large landed estates can be physically
broken up and divided among landless farm workers, as was done
in France during her Revolution in the eighteenth century, in Mexico and Guatemala during this century, in Czechoslovakia and Rumania after World War I, and—on a smaller scale—in Italy after
World War II.

Whether such a breakup of large landed estates is economically
sound or not is highly debatable—in many cases the productivity of
dwarf farms following agrarian reform is lower than it was before on
large farm units. However, a reform government may be ready to pay
the price of lower productivity for the greater social benefit of having
an independent farm class. In any case, the technology of agriculture
is still simple enough so that large units can be broken up, and small
units can be operated with relative efficiency.

In industry, this solution is physically out of the question: an
automobile or aircraft factory cannot be divided up into 10,000
portions, each to be operated by one worker as his personal piece
of property. The technological nature of modern industrial enterprise is such that there is no alternative to collective work and operation. Thus, in facing the task of reuniting work and ownership
in industry, collective ownership seems to socialists the logical
answer, just as the classical liberal deduced the right to individual
ownership from the fact of individual work. In both systems—
classical liberal capitalism and democratic socialism—there is the
underlying assumption that the *right to property ultimately rests on*

work, effort, industry, rather than on formal law, custom, or birth.

John Locke, the founder of modern political and economic liberalism, based the right to property on human labor, and the value of property on the amount of labor "admixed" to nature's resources. The socialists have accepted the Lockean and capitalist rationale of labor. What has changed since Locke is simply the technological character of labor, not its ethical implications: if the logic of capitalism demands individual property for individual work, the logic of socialism demands *collective ownership* for collective work—*provided collective work is the only possible form of managerial organization.*

Where small property has survived as a technologically efficient unit, as in agriculture, the professions, the arts, and some areas of retailing, servicing, and manufacturing, socialists generally agree with adherents of capitalism that private ownership should be kept and strengthened. Thus, socialist governments have enjoyed long tenure in predominantly agrarian countries like Denmark and New Zealand, because farmers in those countries were sympathetic to the socialist program of maintaining their economic integrity and individualism by cheap credits, guaranteed "parity" prices, and other policies designed to protect the small farmer against the threat of domination by banks, insurance companies, and wholesalers.

ROBERT OWEN: CAPITALIST-SOCIALIST

The filial link between socialism and capitalism can be illustrated by the fact that the first modern socialist was a wealthy and successful capitalist. Robert Owen (1771-1858), generally regarded as the founder of British socialism, was the first to use the term "socialism." A self-made capitalist, he had made a fortune by the age of forty. He was a man of sound, practical judgment, and he easily could meet one test of experience frequently described by conservatives as essential whenever a reformer comes forth with some new scheme: "Have you ever met a payroll in your life?" Owen had. In his *A New View of Society* (1813), he describes himself as a "manufacturer for pecuniary profit."

His views were the result, not (like Marx's) of study in the British Museum, but of experience in his own industrial enterprises. Owen dedicated his book to His Royal Highness, the Prince Regent of the British Empire; he was no refugee from his own society, as were Marx and Lenin later, but a respectable, wealthy man, as English as mutton or tea. He considered drink as an incentive to crime and a main source of misery, and his list of virtues and vices would have appealed to Benjamin Franklin.

Far from looking upon capitalist Britain as a dungeon of inhumanity, he described the British constitution as being "among the best devised and most enlightened that have hitherto been established." Refusing to believe that evil can be transformed into good in a day, he advocated "progressive repeal and modification" of unjust laws and conditions; strongly rejecting the alleged blessings of revolutionary change, he felt that "the British constitution, in its present outline, is admirably adapted to effect these changes, without the evils which always accompany a coerced or ill-prepared change."

Realizing that love and fellowship cannot be conceived in hatred and born in strife, Owen appealed to "every rational man, every true friend of humanity," and he hoped for cordial cooperation and unity of action between the Government, Parliament, the Church, and the People.

Owen's rationalism also emerges from the fact that *A New View of Society* discusses one subject more than any other: *education.* Owen believed that the evils of his society were due to circumstances rather than to the depravity of man, and he was convinced that, just as crime and degradation were the result of specific social and economic conditions, education in a new environment could produce human beings endowed with rationality, habits of order, regularity, temperance, and industry.

In his own time, children of six and seven years of age were employed in factories for twelve hours a day and more, and Owen makes the suggestion—bold and radical for the capitalist conscience of 1813 —that a regular workday of thirteen hours from six in the morning to seven in the evening should not be imposed upon *children under twelve,* because at that age "their education might be finished, and their bodies would be more competent to undergo the fatigue and exertions required of them." Human nature, Owen says, is "universally plastic," and if education is the key to make men more rational and cooperative, "the best governed state will be that which shall possess the best national system of education."

Owen was in the true liberal-capitalist tradition of looking to society, rather than to the state, for important change. A century before Keynes and Beveridge, Owen understood the crucial importance of full employment for the maintenance of a civilized society. Yet he was opposed to the dole, or cash relief to the unemployed, on the ground that the "industrious, temperate, and comparatively virtuous" should not be compelled to support the "ignorant, idle, and comparatively vicious." Owen clearly saw the human aspects of unemployment—yet he wished the state not to dispense employment, but to provide an educational system good enough to equip every person with the skills wherewith to find employment in the open market.

A believer in the individualist principle of *self-help,* Owen started the cooperative movement and supported the incipient trade union organizations springing up throughout England and Scotland. For Owen, cooperation was more than selling milk to housewives; he believed that *producers' cooperatives* rather than consumers' cooperatives would establish a new social order. He sank much of his fortune in producers' cooperatives in England, and he also spent several years, and the better part of his wealth, in a cooperative venture in the United States. His best-known experiment, the settlement of New Harmony in Indiana, did not succeed, but his ideas are today more important than ever.

The British experiment of nationalizing selected basic industries and services has raised the fundamental question whether the Owenite method of cooperation outside of the formal machinery of the national government is not preferable to nationalization as effected in Britain since 1945. In the British trade union movement, too, the Owenite bias against the state has strongly survived; if the trade unions have never been overly enthusiastic over nationalization schemes, it is because they dread the growth of the state machinery and the transformation of free trade union officials, responsible to their members, into semi-government officials, responsible to the state.

SOCIALISM AND DEMOCRACY

The link between democracy and socialism is the most important single element in socialist thought and policy. Looking at the history of socialism, it can be quickly seen that *successful socialist movements have grown up only in nations with strong democratic traditions,* such as Great Britain, Scandinavia, Holland, Belgium, Switzerland, Australia, New Zealand and (more recently) Israel.

The reason for this parallelism is simple. Where democratic, constitutional government is generally accepted, socialists can concentrate on their specific program, overambitious as that program may seem, namely: to create more opportunity for the underprivileged classes; to end inequality based on birth rather than service; to open the horizons of education to all the people; to eliminate discriminatory practices based on sex, religion, race, or social class; to regulate and reorganize the economy for the benefit of the whole community; to maintain full employment; to provide adequate social security for the sick, unemployed, and aged; to re-plan the layout of towns and cities; to tear down the slums and build new houses; to provide medical facilities for everybody irrespective of the size of his purse; and finally, to rebuild society on the foundation of cooperation in lieu of competition, incentive, and profit.

All these goals of democratic socialism have one thing in common: to *make democracy more real by broadening the application of democratic principles from the political to the nonpolitical areas of society.*

Historically the first liberties to be conquered, freedom of worship and freedom of political association, are still the most essential foundations of democracy today. Where these foundations exist, therefore, and where democratic principles are firmly rooted in the hearts and minds of the people, socialists can concentrate on the "finer points" of democracy.

By contrast, socialist parties have fought an uphill and generally losing struggle in nations in which democracy is not a living thing, but an aspiration, a hope, an idea yet to be realized. Thus, the Social Democratic Party in Germany always worked under one heavy handicap: in the Second Reich (1870-1918), political autocracy was a reality, and parliamentary institutions were a cover for the virtual dictatorship, first of Bismarck, and then of Kaiser William II. In the eighteen seventies, Bismarck outlawed the Social Democrats as "enemies of the state," and such party leaders as escaped being jailed fled to England and other free nations in Europe or America.

During the Weimar Republic (1919-1933), the German Social

Democratic Party was paralyzed again by the insecurity of democratic institutions; the main issue of the Weimar Republic was not this or that social reform in which the socialists could take a special interest, but something much bigger: the issue of democratic government itself. Whereas in nations with long-established democratic habits socialists could argue over issues *within democracy,* taking the existence of democracy for granted, German socialists constantly had to argue and fight over the *issue of democracy itself.* As fascism grew in the Weimar Republic, the German socialists became increasingly concerned with the defense of republican and democratic institutions rather than with problems of economic reform.

In Russia before 1917, the situation was even simpler. The despotic tsarist regime did not make even the pretense of democracy or self-government; social and economic reform by peaceful means was thus made virtually impossible, and the door for communism was opened.

World War II provides further illustrations of this point. In France, for example, the socialist party had become the strongest political party by 1936, far stronger than the communist party. During World War II, however, under the German occupation, the communists found the political environment of underground and illegal activity much more congenial to them than to the socialists. Democratic socialists in a country like France function best when they carry membership cards rather than high explosives on their bodies. The type of person who joins such a party is well-meaning and stable, probably a family man, in any event a skilled worker or civil servant with a steady job. People of this kind do not readily engage in illegal, terroristic activities such as were necessary in France under German occupation in World War II.

The communists, on the other hand, attract an entirely different type of person, more fanatical, more devoted to his cause, and used to illegality and semi-illegality even in so-called normal times. What the Third French Republic (1870-1940) could never accomplish, four years of German occupation managed to do: at the end of World War II, the communists, polling about twice as many votes as the democratic socialists, emerged as the strongest single party of France.

By contrast, the socialist vote in *the British general election of 1955 was 386 times larger than the communist vote.* The evidence (not only from Great Britain, but also from other democratic countries

with strong socialist movements) indicates that fullest civil liberty
for all ideas and parties, including subversive, revolutionary organizations, seems to be the best antidote against fascism and communism,
and that repression is the natural soil for the growth of revolutionary
movements.

If one were to rank democratic nations today primarily in the
light of their respect for civil liberty, Great Britain, Norway, Denmark, Sweden, Holland, Belgium, Australia, New Zealand, and
Israel would be at the top of the list; and all these countries are, or
recently have been governed by socialist administrations, or by coalition cabinets with strong socialist participation.

The reasons for this parallelism are not too complex. Democratic
socialists are keenly aware of the fact that without the opportunities
provided by liberal, constitutional government they could not get
to first base. Once in control of the government, socialists still maintain the psychology of the opposition, because they know that the
possession of political power does not automatically solve the problems of social and economic organization. In other words, before
socialists take over the government, they are in opposition to the
government *and* to the wealthy classes; after they gain control of
the government, the oppositionist psychology—directed as it is
against the economic status quo—necessarily persists.

Moreover, even in the purely governmental realm, socialists tend
to preserve a certain degree of caution and suspicion after they get
into office, because they realize that, though they can gain control
of the *legislature* in an election, the other sources of political power
—the *civil service* and the *judiciary*—may be hostile to them.

Another factor essential to this discussion is all too frequently
neglected. Examining the remarkably high state of civil liberty in
nations with strong socialist movements, one tends to overlook *the
high respect for civil liberty demonstrated by the opponents of socialism.* After all, if the conservative and propertied classes had
shown less respect for the letter and spirit of constitutional government, the chances of socialist growth would have been very slim.
From the viewpoint of dollars and cents, the conservatives' genuine
acquiescence in socialism meant that they valued their faith in democracy higher than their pocketbooks, and were ready to be heavily
taxed even for programs they considered undesirable or unreasonable.

It can thus be seen that both groups took a gamble: the socialists trusted their opponents not to destroy the processes of democratic government in order to protect their financial interests; the propertied classes trusted the socialists not to abuse electoral victories, and to act reasonably and moderately when in office.

Where the propertied classes were unconvinced by the biblical admonition that it is more blessed to give than to receive, and were unwilling to pay an occasionally higher income tax as an insurance premium for the maintenance and stability of the social order, the natural response to distrust was more distrust. It is in this kind of political atmosphere that democratic socialism has been pushed back in Italy and France, giving way to the more radical demands of communism.

SOCIALISM VERSUS COMMUNISM

Socialism and communism are not two of a kind, but represent two incompatible ways of thought and life, as incompatible as liberalism and totalitarianism.

There are several factors of irreconcilable antagonism between socialists and communists. First, *communists* seek to bring about the end of capitalism by a single act of *revolutionary upheaval and civil war. Socialists,* on the other hand, adhere to *strict constitutional procedures:* they seek power by ballots, rather than bullets; and once in office, they know they are not in for keeps, but are subject to be voted out in the next election.

The British labor movement has at no time approved of any cooperation with communists. In the middle nineteen thirties, when the communists in many countries sponsored Popular Fronts and United Fronts of all antifascist forces against the Berlin-Rome-Tokyo Axis, the British labor movement forbade its members to have anything to do with such efforts, on the grounds that its integrity would be jeopardized by association with communist aims. Members of the Labor Party who violated the ban by cooperating with communists in front organizations or appearing with communist speakers on the same platform were ousted from the party. Among those expelled were such well-known men as Sir Stafford Cripps and Aneurin Bevan. At the time, the Labor Party's policy of not getting tangled up with communists in any shape or form was markedly different from that of antifascist parties, both socialist and nonsocialist, in other countries, and the Labor Party was attacked for being hypocritical, sanctimonious, intransigent, and dogmatic. The passage of time, however, would seem to have fully vindicated the consistent policy of British socialism to have no dealings whatsoever with communism.

In 1945, the Labor government surprised many by allowing the fascists in Britain to reorganize as a political movement, although a number of fascists had committed treason during the war. One of the top fascists, William Joyce (popularly known as Lord Haw-Haw), had spent the war years broadcasting for the nazis in Berlin, for which offense he was executed as a traitor after World War II. The socialists in Britain took the view that the fascists had a right to engage in political propaganda as long as they did not violate any laws; further, they felt that the effectiveness of fascist propaganda depended rather on the common sense of the people than on prohibitory laws. Above all, British socialist leaders saw that if fascism lacks the protective coddling of extreme right-wingers and conservatives, it has no way of permeating larger groups of people.

In most other nations, the political Left fought fascism, whereas the Right concentrated on communism; the division of labor was exactly the opposite in Britain. *Fascism was destroyed by the Conservative Party,* and *communism by the Labor Party.* Both major parties clearly understood that the issue of democracy versus totalitarianism must not be poisoned by partisan arguments, and that it is too big an issue to be dragged into the mud of election campaigns. As a result, there are few (if any) countries in the world in which both fascism and communism are as dead and ineffectual as in Britain.

Moreover, this fight against totalitarianism was primarily carried on by the British people through their party organizations rather than through the strong arm of the government. In the United States, the House Committee on Un-American Activities and the Attorney General of the United States periodically publish lists of subversive organizations and publications for the information of law-enforcement officers as well as interested citizens. In Britain, the Labor Party issues from time to time lists of communist or communist-dominated organizations which no member of the Labor Party is permitted to join. This policing of the communist movement and its network

RELATIVE VOTING STRENGTH OF SOCIALIST AND COMMUNIST PARTIES*
(as of September 1, 1957)

Country	A: Socialist % of total vote	B: Communist % of total vote	C: Relation of A to B
Australia	43.9	1.12	39.2 times
Austria	35	3.6	9.7
Belgium	37.5	3.56	10.5
Canada	11	0.11	100
Denmark	39.4	3.1	12.7
Finland	26.5	21.4	1.2
France	14.8	25.5	0.58
Germany (West)	28.8	2.2	13
Great Britain	46.3	0.12	386
India	14	8.9	1.5
Israel	47.7	4.5	10.6
Italy	4.52	35.3	0.13
Netherlands	33.3	4.75	7
New Zealand	44.1	0.09	490
Norway	46.7	5.1	9
Sweden	44.6	5	8.9
Switzerland	27.1	2.6	10.4

* In the period 1946-1957, socialist voting strength generally remained stable. As to communist voting strength, the only increases were in India (from 3.3% to 8.9%) and Italy (from 29.7% to 35.3%). Major declines of communist voting strength in the period 1946-1957 occurred in Austria (from 5.4% to 3.6%), Belgium (from 12.7% to 3.56%), Germany (from 8.4% to 2.2%), Denmark (from 12.5% to 3.1%), Great Britain (from 0.41% to 0.12%), the Netherlands (from 10.6% to 4.75%), and Norway (from 11.9% to 5.1%). In West Germany, the Communist Party was outlawed in 1956; the figures in the table refer to the election of 1953, the last in which the communists participated.

of front-organizations by the Labor Party is probably more effective than if the same job were done by the government, because it uses publicity—a weapon the communists do not like—rather than the authority of the state. Communists thrive better under persecution than under the full exposure of truth and publicity.

Above all, the British Labor Party has successfully eliminated communism from its main position of influence—labor unions. *If communists are a negligible factor in Britain today, the main credit goes to the organized labor movement.* It has steadily and quietly fought them whenever and wherever they have tried to gain influence. In open elections, the communists are no menace in most democratic nations, but in labor unions the communist technique of infiltration has often been extremely effective. Because of the communist goal of revolution, it is understandable that socialist parties look upon communists as a group of troublemakers who must be kept out of unions or any other organized working-class activity. And because trade unionists have had the most intimate knowledge of communism—based on everyday contacts rather than on a study of ideology—they have generally proved themselves to be the staunchest opponents of communism in the labor movements. The purely political elements of the socialist parties have not always shown the same steadiness and vigor.

It is understandable why the communists work with such desperate energy for the control of organized labor: they know that no amount of propaganda will convert the middle and wealthier classes to communism. By contrast, the socialists have learned from elementary electoral statistics that parliamentary majorities cannot be obtained by appealing to one class only; a considerable proportion of the working class (in England about 40 per cent) does not vote Labor, and if the Labor Party is to obtain a majority, it must appeal to other groups. The communists, prisoners of their dogmas, can only think in terms of class and class antagonisms; the socialists have learned to think in terms of parliamentary majorities.

On the crucial issue of public ownership, the gap that separates socialists from communists is unbridgeable. Communists visualize the transition from capitalist enterprise to public ownership as sudden and complete. There is no payment for expropriated property, because communists consider capitalist property no better than theft. By contrast, socialists do not believe that the transition from capitalism to public ownership of the means of production can be either sudden or complete. Most socialists believe in the instalment plan: public ownership of the means of production is to be built up gradually, by instalments; if one phase works, then the next will be tackled. Responsible socialists feel that they must prove pragmatically, through actual accomplishments, the usefulness and practicality of public ownership in particular industries or services.

Even Bevanites believe in gradual nationalization. On that, they agree with the majority led by Gaitskell and Morrison. The difference is with regard to the amount of nationalization in a mixed economy: the majority accepts, for a very long time to come, a mixed economy in which the element of private enterprise is predominant, or about evenly balanced with that of nationalization. By contrast, the Bevanites are willing to accept a mixed economy, provided the nationalized sector of the economy is preponderant in the not too distant future.

As to compensation, socialists tend to share the general democratic conviction that no citizen may be deprived of his property without due process and compensation. Important as public ownership of the basic industries is to their plans, socialists consider public ownership not as an end, but as a means to an end, and a means that does not justify the violation of property rights.

There is another vital difference with regard to public ownership. Communists seek to transfer all means of production, distribution, and exchange to the state, leaving to the individual only the free discretion over consumer goods. Communists insist on *total nationalization*, because their dogma tells them that publicly owned property is always preferable to private enterprise.

By contrast, socialists seek to work out a set of empirical principles that will indicate in a *particular* instance whether a specific *industry or service* is to be transferred to public ownership and control. The socialists' criterion may be that the industry under examination is a monopoly (such as gas and light, telephone, and other utilities tend to become); or that the industry is sick, as the British coal industry was before its nationalization; or that the industry, although neither inefficient nor monopolistic, is of such vital importance to the national economy in peace and war that it seems socially undesirable to leave its operation in private hands (the British iron and steel industry was nationalized on these grounds).

The British Conservatives are in substantial agreement with Labor on the first two criteria; on the third the two parties are in partial disagreement. Clearly, the irreconcilable difference of viewpoint with regard to private property is not between conservatives and socialists, but between democrats (conservatives, liberals, or socialists) and totalitarians (fascists or communists).

Philosophically and politically, the difference between communists and socialists goes to the root of things. As we saw earlier, Lenin's theory of the professional revolutionary is based on the assumption that the majority of the people (or the working class) are unable to think for themselves; that a minority, the communist party, has the job of leading the proletariat; and that within the minority a small group of men, the professional revolutionaries, are to formulate policies and assume leadership. Thus, in Leninist theory (and in communist practice), a small minority within a minority is to be the ruling elite.

This elite concept is totally rejected by socialists, who believe in democracy and majority rule within their own party as much as in their own nation. Clement Attlee, British Prime Minister from 1945-1951 and leader of the Labor Party from 1935 to 1955, writes in his book *The Labour Party in Perspective* (1937) that his party's strength depends, "not on the brilliance of individuals, but on the quality of the rank and file." Attlee's own career confirms this diagnosis—brilliance is not his *forte,* and he lacks the dynamic leadership qualities of a Churchill or a Roosevelt.

Contrary to the communists, socialists believe in peaceful persuasion as the only method of promoting their program. Communists feel that it is useless to seek change by persuasion, because all means of communication, education, and propaganda are biased in favor of the capitalist *status quo,* and that freedom of the press amounts to little if one lacks the necessary funds to start a newspaper. For this reason the communists were stunned when the British Labor Party polled its electoral victory in 1945, and again in 1950.

According to orthodox Marxism-Leninism, such victories were impossible: since the British press was overwhelmingly in favor of the Conservative Party, how could the voters, who presumably had been reading the pro-conservative papers daily for years, vote Labor? According to Lenin, workers under capitalism are mentally enslaved to capitalist ideology, and cannot therefore be peacefully converted to socialist thinking until there has been a change in the economic structure of society. Only *after* capitalism has been destroyed, Lenin argues, will the workers be able to think along anti-capitalist lines, because (as Marx said) it is the conditions of man's life that determine his thinking.

To the communist, every capitalist system, whether democratic, authoritarian, or fascist, is a bourgeois dictatorship; specifically, democratic institutions in a capitalist system are considered as so much façade and hypocrisy, which do not make the capitalist system any less dictatorial. Once capitalism—even liberal capitalism—

is identified with dictatorship, the communist insistence on violence as the sole means of change is a logical conclusion.

Socialists, on the other hand, draw a fundamental distinction between two types of capitalist system, the political dictatorship and the liberal democracy. In a liberal democracy socialists generally believe in playing according to the rules of the game—provided, of course, the other side does the same.

Finally, *socialists reject the communist thesis that the choice in a democracy is between full capitalism and full collectivism.* Democratic parties do not concern themselves with bringing about the millennium as of a certain date, but seek to tackle issues that are comparatively manageable and to avoid definitive solutions that are irrevocable.

Socialists therefore envisage the transition from a predominantly capitalist economy (a purely capitalist economy exists and has existed only in the minds of the extreme Right and the extreme Left) to a predominantly socialist economy, not as a result of a sudden revolutionary *coup* that makes the return to private enterprise impossible, but as the result of gradual measures, none of which by itself irrevocably alters the nature of the whole economy.

Whereas the communists think in terms of three absolutes—capitalism, revolution, communist dictatorship—socialists think in terms of three *relative* concepts: a predominantly capitalist economy as the starting point, a long period of gradual change, and finally a predominantly socialized economy.

ELEMENTS OF SOCIALIST THOUGHT AND POLICY

The totalitarians of all shades have authoritative statements of doctrine, such as the *Communist Manifesto* or Hitler's *Mein Kampf*. Socialism, on the other hand, like many other liberal movements and ideas, has no Bible, because liberals generally cannot agree to their beliefs and doctrines, and are better at criticizing Bibles than at writing them. Moreover, socialism has developed in different countries in accordance with different national traditions, and there has never been any central authority—such as world communism possesses in Moscow—to lay down a socialist party line.

Yet despite the absence of such authoritative statements of socialist doctrine, it is not too difficult to cull from socialist writings, and from the policies of socialist parties, the outlines of socialist thought and policy. What emerges, however, is not a consistent body of ideas and policies. It has been the main strength—and weakness—of socialism that it has had no clear-cut body of doctrine, and that it has fed on contradictory sources, sources that reflect the contradictions of the societies in which socialism has developed.

The complex, and frequently self-contradictory, elements of socialist thought and policy can best be illustrated from the British socialist movement, the most influential in the world. The elements that stand out in the British movement are:

> (1) religion
> (2) ethical and esthetic idealism
> (3) fabian empiricism
> (4) Liberalism

(1) In *The Labour Party in Perspective,* Attlee writes that "the first place in the influences that built up the Socialist movement must be given to religion. England in the nineteenth century was still a nation of Bible readers. To put the Bible into the hands of an Englishman is to do a very dangerous thing. He will find there material which may send him out as a preacher of some religious, social, or economic doctrine. The large number of religious sects in this country, and the various tenets that many of them hold, illustrates this."

The *Christian Socialist movement,* headed by two clergymen, Frederick Maurice and Charles Kingsley, reached its peak in the middle of the nineteenth century, and was an important source for the later development of working-class and socialist organizations. The Christian Socialists had as their guiding principle the concept that *socialism must be Christianized, and Christianity socialized.*

George Lansbury, Attlee's predecessor as the leader of the Labor Party, writes in *My England* (1934) as follows: "Socialism, which means love, cooperation, and brotherhood in every department of human affairs, is the only outward expression of a Christian's faith. I am firmly convinced that whether they know it or not, all who approve and accept competition and struggle against each other as the means whereby we gain our daily bread, do indeed betray and make of no effect the 'will of God.' " The late Archbishop of Canterbury, William Temple, came very close to socialism in his *Chris-*

tianity and the Social Order (1942). Temple holds that every economic system is, for good or ill, an immense educative influence, and that therefore the church must be concerned with it. The church is thus bound to ask "whether that influence is one tending to develop Christian character, and if the answer is partly or wholly negative the church must do its utmost to secure a change in the economic system so that it may find in that system an ally and not an enemy."

This practical concern of Christianity was particularly strong in Victorian England, throughout the whole second half of the nineteenth century. A sense of moral seriousness and dedicated disinterestedness characterized the Victorian period, and Victorian religion, while conceding that grace and faith were essential to salvation, nevertheless emphasized conduct and *salvation by works* Many socialist leaders of the older generation who (like Attlee and Cripps) came from upper-class homes were steeped in an atmosphere in which religion was taken seriously.

Another religious influence of profound influence in Britain was the tradition of religious dissent, of *nonconformity*. In other European states, Protestantism had resulted in freedom *of* the church in relation to Rome, but not necessarily in freedom *within* the church in matters of doctrine and church government. To the nonconformist, Protestantism meant freedom of individual conscience, and the freedom to organize voluntarily in associations of like-minded believers. This principle of *voluntary association* was later translated from religion into politics, where it became the life principle of the free, democratic society.

It was in the village chapels of the eighteenth and nineteenth centuries that many local leaders of working-class organizations learned to think for themselves, as well as to conduct public meetings and administer finances. *Wherever nonconformity was strong, labor unions and cooperatives were strong;* in fact, the trade unions have been aptly called the present-day descendants of the earlier nonconformist congregations. Nonconformity supplied more than a particular religious outlook: it was also the source, in the labor movement, of the idealism, the moral dedication, and of the seriousness that have characterized the movement and its leaders.

If one studies the internal organization of some nonconformist churches, one is struck by its similarity with the organization of trade unions: both are loosely federated unions of voluntary bodies freely associating with each other. The Labor Party today is also a federal union, made up of three main bodies—trade unions, co-operatives, and local constituency organizations—each of which is in turn made up of loosely federated organizations. Because the Labor Party has this federal character, its internal structure resembles more the American federal system than the much simpler and more streamlined political system of Britain itself.

The complexity of the religious root of modern socialism becomes apparent in the fact that *nonreligious, rational humanism* has also played a vital role in the evolution of socialist thought and action. Robert Owen was a rationalist, and among more modern socialist leaders in Britain Sidney and Beatrice Webb, Harold J. Laski, and G. D. H. Cole, to mention but a few, have not been much inspired by formal religious beliefs. It remains, however, of some interest that the political leaders of the labor movement, men like George Lansbury, Clement Attlee, and Sir Stafford Cripps, have been profoundly religious, whereas the principal intellectual figures, the men who formulate ideas rather than policies, tend to represent the *rationalist* root of socialism.

In the United States, too, religion has played an important part, in the cooperative and communal settlements established in the eighteenth and nineteenth centuries as well as in the more recent socialist activities of a political and propagandistic nature. In the twentieth century, democratic socialism in the United States has been symbolized above all by Norman Thomas, who was a minister of religion before he took up the cause of socialism as his life's mission.

By contrast, religion has played a much smaller part in Continental European and Latin American socialism. Whereas in England religious dissent was the bridge between religious and political unorthodoxy, with the virtual absence of nonconformity outside of the English-speaking world dissent from the established social and political order has generally also included dissent from the established church, or from religion itself.

Before World War II, there were small groups of religious socialists in countries like France or Germany, but on the whole socialists tended to be anticlerical, or at least indifferent toward religion, because most churches in Continental Europe openly supported the political and economic *status quo*. During World War II, the heroic struggle of many priests and ministers against nazi-fascist oppression brought about a closer understanding between churches and most socialist parties. Since then, the churches have become less committed to one particular set of social and economic theories, and the socialists have abandoned much of their earlier agnosticism and anticlericalism. Also, the success of British socialism has proved to many socialists in other lands that socialism and religion do mix, provided the mixture is accomplished in the right spirit.

(2) *Ethical and esthetic idealism* is another important source of British socialism, although its impact cannot be measured in votes and membership cards. Expressed by poets like John Ruskin and William Morris, ethical idealism was not a political or economic program, but a revolt against the squalor, drabness, and poverty of life under industrial capitalism. Developing first in England, capitalism probably produced more ugliness there than anywhere else, because English industrialists had no way of imagining what the new way of life would do to the beauty of the English countryside, no way of foreseeing the rapid disfigurement of lovely old towns and villages by slums and factory centers.

Whereas Marx approached industrial capitalism in terms of cosmic laws—the development of world history according to inevitable social laws, philosophical materialism, the law of the falling profit rate, to name but a few—Morris kept his gaze closer to the ground. He saw around him ugly household goods and furnishings, and men and women who lacked joy and beauty in their daily lives. When once asked in a public meeting what he thought of Marx, Morris said: "I am asked if I believe in Marx' theory of value. To speak quite frankly, I do not know what Marx' theory of value is, and I'm damned if I want to know." What Morris cared about was human beings, not this or that "system." He felt intensely that the arts must be brought back again into everyday life, and that people's creative impulses should be given expression in their daily life and work.

The influence of Ruskin and Morris was more negative than positive: they showed what was wrong with a civilization—physically and morally—that was built on strife and squalor, but they did not formulate any specific program to improve the specific conditions to which they objected. Nevertheless, this esthetic and ethical revolt was important in preparing the intellectual environment in which socialism could later find a sympathetic response.

Ruskin and Morris were mainly read by the more educated class, which absorbed from them (and other writers, like Charles Dickens and Thomas Carlyle) a groping understanding of what industrial civilization does to man, not only as a worker, but as a human being. The esthetic and ethical rebels of Victorian England undermined the self-confidence that then prevailed and fostered self-criticism; out of that doubt and self-criticism more positive socialist ideas could later be developed step by step.

In one particular field—town and country planning—the Labor Party reflects directly and explicitly the message of Ruskin and Morris. The whole concept of community planning—which is more than tearing down slums and building neat little row houses of uniform size and style—owes much to the outlook of the early pioneers of socialist thought, for whom problems of industry merged with more general problems of creating a community in which each member would have access to the means of civilized enjoyment.

(3) *Fabian empiricism* is perhaps the most characteristically *British* aspect of the British labor movement. The Fabian Society, founded in 1884, was named after a Roman general, Quintus Fabius Maximus Cunctator—the "delayer." The early motto of the society was: "For the right moment you must wait, as Fabius did; but when the right moment comes you must strike hard, or your waiting will have been vain and fruitless."

The founders and early members of the Fabian Society included George Bernard Shaw, Sidney and Beatrice Webb, H. G. Wells, and Graham Wallas. It was noteworthy that none of them came from the poorer classes, and that there was a sizable portion of writers in the group.

In Sidney Webb's historical survey of the basis of socialism, included in the *Fabian Essays* (1889), we find what is still the basic philosophy of Fabianism, and, more generally, of British socialism. Webb looked upon socialism (eleven years before the foundation of the Labor Party) as an inevitable outcome of the full fruition of democracy, but he insisted that his "inevitability of gradualness" was sharply different from the Marxian inevitability of revolutionary, catastrophic change.

Webb emphasized in the *Fabian Essays* that social organization can only come bit by bit, and that important "organic changes" can only take place, in England at least, under four conditions: first, such changes must be *democratic,* acceptable to a popular majority, and "prepared for in the minds of all"; second, they must be *gradual,* causing no dislocation; third, they must *not* be regarded as *immoral* by the people; fourth, they must be *constitutional and peaceful.*

Marxians on the Continent and elsewhere aimed their propaganda at the proletariat. As to the middle and upper classes, the job at hand was to liquidate them, not to convert them to socialism. Because the propaganda was thus exclusively aimed at the proletariat, it tended to be highly emotional and sloganized, taking into consideration not only the low educational level of the workers, but also the fact that they were expected to be half converted before they were ever exposed to communist agitation.

The Fabian Society started from the assumption that there could be *no progress toward a just social order in Britain unless the middle and upper classes could be shown the reasonableness and equity of the basic claims of socialist thought and policy.* Since government in Britain was government by persuasion and consent, and since the governing classes of Britain were largely recruited from the middle and upper classes, there could be no change of policy in Britain without the preliminary consent of those classes. It was fortunate for the Fabians in a country like England that they spoke the same language—literally and metaphorically—as did the governing classes, and knew how to *permeate* the latter in ways which would have been closed to formal propaganda from persons outside of the same class.

The Fabian technique of permeation was based on the premise that you do not change a reasonable person through a one-time brilliant argument, lecture, or emotional appeal. It was the Fabian policy to work on the minds and feelings of their hearers in a slow, gradual process rather than in one sudden act of conversion, and preferably on social, informal occasions rather than on formal, official ones.

An emotional appeal to a high British civil servant, telling him that according to the Marxian dialectic the capitalist system is doomed, and that such doom will be followed by the classless proletarian society, was likely to have less effect than a casual reference at luncheon to a new government report, written by a fellow bureaucrat, on the incidence of disease and crime in slum areas. Similarly, serious discussion of a recent book by a scholarly economist of good repute on changes in the distribution of income among various social and economic groups was likely to have more effect on a conservative political leader than the shorter appeals of "Down with Capitalism" and "Long Live Proletarian Solidarity."

Permeation had also another side: the Fabians did not consider it their job to pass resolutions, make appeals to kings and parliaments, or address themselves to the masses of the people. They were interested in convincing a small group of persons, regardless of party affiliation as long as they had two qualifications: first, they had to be persons of *continuous* influence in public life, so that the long process of permeation, if successful, would pay off; second, such persons would have to be *reasonable,* by which the Fabians meant not partisan extremists. Since such persons could be found in all political parties, the Fabians cultivated conservatives, who met their qualifications, as well as liberals.

This sort of Fabianism assumes a *Fabianism in reverse,* or else it would not stand a chance of success. For example, Fabians and other socialists in England religiously read *The Times,* not because they agree with its editorial viewpoint (*The Times* is generally conservative), but because *The Times* is "a good paper." In most other countries socialists consider the local substitute for *The Times* a source of bourgeois contamination, from which they should steer clear.

The difference between the Fabian and Marxian-communist approach can best be seen by contrasting the writings of the two groups. Marx was little interested in the minutiae of life; his *magnum opus, Das Kapital,* is an attempt to give meaning to history as a whole, and much of his thought was devoted to fundamentals of philosophy. Lenin wrote volumes and volumes on such subjects as *Materialism and Empirio-Criticism.* By contrast, over 95 per cent of all Fabian publications have been pamphlets rather than heavy tomes, and pamphlets lend themselves more to small subjects like *Municipal Milk and Public Health* (Fabian Tract No. 122) than to the future of western civilization. The Fabian Society is rarely to be found in high intellectual altitudes, sniffing the thin air surrounding the metaphysical peaks; it is more often found "nosing about in the drains," seeking to remedy some immediate and *specific* condition.

Early in the history of the Fabian Society, Fabian Tract No. 70 (written by George Bernard Shaw) made it plain that Fabianism was no rival to existing philosophies trying to explain the whole cosmos, and that it had "no distinctive opinion on the Marriage Question, Religion, Art, abstract Economics, historic Evolution, Currency, or any other subject than its own special business of practical Democracy and Socialism." This sense of practicality and concreteness is indicated by typical titles of Fabian Tracts and other pamphlets: *Liquor Licensing at Home and Abroad; Life in the Laundry; Public Control of Electrical Power and Transit; The Case for School Nurseries; The Endowment of Motherhood; The Reform of the House of Lords;* and *The British Cabinet: A Study of Its Personnel, 1901-1924.*

Two Fabian pamphlets, *Metropolitan Borough Councils: Their Constitution, Powers, and Duties* and, *Borough Councils: Their Constitution, Powers, and Duties,* were written by Clement R. Attlee in the spring of 1920, when Lenin was busy, not with the reform of borough councils, but with the destruction of states and empires.

The Fabian approach can perhaps best be shown in a simple illustration: if a slum clearance project is debated in terms of fundamental issues—such as socialism versus capitalism—agreement between advocates of the project and their opponents is unlikely. However, if the pertinent facts can be clearly brought out—the cost (in dollars and cents) of a slum area in terms of disease, crime protection, fire hazards, as compared with the cost of building new houses with public assistance—the original gap has been considerably narrowed, and agreement will be likelier than it was when the argument centered on issues of apparently irreconcilable ultimate values.

The successes of Fabianism have probably stemmed chiefly from this concern with *reducing questions of principle to questions of fact.* Fabians gambled on the notion that facts do matter, and that the impact of facts ultimately determines how people will think and act.

In his autobiography, *Power and Influence* (1953), Lord Beveridge has an interesting sidelight on the Fabian faith in facts. One of the greatest contributions of Sidney and Beatrice Webb was the creation of the London School of Economics and Political Science in 1895, in order to provide an adequate opportunity for the study of economics and allied subjects. The Webbs themselves chose the first four Directors of the London School. Of the four, Beveridge tells us, the first two became Conservative Members of Parliament, the third had socialist sympathies, and the fourth (Beveridge himself) was a Liberal. The Webbs, Beveridge says, "believed that the impartial study of society would further the Socialism which was their practical aim, but they were prepared to take the risk of being wrong in that belief."

The Fabian technique of trying to reduce apparently irreconcilable differences of principle to negotiable disagreements over facts is no invention or novelty, but is implicit in the very nature of the democratic society. We have peace in a free society to the extent that people are willing to keep to themselves conflicting fundamentals in religion, morals, and philosophy. It is for this reason that there is separation of state and church in the United States: not because Americans are indifferent to religion, but because the framers of the Constitution felt that it is wiser to keep a fundamental issue like religion out of politics, and concentrate on issues in which people of all religions can cooperate without injury to their religious belief.

Fabianism has frequently been described as reform without resentment, social reconstruction without class war, political empiricism without dogma or fanaticism. Despite its small size (its membership never exceeded a few thousand), the Fabian Society has had an enormous impact. In the 1945 election, which led to the first Labor government based on a substantial parliamentary majority, 229 of the 394 Labor Members of Parliament were Fabians, and more than half of the Government, including Attlee (the Prime Minister from 1945-1951), was Fabian.

(4) *Liberalism* has become an increasingly important source of socialism, particularly since Liberal parties have dwindled to insignificance in many countries. In England, the Liberal Party has virtually disappeared, and the Labor Party seems to have inherited almost two-fifths of the estate. Temperamentally, many Liberals do not find it easy to join a socialist movement, because the passion for individual liberty and individual difference is still the most distinguishing trait of the Liberal.

Apart from the tendency toward red tape and regulation for the sake of regulation, there is also in socialism a tendency toward the state, the mass, the collectivity. Both tendencies are repugnant to the true Liberal—the man who occasionally still likes to be himself, and not just a number in the National Register. Yet, during the last thirty years, more and more Liberals have joined the Labor Party. Why?

In the first place, the disappearance of the British *Liberal Party* is due to the fact, not that it has failed, but that *its success has made it unnecessary*. Both the Conservative Party and the Labor Party are now thoroughly committed to the Liberal principles of respect for individual freedom of worship, thought, speech, and association. Liberalism as a protest against clericalism is no longer a live issue in England (or in most other countries).

Free trade, another great ideal of nineteenth-century British Liberalism, no longer arouses passionate political interest, and is now the concern of experts rather than politicians. With both Conservatives and socialists committed to some form of tariff protection, even the Liberals realize that free trade no longer has the importance it once had.

The specific issues gone, many liberals have joined the Labor Party, or vote Labor, or think of themselves as vaguely socialist. Liberalism has generally been to the Left of the Conservatives; and in a country with a two-party system, like Britain, if one wishes to stand to the Left of Conservatism, the Labor Party is now the only platform to stand on.

On issues of public ownership, the Liberal elements in the Labor Party are opposed to doctrinaire policies of nationalizing for the sake of nationalizing—*i.e.,* the Liberals in the Labor Party generally are on its Right wing, just as the Liberals in the Conservative Party are its Left wing. The Right-wing Laborite is so close to the Left-wing Conservative—in mentality, outlook, temperament, and policies —that it takes a pencil of electronic sharpness to draw the line of demarcation between the two. The London *Economist* has coined the phrase "Butskell," a composite of R. A. Butler, a leading Conservative of reformist leanings, and Hugh Gaitskell, the moderate Labor leader. "Butskellism" is a symbol of the closeness of both major British parties on major issues.

Liberalism has contributed much that is lasting in British socialism. Because of the Liberal influence, socialist leaders are more moderate and less doctrinaire than they might otherwise have been, and have a deeper respect for individual liberty. Liberalism has turned the Labor Party into a national party, rather than one based on class, and it has bequeathed to the Labor Party the Liberal message that there can be reform without bitterness and hatred.

SOCIAL-ECONOMIC CHANGES AND REFORMS

The victory of the democratic nations in World War I provided a strong stimulus for the growth of socialist parties throughout the world. The war had been fought in defense of the ideals of liberty and social justice against the authoritarian imperialism of Germany and her allies, and during the war promises were made to the peoples of the major democratic belligerents that military victory would be followed by the establishment of a new social order based on greater opportunity and equality.

In England, the Labor Party reflected in its growth and development the protest against the old social order. Founded in 1900, the Labor Party polled only two seats in the Parliamentary elections of that year. By 1910 forty Laborites sat in the House of Commons, and the party had ceased to be a negligible factor. In 1918 the parliamentary representation rose to 57, and in 1922 the Labor Party obtained 142 seats out of 615, replacing the fading Liberal Party as the second strongest party in the country. In 1924, the Labor Party, though still a minority, formed a government with the tacit support of the Liberal Party, but the experiment lasted only for ten months, because the Liberals finally decided that they could not go along with a socialist program.

In 1929, the Labor Party became for the first time in its history the largest single party in Britain, obtaining in the general election 288 out of 615 seats in Parliament. Although lacking an absolute majority in the House of Commons, the Labor Party formed a government that lasted until the summer of 1931. The coming of the world depression in 1929 weakened Britain economically, and the Labor government, being unable to follow socialist policies to cure the depression and unwilling to adopt conservative remedies, resigned in the summer of 1931. In the ensuing election the parliamentary representation of the Labor Party dropped to 52 out of 615, but by 1935, the last election before World War II, its strength in the House of Commons had risen again to 154. As long as the shadow of nazi-fascist aggression hung over Britain, however, there was little chance for embarking upon a major experiment of social and economic reform.

Between 1935 and the end of the war in Europe there was no general election. In the first postwar general elections, held on July 5, 1945, the Labor Party obtained 394 out of 640 seats, with the result that for the first time in British history a Labor government was formed with a clear majority in the House of Commons. In 1950, the Labor majority fell to a bare 315 out of 625 seats, and because of the narrow margin and the resulting instability of government, a new election was held in 1951. Although the Labor Party received more votes than the Conservatives in the 1951 election, it lost its parliamentary majority to the Conservatives, 321 seats to 295. In the elections of 1955, the Conservatives polled more votes than Labor, winning a comfortable parliamentary majority of 345 seats against Labor's 277, with the remaining 8 seats distributed among the Liberals and other small splinter groups.

British politics has thus been reduced again to the classical two-party pattern; the Liberals have virtually disappeared as a factor in public life, and the choice is now between Conservative and Labor.

Between 1900 and 1918, the Labor Party was not officially committed to socialism, although it included, of course, many individual socialists. In 1918, when the party adopted socialism in its program, its commitment to the nationalization of industry was just about complete. But as the party learned the facts of life it changed its outlook drastically, and now it is urging nationalization only where it has been proved pragmatically that public ownership will do more for the welfare of the nation than private ownership. In the election of 1945, for example, the Labor Party did *not* enter the campaign with a program of "socialism" in the abstract, but promised to nationalize specifically listed industries and services, if elected to office.

In each case, it explained why nationalization was necessary. For gas and light, water, telephone and telegraph, and other utilities, the criterion of nationalization was the existence of a *natural monopoly*. On the coal industry, there was general agreement in Britain, regardless of party, that the industry was so sick and inefficient that it could not be put on its feet except through nationalization. The iron and steel industries were declared to be so *vital to the nation*, in peace and in war, that their management could not safely be subject to the decisions of private persons. The nationalization of all inland transportation, by rail, road, and air, was proposed on the ground that *wasteful competition* could best be avoided by a *coordinated*

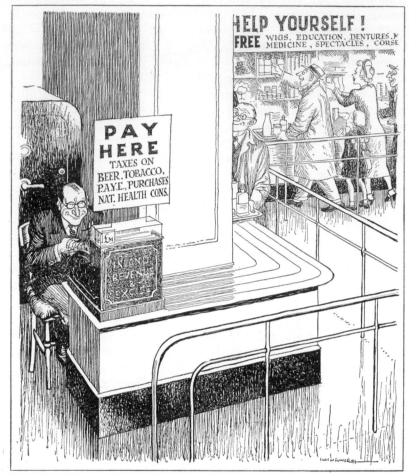

Reproduced by permission of the Proprietors of Punch

ROUND THE CORNER

scheme of transportation owned and managed by public authorities. The Bank of England was also proposed for nationalization on the ground that its purpose was so obviously public. Finally, the election program of 1945 also promised the setting up of a National Health Service, so that the best possible health and medical facilities might be available to every person without regard to his ability to pay.

After the electoral triumph of 1945, the Labor Party methodically carried out its program. With one exception, there was little argument over nationalization. On the exception, iron and steel, the Conservatives argued that the industry was highly efficient, and that the needs of the national welfare could be accommodated without nationalization.

The attitude of the British public toward nationalization was generally one of indifference. The exception was, and is, the National Health Service, because of its direct effect on the everyday life of the individual citizen. Although no one was compelled to join the National Health Service, 97 per cent of the population and over 96 per cent of the doctors and physicians are in it. At first there was considerable delay and confusion arising out of the administrative and technical difficulties experienced in setting up the necessary machinery, and a number of barbs—some good-natured, others not so good-natured—were leveled at the program by the press of Britain (see cartoon) and the United States. As the program began to hit its stride, however, adverse criticism (in Britain, at least) died down, until now the National Health Service seems to have established itself as a part of British life. The Conservative Party, like the Labor Party is fully committed to the program.

The Labor Government elected in 1945 also set up a comprehensive cradle-to-grave scheme of social security. The system provides protection against sickness, unemployment, and old age, supplemented by maternity grants, widows' pensions, and family allowances. Social security as set up by the Labor Government was no invention of the Labor Party, but the culmination of several decades of social legislation, enacted by Conservative and Liberal governments. A fully integrated system of social security was first proposed during World War II in the *Beveridge Report* (1942); in the middle of the war, both the Conservative Party and the Labor Party pledged themselves, if elected to office after the war, to introduce a comprehensive system of social security.

A further policy of the Labor Government in the years 1945-1951 aimed at greater social equality. The setting up of the basic institutions of the welfare state in itself contributed to greater social equality, by bringing within the reach of large sections of the population many facilities and services that hitherto had not been available to those sections. *Educational opportunities* on the secondary and university levels, for example, were opened up to children of lower-income families.

Taxation was the greatest leveler. Thus, a person with an income of £100,000 retained in 1910, after payment of taxes, about £94,000. In 1953, the net income on £100,000 after payment of taxes had shrunk to about £6,000. Inheritance taxes took about 50 per cent of bigger fortunes in 1938, about 80 per cent after World War II. In 1938, the last normal prewar year, there were 6,600 persons in Britain whose income was over £6,000 after payment of taxes. By 1949, that number had dwindled to 60, to rise again to 500 in 1955, although the value of the pound had been cut to about one-third of its prewar purchasing power. At the same time, there was a sharp increase in the middle-income groups.

Putting the trend toward equality in Britain in another way, it can be seen that the proportion of the national income paid in wages and salaries was 60 per cent in 1938 and rose to 69 per cent in 1955 (after payment of taxes), whereas the share of dividends and interest in the national income dropped from 34 per cent to 20 per cent during the same period. Although all these policies have by no means brought about absolute equality, they have gone a long way toward the elimination of extremes of inequality.

One of the remarkable results of the victories of democratic socialism was the elimination of communism as an important factor in British politics. In the years between World War I and II, the communists usually had one representative in the House of Commons; in the election of 1945, the communists obtained two seats out of 640 in the House of Commons; in the election of 1950, after five years of vigorous Labor administration, the communists were unable to elect a single candidate, and they repeated this failure in 1951 and 1955. *Far from being the first step to communism, democratic socialism thus proved itself to be the high road to the grave of communism.* By contrast, where socialism declined after World War II, as in France and Italy, communism gained control of organized labor, thus threatening the very existence of state and society.

The record of the Labor Government in the years 1945-1951 does not conclusively prove nor disprove whether nationalization, or how much nationalization, is the cure for the social and economic ills of modern industrial society. The British voting public has been more impressed by the greater social equality of the welfare state than by nationalization. Even if it were conceded that the nationalized industries and services seem to have worked out fairly satisfactorily on the whole, no one claims that they have solved Britain's basic economic problem of earning enough abroad with which to buy the foodstuffs and raw materials necessary to maintain her industries and feed her people. Before embarking upon further measures of nationalization, the British people want to see how the industries and services so far transferred to public ownership will work out, and the Labor Party reflected these doubts by proposing only very moderate schemes of nationalization in the elections of 1950, 1951, and 1955. As to the next general election, the Labor Party announced in 1957 that its chief domestic policy issues would be a thorough reform of housing conditions and sharply increased benefits for the old, and not further major experiments in nationalization.

A small group of extreme socialists, led by Aneurin Bevan, want to push nationalization further, regardless of the possible results, but most members of the Labor Party feel that nationalization can appeal to the British electorate only as a pragmatic policy, the success of which must be determined by further experience.

Dropping much of the traditional socialist belief in nationalization, the Labor Party has come close to the Conservative Party, which in turn no longer opposes the basic principles of the welfare state. Inasmuch as both parties seem to be united on kindred principles of social policy, and because so much of the British economy depends upon factors external to it (such as prosperity in the United States), there is little room left for such differences in principle as characterized the classic nineteenth-century struggles between the Whigs and the Tories.

In the late nineteen fifties, British politics thus gives the impression of ideological peace and near-uniformity. The Labor Party, in particular, is in search of a new program and set of principles that can inspire the country, for the *impulse of early socialism*—nationalization plus social security—*has been largely spent*. The very success of democratic socialism has thus become the main source of its hesitation and stagnation.

On the European Continent, the Scandinavian countries have had the most impressive record of social reform, both in the interwar years and after World War II. From the early nineteen thirties onward, the Scandinavian countries have been governed by socialist administrations based on parliamentary majorities, and as a result communism has been kept down to minor proportions in all three countries (Norway, Denmark, Sweden). The Scandinavian socialist movements emphasized economic development and social security rather than nationalization, and their economic policies were centered on fiscal measures (such as cheap money) and taxation rather than on public ownership. Full employment was a major point in Scandinavian (as in British) socialism.

One of the important lessons of the social and economic reform in Scandinavia in the last thirty years is the emphasis on *socialization rather than nationalization*. One of the most serious political weaknesses of the British program of economic change has been the tendency to substitute *state* ownership and management for private ownership, thus increasing the tendency toward governmental centralization. By contrast, the Scandinavian reform programs have experimented with other types of social ownership in lieu of private ownership.

The most significant contribution of Scandinavia to social reform is the use of the *cooperative movement* rather than the state as the agent of social and economic reform. Whereas in Britain the cooperative movement has been largely confined, as in most other countries, to retail and wholesale trading in a selected group of articles, the Scandinavians have set up cooperatives for slum clearance, health insurance, and industrial production. This Scandinavian *middle way* avoids the evils of unbridled capitalism, and steers clear, at the same time, of the dangers of statism.

PROBLEMS OF NATIONALIZATION

Socialist theory and practice have undergone drastic changes on the issue of nationalization in the last forty years. When the British Labor Party adopted a socialist platform in 1918, it demanded the "nationalization of all the means of production, distribution, and exchange." At that time, the formula expressed the prevailing socialist orthodoxy.

Today, there is not a single socialist party in the world, nor a single socialist leader of repute and responsibility still adhering to the old formula of nationalizing all the means of production, distribution, and exchange. In July 1951, the Socialist International, speaking for over thirty socialist parties throughout the world, adopted a program that specifically rejected the older doctrine of total nationalization, and conceded that socialist planning is com-

Herblock in the *Washington Post*

"I GUESS THEY'RE TRYING TO SELL US ON SOCIALISM"

patible with private ownership in agriculture, handicrafts, retail trade, and small and medium-sized industries.

Moreover, nationalization is now increasingly rejected as the only alternative to private capitalism. In his *Democratic Socialism: A New Appraisal* (1953), Norman Thomas, the leader of American socialism during the last thirty years, writes that "the state under the most democratic theory and practice will become too huge, too cumbersome, if it seeks to control directly all economic activity." Thomas speaks of the *dangers of statism* inherent in total nationalization, and like most thoughful socialists today he stresses that the alternative to private capitalism is *socialization, not nationalization.*

Freedom is inextricably linked to the *diffusion of power;* this truism has always been admitted by socialists to apply to political government. They are now finally coming around to the idea that *in the economic realm, too, there can be no freedom unless there is diffusion of economic power.*

Total nationalization—even under the most democratic safeguards —is bound to lead to the all-powerful state, and such a state is a threat to liberty even if it uses its powers benevolently.

The concept of socialization, by contrast, implies the diffusion of publicly owned property: property is owned and managed not by the state but by producer or consumer cooperatives, trade unions, churches, educational institutions, public corporations, and other organizations, with these organizations deriving their powers from voluntary association rather than from the sovereign authority of the state. In such organizations, there is also much more room for the direct representation of workers and consumers than in nationalized industries and services.

This approach has been successfully tried in Israel as well as in Scandinavia. In Scandinavia, most public housing has been built, not by the state, but by corporations that combine individual ownership and management with financial assistance from housing cooperatives and municipal agencies. In Scandinavia, too, as mentioned earlier, cooperatives are not confined to the retail business, as in many other countries, but are common in the field of manufacturing and wholesaling. In Israel, the Federation of Labor is the largest employer in the nation, and it has a considerable share in the ownership and control of such basic industries as transportation, building, foundries, heavy machinery, cement, glass, and rubber. Also, a sizable proportion of Israel's agricultural production is in cooperative farm communities.

None of these solutions are final, and mistakes are constantly made, but these forms of socialization do seem to their advocates to avoid the worst evil of nationalization: monopoly, and the resulting concentration of economic and political power. In a capitalist democracy, the economic power of private monopolies can at least be opposed by the political power of the state. *When the monopolist is the state itself, who will protect the citizen against the state?*

Today, then, no socialist party advocates any longer that *all* industries be collectivized—nationalization is recommended only for *some* industries. How many is "some"? There is no clear-cut answer, but there seems to be universal acceptance among socialists of the idea that natural monopolies in the public utilities field be publicly owned and managed. The concept of the "sick industry" (*e.g.,* the British coal industry) and the criterion of the "key industry" (*e.g.,* the British steel industry) have also been widely accepted as standards upon which nationalization may be based.

As has been seen in the case of British steel, the difference between the socialist and nonsocialist viewpoint is less real than both parties believe it is. The socialists were willing to make one big concession when they nationalized steel: to leave the individual steel firms intact, so that their name, management, and traditions might be preserved in a highly competitive market, in which intangible assets are important. The only major change in the steel industry would have been that the stockholders of steel companies would *exchange their shares for state bonds with fixed income.*

When the Conservatives got into office, they were willing, on their part, to make a big concession: while "denationalizing" the iron and steel industry, and returning the property to private ownership (thus transforming bonds again into shares), they set up a national *Iron and Steel Board,* designed to protect the national interest. On this board, in addition to the representatives of management, there are representatives of the state and of the steel workers (a former secretary of the steel workers' union was appointed as the first vice-chairman of the board).

The socialists have announced that, when next in office, they are going to "renationalize," or "un-denationalize," the steel industry. It remains to be seen whether the limits of English language will be reached before the patience of the English voters is exhausted.

It appears that *nationalization lends itself best to industries or services that are highly standardized—i.e.,* where *uniform rules of administration* can be easily applied (this is the thesis of "gas and water socialism").

But when it comes to industries that demand high adaptability to changing conditions—industries, for example, producing largely for export—or industries operating with a considerable element of risk, the case against nationalization or socialization is strong. The tendency of a bureaucratically run enterprise to put security above adventure and risk is incompatible with rapid industrial expansion. The automobile industry a generation ago and the air conditioning industry today are the products, not of the pre-existing giant enterprises, but of relatively small corporations that were willing to put risk capital into new products.

It remains to be proved that this same spirit of adventure, risk, and experimentation can be shown by publicly owned enterprises. After all, it is one thing to risk, and speculate with, one's own money, and quite another thing to use the public treasury for questionable ventures.

The traditional concern of socialists has always been with *distribution* rather than *production*. The most creative contribution of socialism has therefore been its revision of the internal social structure of nations in the direction of equality. Many countries with strong socialist parties exhibit a tremendous internal cohesion and unity, the direct result, according to socialist leaders, of a high degree of social justice, based on the concept of "fair shares for all." By contrast, these leaders point out, where socialism has recently been weak, as in France and Italy, the people are torn and disunited among themselves, and there is a general feeling of frustration, resentment, and stagnation.

When it comes to production, it has not been shown so far that publicly owned enterprise is any more efficient than private enterprise. There are three problems here. First, there is the *managerial problem* of administering vast public enterprises with flexibility and initiative, and at a low cost. The excessive tendency toward centralization and playing it safe is one serious matter. Moreover, it is not certain that the managerial situation will improve as nationalization continues. In the first phase of public ownership, the public corporation can draw upon managerial talent which has been trained in the tough environment of private competition; but if nationalization goes on, management of public enterprises will have to draw its top personnel from among its own ranks. It will then be seen whether persons trained and bred in the secure, sheltered atmosphere of bureaucratic monopoly will possess as great a capacity to operate large undertakings as is shown by graduates from the hard school of private competitive business.

This problem is closely tied to a second problem. In private business, the *system of profits and losses* operates in a crude but effective way to keep efficiency at a relatively high level, and the threat of bankruptcy is always real. In a public enterprise, this system no longer operates to the same extent; if there are losses, no one goes bankrupt, and the losses of one division can be passed on to the whole enterprise. Even if the whole enterprise or industry is in the red, management can, because it has a monopoly, either increase prices or receive subsidies from general taxation.

Third, there is the *political difficulty.* How are public corporations to be related to the elected representatives of the people? If the public corporation is too closely supervised by parliament or congress, its management may become demoralized and lose in efficiency. If parliamentary control is relaxed, on the other hand, up goes the cry that there is not much difference between the old and the new system (since if management can do more or less as it pleases, what has nationalization changed?).

THE IMPASSE OF SOCIALISM TODAY

Socialists today find themselves bewildered, taking stock, and uncertain of the future. For over half a century, the socialist movement was almost entirely devoted to propaganda and organization outside the framework of governmental responsibility. Now that so much of the socialist program has been realized, however, socialism faces a fate similar to that of organized political Liberalism.

Just as political Liberalism has passed away largely because some of the causes it championed have died a natural death while others have been solved by conservatives and socialists along liberal lines, socialism too may gradually pass away, as far as its original program is concerned, even though political parties with the socialist label may continue for a long time.

In the field of international politics, the main weakness of socialists has been the *failure to understand the role of power.* This intellectual failure was based on an admirable emotion: the desire to remove power from the society of nations and establish a world commonwealth based on peace and justice. Desirable as this goal may be, however, specific international problems cannot be solved by it or any other abstraction. Moreover, the practical realities of national economic planning have frequently given socialist foreign policies a strong element of *isolationism,* which is in sharp contrast with the traditional socialist slogan of international brotherhood.

Thus the foreign policy of the Labor Government during the years 1945-1951 was discouraging to all those, in Europe and America, who believed that Britain would be the natural leader in a movement for a united Europe. In fairness to the Labor government, however, it should be noted that the Conservative government that followed it into power has pursued the same negative policies with regard to European federation, as well as roughly the same policies on the other main issues of foreign affairs.

In Norway, the socialist government has been in favor of a strong alliance with the North Atlantic treaty powers, whereas in Sweden the socialists have been in favor of neutrality and avoiding advance commitments. In the Middle East, the socialist-dominated government of Israel is strongly associated with the United States and her allies, but India's Premier Pandit Nehru, also a socialist, is trying to maintain complete neutrality between East and West. All these policies have little to do with socialism and are based primarily on national interests, attitudes, and traditions.

In sum, therefore, it can be said that from the viewpoint of ideology the pacifist heritage of socialism has frequently paralyzed its ability to solve international problems realistically, and that, taking the picture as a whole, the foreign policies of socialist governments in recent years have been no better and no worse than those of nonsocialist governments in the same countries. The quality of a particular government depended on how intelligent and far-sighted that particular government was, rather than on whether it was socialist, liberal, or conservative.

In July, 1951, The Socialist International was re-established. At its first congress, over thirty socialist parties committed themselves to support the rearmament of their countries for collective defense against communist aggression. That resolution, an expression of realism and common sense rather than of socialism as such, is primarily of interest as reflecting a definite change of socialist outlook on the nature of war.

A generation ago, socialists looked upon capitalism as *the* cause of war, and upon universal socialism as the only guarantee for peace. From experience with both fascist and communist imperialism, socialists have learned that war is a much more complex problem, and that the forces of imperialism can be tied to any system of economic organization, not just the capitalist system.

The older, unsophisticated view that international problems can be solved with a mixture of good will, soft soap, and improved old-age benefits still survives in some quarters of the socialist movement. The neutralism of the Bevanites in England and similar tendencies in France, Germany, and Italy are the result not so much of communist sympathies as of a failure to understand the realities of power behind the threat of communist aggression. Some of these socialist neutralists appear to nourish the hope that free school lunches and shorter workdays in their countries will not only discourage communism at home, but also so impress the men in the Kremlin that they will drop their aggressive plans for world domination.

When it comes to the economic program of socialism, the present difficulties are not likely to be resolved so soon. One great objective of socialism, the *welfare state*—i.e., the responsibility of the community for a minimum standard of social and economic security for every person—is *no longer a monopoly of socialist parties*. All other parties in democratic nations, with the exception of ultraconservative diehards, are also in favor of the welfare state. Some parties are more warmly for it than others, and some parties recommend more benefits than others; but as a general principle, the welfare state (in the minimum sense) is accepted by reasonable persons in all parties, and is no longer a matter of partisan controversy.

The concept of the welfare state no longer requires a separate political party. In fact, much of the welfare state in England was historically the work of the Conservative Party, and the limits of the welfare state are increasingly set by the ability to pay for its benefits rather than by differences of ideology.

Finally, as to the argument that *nationalization* would bring about a *more equal society:* in a democratic society, owners *of property* that is to be nationalized or socialized receive adequate compensation. There is thus no change in property relations, except that shareholders become bondholders with a fixed income, which is theoretically supposed to be equivalent to their former income as shareholders. There is, of course, an easy way of reducing the real value of this new fixed income of the bondholders of nationalized enterprises: inflation. But if inflation is to do the job, it can be accomplished without the roundabout way of nationalization. Moreover, there are better methods than inflation, such as *high inheritance taxes* and *high income taxes,* which are less dramatic and more effective than nationalization.

Because of all these difficulties, socialists have therefore given up any leaning, if they ever had one, toward absolute equality. They are now satisfied with *reasonable equality,* provided there is a minimum income and living standard for every family. A moderate conservative would probably put it somewhat differently: he would argue in favor of *reasonable inequality,* provided opportunity for advancement is kept open for everybody.

When members of the Socialist International voted in July 1951 for a program of "full employment, increased production, social security, and a just distribution of incomes and property," they only echoed their support of what reasonable people in all parties believe in nowadays. The very fact that after two generations of socialist propaganda and accomplishment the main principles of the welfare state have been accepted by all parties in democratic states has created a real dilemma for the future of socialism: if it keeps on trying to convert the converted, it will lose the old fire and enthusiasm that made it a distinctive movement in the western world in the last three generations. If its leaders are unable to formulate a new program, adapted to the needs of the second half of the twentieth century, the party may simply settle down to a fixed position slightly to the Left of the conservative parties, separated from the latter not by a basically different economic or political philosophy, but simply by its concentration on translating the conception of the welfare state into a reality at the earliest possible moment.

FOR FURTHER READING

Attlee, Clement R., *As It Happened* (Viking, 1954)
Blum, Leon, *For All Mankind* (Viking, 1946)
Buber, Martin, *Paths in Utopia* (Macmillan, 1949)
Cole, G. D. H., *The Post-War Condition of Britain* (Praeger, 1957)

Cole, Margaret (ed.), *The Webbs and Their Work* (Frederick Muller, 1949)

Crosland, C. A. R., *The Future of Socialism* (Macmillan, 1957)

Crossman, R. H. S. (ed.), *New Fabian Essays* (Praeger, 1952)

Durbin, E. F. M., *The Politics of Democratic Socialism* (Routledge, 1940)

Ebenstein, William, *Modern Political Thought* (Rinehart, 1954), ch. 11

———, *Political Thought in Perspective* (McGraw-Hill, 1957), ch. 21

Egbert, Donald Drew, and Stow Persons (eds.), *Socialism and American Life*, 2 vols. (Princeton University Press, 1952)

Gaitskell, Hugh, *Socialism and Nationalisation* (Fabian Society, 1956)

Galenson, Walter (ed.), *Comparative Labor Movements* (Prentice-Hall, 1952)

Hayek, Friedrich A., *The Road to Serfdom* (University of Chicago Press, 1944)

Kautsky, Karl, *Social Democracy versus Communism* (Rand School Press, 1946)

Lewis, W. Arthur, *The Principles of Economic Planning* (Public Affairs Press, 1949)

Mises, Ludwig von, *Socialism* (Yale University Press, 1951)

Morris, William Dale, *The Christian Origins of Social Revolt* (Macmillan, 1949)

Pigou, A. C., *Socialism versus Capitalism* (Macmillan, 1937)

Schumpeter, Joseph A., *Capitalism, Socialism, and Democracy*, 3rd ed. (Harper, 1950)

Socialist Union, *Twentieth Century Socialism* (Penguin Books, 1956)

Sturmthal, Adolf, *Unity and Diversity in European Labor* (Free Press, 1953)

Ulam, Adam B., *Philosophical Foundations of English Socialism* (Harvard University Press, 1951)

index

INDEX

C